Moody

Moody

by

John Pollock

Foreword by
Luis Palau

MOODY PRESS
CHICAGO

Library of Congress Cataloging in Publication Data

Pollock, John Charles.
  Moody.

  Originally published: Moody without Sankey. London:
Hodder & Stoughton, 1966.
  Bibliography: p. 346

  1. Moody, Dwight Lyman, 1837-1899.   2. Evangelists—
United States—Biography.   I. Title.
BV3785.M7P6 1984   269'.2'0924 [B]   83-23807
ISBN:0-8024-0269-0

   1 2 3 4 5 6 7 Printing/MG/Year 88 87 86 85 84

Printed in the United States of America

Contents

CHAPTER   PAGE

Foreword   vii
Preface   xi
Acknowledgments   xiii

PART ONE: CRAZY MOODY, 1837-1871

 1. The Boy with the Crooked Finger   17
 2. Boston Sunrise   21
 3. Chicago Moneymaker   31
 4. "Go Fast or Burst"   37
 5. The Children's Friend   49
 6. Drums in Tennessee   57
 7. The Rescue Shop   67
 8. "Brutally Ridiculed"   75
 9. The Little Lancashire Lad   81
10. Sankey on a Soapbox   93
11. Fire   99

PART TWO: THE MAN FROM THE WEST, 1872-1875

12. The Unanswered Letter   111
13. White Elephants   121
14. Surprise in the North   129

15. Glasgow Conquered   137
16. Racked Hearts   147
17. The Road to London   155
18. Dockers and Duchesses   165
19. Climax in Britain   175

PART THREE: REMAKING AMERICA, 1875-1881

20. Chickens at Northfield   187
21. All America Stirred   201
22. Moody's Dilemma   213
23. The School on the Hill   223
24. Both Sides of the River   235

PART FOUR: "THE POWER OF CHRISTIAN UNION,"
1882-1899

25. Dan'l at Cambridge   249
26. Seedbed of a World Movement   263
27. Student Volunteers   273
28. Slow Birth of the Bible Institute   285
29. A Dark Valley and the Sea   297
30. The Incomparable Moody   309
31. Northfield   321
32. The Grandchildren   331
33. Heaven Opens   337

    List of Principal Sources   346

Foreword

Every Christian should read *Moody*. I have read it at least a half dozen times! No one can read this book without becoming tremendously excited, motivated, and deeply moved by God. It is one of the few books that I say are "must reading for every Christian."

This book records the life story of one of the greatest heroes of the Christian faith. Such books thrill me because they reveal how God can and does use ordinary men like D. L. Moody to accomplish great tasks—ordinary people whose lives have shared particular characteristics: personal holiness, sensitivity to God, much prayer and in-depth study of God's Word, humility, a consuming passion for the salvation of the lost, and a definite indication of the power of God in the life.

The influence men like D. L. Moody have had upon society is still felt today through their converts, their writings, their courageous stand for the authority of the Word of God, and their personal relationship to Jesus Christ.

Unfortunately, we do not study church history and the heroes of the faith, who are wrapped up in that history, as we should.

I remember wondering in school how certain teachers could make something as exciting as history so boring. Did you ever have teachers like that? History is *not* boring, especially church history. Church history is people—ordinary people used mightily by God—people like D. L. Moody. It is the stimulating and far-reaching events that impacted the lives of such people.

In *Moody,* author John Pollock gives us one of the most accurate and detailed studies of Moody's life ever made. Here is the story of a man who rose from poverty with only a minimum of education to bring two continents to repentance. Here's the story of a warm-hearted, unpretentious heavyweight who rose from obscurity to work with as much ease among ragamuffins as he did among millionaires, royalty, and the ecclesiastical and political leaders of the world.

Dwight L. Moody was an evangelist to the masses. He was the pacesetter in methodology. It has been said that Moody traveled over a million miles in his lifetime and preached the gospel to over 100 million people.

In John Pollock's electrifying book we see some of the secrets as to why God was able to use Moody with such incredible power: he was 100 percent committed to reaching as many people as possible in his lifetime for Jesus Christ; he was in the deepest sense a man of prayer and a student of the Bible; he did not question the authority of God's Word; he was incredibly humble; he was free from the lust of money (although he could have been a very successful business-man); and he fully understood the meaning of Galatians 2:20: "It is no longer I who live, but Christ lives in me."

God desires to use you and me with "power from on high," as He used D. L. Moody. I believe that if you read this book with clear eyes and an open heart you will realize your accountability before God to help our generation to hear the gospel and the voice of God.

Moody may have lived a hundred years ago, but his life story speaks to this generation with the same power that it did in the nineteenth century. The great city masses that Moody loved so much are with us on an even greater scale today, three generations later.

The consuming passion that Moody had for the salvation of the lost should inspire us today. His strategy, "Reach the big cities and you reach a nation," is even more valid today because the centers of influence (such as the media) are housed in our metropolitan areas.

As you can see, I have a natural interest in this man, D. L. Moody, because I believe that our evangelistic team has profited immensely from his example. We are trying to follow in his footsteps by preaching the gospel to the masses in our generation.

Everywhere Moody went he delighted audiences, whether he was in a mass rally or a personal interview with some head of state. University students were held spellbound by this man, who went to school only from age five to thirteen. Corporate executives were touched by the authority and power that they saw in him. Tough street kids were literally disarmed by this man's compassion for all people.

Moody was more than a humble Bible teacher. He had the genius of a military strategist. As Christians, we find ourselves involved in a spiritual war. This book, I believe, can inspire the most educated Christian and the humblest believer to move out into the front lines with greater confidence, boldness, and faith.

As I have studied the life of D. L. Moody, I have been impressed by three events that seem to have prepared him for his famous international campaigns.

First, in February 1868, Harry Moorhouse was invited to the pulpit at Moody's church. For seven nights he preached from John 3:16, "For God so loved the world, that He gave His only begotten Son, that whoever believes in Him should not perish, but have eternal life." Night after night, Moorhouse gave proof from the Bible that God loves sinners. In private counseling he told Moody, "Teach what the Bible says, not your own words, and show people how much God loves them."

That teaching shattered Moody's belief that God hates the sinner, as well as the sin. "I never knew up to that time that God loved us so much," said Moody. "This heart of mine began to thaw out. I could not keep back the tears."

A second incident occurred at the 1870 annual convention of the YMCA, of which Moody was president from 1866 to 1869. During the 1870 meeting, Moody, while directing a prayer meeting that lacked enthusiasm, asked for a volunteer to sing. Ira David Sankey, a twenty-nine-year-old delegate from Pennsylvania, stood up and sang, "There Is a Fountain Filled with Blood." Moody was so impressed by Sankey's voice that he asked him to come to Chicago and help in the work of campaign evangelism. Sankey left his post office job in Pennsylvania and joined Moody in early 1871.

The third incident took place on October 8, 1871. While preaching at Farwell Hall, Moody asked the members of the congregation to evaluate their relationship to the Lord and to return the following week to make their decisions for Christ. That crowd never regathered, for within minutes the great Chicago fire erupted, destroying the entire city. That incident so devastated Moody that he vowed he would never again close a meeting without inviting people to receive Christ as their Savior.

Among the thousands of anecdotes written about Moody, one that has remained with me over the years is the account of a meeting between young Moody and an evangelist named Henry Varley, who met Moody during his visit to the British Isles in 1872.

Moody and Varley were sitting on a park bench in Dublin—I believe—and Varley remarked, "Moody, the world has yet to see what God will do with a man fully consecrated to Him."

The remark was made casually, and Moody did not comment, but for days the words burned inside him. *The world has yet to see what God can do with and for and through a man who is fully consecrated to Him,* Moody kept repeating to himself. *Varley was referring to any man. He didn't say he had to be educated or scholarly. Just a man. Well, by the Holy Spirit in me, I'll be that man.*

"The eyes of the Lord are toward the righteous, and His ears are open to their cry" (Psalm 34:15).

Moody later commented that Varley's remark and Charles H. Spurgeon's preaching (which he also heard in Britain) focused on something he had never realized before. "It was not Spurgeon who was doing that work; it was God. And if God could use Spurgeon, why should He not use me?"

After reading this book, you will realize, I believe, how God can use you as well. God is not looking for saints, scholars, and superheroes. He simply wants to use ordinary people like you and me.

The requirement? Full consecration.

Has the world yet seen what God can do through you?

LUIS PALAU
President
Luis Palau Evangelistic Team

Preface

More than eighty years after his death, D. L. Moody remains a towering figure in history. The influence of his evangelism is still felt; the institutions he founded in America continue to flourish; and his position in history is secure. But it is his personality that commands attention: rugged, delightful, compassionate—a man of total integrity, with a supreme gift for bringing Christianity before the whole range of contemporary hearers and putting them to work for God.

When this book was first published, more than twenty years ago, the *New York Times* was kind enough to say, "By the time a reader has finished this book he has the impression that he knows Moody, has heard him and even shaken hands with him." That was certainly my aim, to bring to life a unique figure who "put one hand on Britain and the other on America and lifted them both nearer to God."

Acknowledgments

From the moment we landed in California until we sailed for England my wife and I received great kindness.

At Pasadena, the late Dr. Wilbur M. Smith, of Fuller Theological Seminary, compiler of the *Annotated Bibliography of D. L. Moody*, who for years had been encouraging me to undertake this biography, gave us hospitality and much advice. In Chicago, Dr. William A. Culbertson, then the president of Moody Bible Institute, and his faculty and staff were most hospitable and helpful. In particular, Mr. Bernard R. DeRemer of the Moodyana section put aside a great deal of time during our weeks of research in the MBI archives.

At Northfield, we were welcomed by the Moody family and the schools and given every possible assistance, especially by the late Mrs. W. R. Moody, with her most helpful cooperation and kindness. Mrs. Moody, who had recently celebrated her ninety-first birthday, was the only person living who knew Moody well. As the wife of Moody's eldest son and daughter of his greatest friend, D. W. Whittle, her memories covered the last twenty-five years of his life. She also made available to me her valuable collection of manuscripts. Mrs. Emma Moody Powell, who maintained and enlarged the Moody collection of her parents, the late Mr. and Mrs.

A. P. Fitt, allowed me unrestricted access to her manuscripts and to her own research notes, and gave me childhood memories of her grandfather. The patience and interest of the late Frank W. Pearsall, former Director of Public Relations of the Northfield Schools, smoothed my path.

I should also like to thank the following people: Her Majesty the Queen for her gracious permission to print the letter from the Countess of Gainsborough to Queen Victoria, and the Librarian, Windsor Castle (Sir Robert Mackworth-Young); the late Admiral of the Fleet the Earl Mountbatten of Burma, K.G., for allowing me to see and quote from papers in the Broadland Archives, and Lord Brabourne; Canon T. C. F. Bewes; the Bucknell Librarian, Crozier Theological Seminary, Chester, Pennsylvania; Mr. Charles Cleall and Mr. Robin Sheldon for helping me with technical aspects of Sankey's music; the president of the Railway and Locomotive Historical Society, Boston, Massachusetts; and Mr. and Mrs. Daniel F. Sutherland, of Northfield.

I am grateful also to the Moody Bible Institute for permission to quote from material that appeared from time to time in *Moody Monthly*, as well as from *Heavenly Destiny*, by Emma Moody Powell.

To all others who helped this book forward, my warm thanks.

PART ONE

Crazy Moody, 1837-1871

1

The Boy with the Crooked Finger

From the round-topped hill a muscular youth took a last look at the majestic curve of the Connecticut River. Although he was seventeen, his eyes filled with tears.

He was sorry to leave the Valley, perhaps never again to climb the little hill (he called it a "mountain") and watch the sunset, the colors reflecting on the curve of the river, and the strong evening light on Brattleboro Mountain.

Dwight Lyman Moody turned, and gazed, and gazed again, at the fields and woods and houses of Northfield, where snow patches still lurked in dips and corners on this March day of 1854. He could see smoke curling from the white frame cottage where he had been born on February 5, 1837.

Northfield, Massachusetts, on the New Hampshire and Vermont borders, once a last outpost in dread of Indian attacks, was now no primitive community but a typical New England rural township with about a thousand souls. It was a place of clapboard houses set roomily in their own gardens along a wide main street, graced by a double avenue of elms and rock maples, and of farms scattered on both sides of the Great River and up into the pine-clad hills. Proud and cultured, Northfield's roots and concerns lay south and north along the valley rather than eastward to distant Boston.

The township was peopled with Moody's relations to the third and fourth generation. The Moodys and the Holtons, his mother's family, had been among the seventeenth-century pioneers of the Connecticut Valley. D. L. Moody was kin to a dozen New England worthies—past, present, and future—including Jonathan Edwards, Harriet Beecher Stowe, Oliver Wendell Holmes, and President Cleveland; Franklin Delano Roosevelt, by his Lyman grandmother, was descended, like Moody, from William Holton, one of the first settlers of Northfield (then called Squakheag) in 1672.

Dwight Moody knew nothing about that. His boyhood, as he remembered it on the day when he was leaving all behind to make his fortune in Boston, had been dominated by the effects of his father's premature death.

Edwin Moody, a stonemason with a small farm in the northern area of the town, was a genial, shiftless, lazy fellow, adored by his wife, Betsey, and their numerous offspring, and popular with the neighbors, but addicted to more whiskey than was good for his heart. He died suddenly in May 1841, when Dwight was four, and he died bankrupt. The creditor, Richard Colton, swept in and seized everything he could, including most of the furniture, the horse and buggy, and the cows, except for one calf that he did not discover. The older boys hid their father's tools, and the dower law of Massachusetts prevented Colton turning the widow out of the house.

The month after she was widowed, Betsey bore twins, Sam and Lizzie, making nine children, of which Dwight was the fifth son. He now had six brothers and two sisters.

Four days after the twins' birth, the mortgage on the farm fell due, and rich Ezra Purple from across the river came to collect. "Betsey wasn't up since the birth of her twins," recorded her brother Charles Holton,

> but she had him come to her bedroom, and told him that the money was not ready, but she would get it for him as soon as she could. Purple expressed his disappointment in unkind language, and soon left the house. Going down the hill the harness broke, and he was thrown out on the ground—uninjured. Some of the townspeople, knowing the reason for his visit to Betsey, were so unkind as to say, "It was a pity he didn't break his neck." Hearing of the straits Betsey was in, Cyrus and I, the two brothers living near her, managed to raise the money that year.

D. L. Moody, forty years on, took an apt revenge on the Purples. Betsey's next sorrow was the disappearance of Isaiah, her eldest son and at fifteen her mainstay. He ran away, she knew neither why nor where.

Her hair had turned white, but she set herself to make what she could of the poor farm, "a regular sand heap" as her family thought, and of the trivial earnings of her sons. Dwight's boyish memories were of this tight-lipped yet cheerful mother in her gray homespun, who whipped her children hard but held their ardent devotion. She could milk the cows, "made our clothes, and wove the cloth, and spun the yarn, and darned our stockings." She bade her sons swear vengeance on whiskey.

She sent them to school, but their schooling was erratic because of the need to earn money in the fields and Dwight's own impatience at books. She sent them to Sunday school and church— the First Congregational Church, which had turned Unitarian, as in most towns of New England in the early nineteenth century. Everett, the minister, was a pious, kindly man, a widow's friend, and his Unitarianism was moderate (he baptized the Moodys at one batch in 1842, in the name of the Trinity he denied).

A reaction from the bleak systematized high Calvinism of the Puritans, Unitarianism had not shed Puritan ethics. Betsey Moody's standards were strict; she reared her brood to do their duty to God and their neighbor and behave—or try to behave—as their Puritan ancestors had laid down the rules. The Sabbath was kept from sundown Saturday to sundown Sunday when "we would run out and throw up our caps and let off our jubilant spirits."

Dwight was taught that he must be good—that he could be good if he tried. Their religion was without warmth, irksome, and thought about only on the long Sabbath. Farmwork was irksome, too. Dwight loved to be free on the hills. He loved to run ("and I could run like a deer"), to fight other boys, to swim in the cold water of the Great River, and to be the leader in practical jokes, such as stampeding a farmer's cattle with Indian war whoops or snowballing innocent riders.

By seventeen he was a broad, sloping-shouldered youth with plenty of muscle and stamina, of medium height (growing to five feet ten). His tendency to let his head hang forward as if too heavy for his body made him look stocky. His eyes were darkish gray, and his hair was a rich dark brown, almost black. His lips had rather a pout. And the last joint of both little fingers had a crook inwards so that the tips rested on the next.

With the boys able to earn, food cheap, and firewood free, the crowded family made the little frame house echo with laughter. But Moody hated hoeing fields and husking corn barefoot. When carting, the slow gait of the old horse, Ring, maddened him. Chopping wood against the snowbound winter was a dreary chore, and he was "sick and tired" of doing it all for nothing. He did not grudge his mother a penny but wanted money to spend some on himself, too.

The railroad had come to Northfield when Dwight was eleven. Soon there were two lines. The junction of the Vermont and Massachusetts and the River Road lay just across the Connecticut, almost opposite the Moody Homestead, and the Boston-bound trains clanking across the new bridge sang of a wider world until, from Northfield as from all rural New England, boys and young men drifted eastward into the cities or struck westward to pioneer lands. By the winter of 1853-1854, D. L. Moody was decided. When the snows cleared he put his few belongings in a carpetbag.

His mother grieved, and his older brothers, George, Edwin, and Luther, reminded him brutally that his two previous absences, brief and dismal, had ended abruptly. Young Dwight did not listen, hateful as it was to leave home. He had no trace of doubt that one day he would be famous.

Moody was Yankee to the core. His blood was pure Anglo-Saxon like many of the local place-names, Warwick, Northampton, Winchendon; but he was bred to that smoldering distrust of England left by the War of Independence and of 1812. He would have dismissed as a joke in poor taste any prophecy that fame should first come in Great Britain, that Scotland and England would be loved dearly.

Indeed, anyone who had told him exactly how it would happen would have been answered by a choice Yankee oath.

2
Boston Sunrise

Samuel Socrates Holton, a prosperous shoe craftsman aged thirty-seven, was presiding over his shop on Court Street in Boston, just off Scollay Square, when to his surprise and alarm his nephew Dwight swaggered in.

Dwight had broached the subject of taking a post in the Holton shop on the previous Thanksgiving Day in Northfield. Holton had made no reply. Later he questioned George, the eldest Moody brother at home, and what he heard about Dwight was not to his taste. Therefore, on seeing his nephew six months later in the middle of the boots and shoes, he invited him into the office, chatted pleasantly about the family and then, making plain that he had no more time, asked what Dwight proposed to do in Boston. Dwight, shaken, answered that he had come to find a position. Uncle Samuel Socrates said nothing. Uncle Lemuel, the younger partner, who looked after the second shop farther up the street, suggested Dwight had better stay with him in his Winchester surburban house while looking for work.

Moody walked out of Holton and Company, certain that he would soon gloat over his uncles' chagrin at missing a good assistant.

Up and down the hilly curving streets of a Boston still largely cooped on its original peninsula, he called at shops and offices. Boston was filling fast; the Irish influx following the potato famine had not slacked, and if many immigrants went westward or could not read or write, enough clerks were available to fill every vacancy twice. Moody's confidence seeped.

By the afternoon of the second day Moody was miserable. "The feeling . . . that no one wanted you. I shall never forget those two dark days. Oh, the sadness, the loneliness." He drifted to the docks and toyed with signing on as a sailor. He badgered the post office, although he knew the Northfield mail came only daily, until he got a letter—from little Lizzie, aged twelve, warning him against pickpockets; he shook his empty pockets ruefully, and as he trudged back to meet Uncle Lemuel made a boyish vow, quickly forgotten, promising God, "If He would give me some work, I would serve and love Him."

Moody greeted Lemuel defiantly. "I am going to walk to New York!"

Lemuel judged that pride had nearly cracked. "Ask your uncle for a job, direct," he said.

Dwight refused. "He knows perfectly well what I want."

"Go on, ask him!"

Lemuel won. A chastened Dwight approached Uncle S. S.—as Samuel Socrates was known in the family—who gave him a long, silent, avuncular look.

"Dwight," he said at last, "I'm afraid that if you come in here you will soon want to run the store yourself. Now my men here do the work as *I* want it done." He read his nephew a homily, laid down certain conditions, and offered him the weekend to think them over.

Dwight blurted out, "I don't want till Monday. I promise now."

Moody was genuinely grateful for the break. Twenty-four years later, when Samuel Socrates in "great necessity" appealed to his newly famous nephew, Moody wrote, "You gave me work & good advice & I look back to that hour as the turning point in my life & I feel as if I owe you a debt I can never pay so the money I send you is not a loan but a part payment of what I owe you."

During the following week, Dwight wrote home laboriously: "I do not bord out to Uncle SS now I bord in the city Calvin and I are

going to room together bimb bi that word is not spelt rite I guess."
He intended the good Yankee phrase "by 'n' by." He wrote a hand
that became, for a time, reasonably legible ("if you can read it you
can do peter than I can"), but he spelled as he spoke, in the dialect
and idiom of the Connecticut Valley; and he had inherited from his
mother the peculiar habit of never inserting punctuation—the
words tumbled onto paper as, when he talked, they tumbled from
his mouth.

He slept over the shop. "I have a room up in the third story and I
can open my winder and there is 3 grat buildings full of girls the
handsomest thare is in the city they will swar like parrets." He had
his meals at a hostel "where there is about twenty-five clurcks and
some girls we have a jolly time."

He decided to join what he called "the Christian saciation," the
Young Men's Christian Association of Boston. Founded less than
three years earlier, it was the first YMCA in the United States and
only a week junior to the earliest in North America, the one in
Montreal. It gave him, at a dollar a year, a place where he could get
away on his own. "I can have all the books I want to read free of
expense," Moody recounted. "They have a large room and the
smart men of Boston lecter to them for nothing and they get up a
question."

Moody went to some of the lectures, having quickly discovered
that to be a smart clerk he must not only read books but learn from
the learned. Almost certainly he would have laughed with Oliver
Wendell Holmes, who loved lecturing. He may have heard
Longfellow declaim and John Lothrop Motley read turgid manu-
script pages of the long book he was writing on the rise of the Dutch
Republic. The Boston neighborhood in 1854 teemed with intellec-
tual life. Any day Moody might sell shoes to Emerson or Lowell,
Dana or Whittier, or Julia Ward Howe, or those cultured young
Bostonians Henry and William James and Phillips Brooks.

There were excitements: an accidental explosion on the Common, a dreadful fire at Sargent's Wharf, and, above all, the riots in
which abolitionists attempted to prevent the extradition of the
fugitive slave Burns to the southern states. The final drama could
be viewed from a precarious perch over the Holton store.

I got up in to the secont story right over our shade and thare I stade
un till it was over with all the compineys was out and thare was all of 35

difrent compineys Geo Beans and my self got up there a bout 10 aclock
and thare we sat un till 3 in the afternoon—thay tock him out a bout
2½ to such groaning and hising you never hird
   I was all burnt up in the son the polis came up to the store when he
was clearing the street and told us to com down but we was up so he
could not reach us and he told us to come down the secont time but we
would not com so he at to let us be and so I see it all.

In his scant leisure, Moody loved the open. In the summer he
would run hard round Boston Common or penetrate the long
passageways and gangplanks to Braman's Baths, the basin at the
foot of Chestnut Street, where he could swim in the salty waters of
the Charles and gorge himself afterwards, so far as pocket allowed,
on black mince slugs and apple doughbats. When winter came, he
joined the great toboggan run or watched rich boys race their
highly polished sleds. He scrapped lustily too. "I used to have a
terrible habit of swearing. Whenever I would get mad, out would
come the oaths"—and up would come his fists.
   Best of all was his practical joking.

   I was full of animal life, and shut up in the store through the day and
   sleeping there at night I had to have some vent, and used to lie awake
   at nights to think of some new joke to play upon somebody. My first
   victim was the cobbler employed in the store. He was an Italian
   however and although he liked me he had such an awful temper that
   my joking him came near costing my life. One day I fitted a lady with
   an expensive pair of shoes and he was changing the buttons when
   enraged by some trick I played upon him he took his knife and cut the
   shoe he held into pieces. Another time—and this was the last trick I
   played upon him—he seized the knife and sprang at me, and for a few
   minutes I had all I could do to keep out of his reach.

Moody had no regrets that he had left farming to be a salesman;
instead of mucking unresponsive weeds he was persuading people,
charming them and molding their wills to buy more and costlier
shoes. He reveled in the battle to trade better than the other clerks.
And he had money, though little enough. He sent some to his
mother, but "I would not go back a gain to liv for nothing," he told
her rather unkindly in midsummer. "I never enjoyed myself so well
be for in my life   the time goes like a whirl wind."
   He would not admit it, but he was lonely. "I wish the duse you
would some of you write to me," he scolded his brother George.

What in thunder the reason was I did not get a letter this morning I could not make out. . . . I should like to go home this year if I could git away but it is all in vain cant wright any more so goodby resp. yours Dwight L. Moody HO GEO tell me what kind of a crop of corn this year and potatos.

"I go to meating at Mount Vernon St. Othedx I dont know how it is spelt but you will know what I mean." Betsey did indeed.

Samuel Socrates was not a Unitarian. And he had made Dwight promise, as one of the conditions, that he should attend the Mount Vernon Church and Sunday school, which was Trinitarian or Orthodox Congregationalist. He did this in no partisan spirit, but as a way of keeping his nephew out of mischief.

To Dwight church was church whatever its name, and he reported in a customary mood of dutiful boredom to the Sunday school superintendent. Superintendent Palmer had two claims to minor fame: First, he was a brother of Ray Palmer, who had written "My Faith Looks Up to Thee" at the age of twenty-one, and many hymns since; and second, after a few moments' interrogation following school assembly that Sunday, he assigned D. L. Moody to the class of Edward Kimball. Had Palmer chosen a tight-lipped, insensitive, or even older teacher, the story might have been different.

Moody followed Palmer to the class, already in session, and saw a strikingly tall man of thirty, a salesman in McGilvray's dry-goods store. Kimball smiled at the newcomer, handed him a Bible, and told him to sit down and that they were on a lesson from the gospel of John. Moody began thumbing hastily through Genesis. "Out of the corner of their eyes the boys saw what he was doing," Kimball records, "and, detecting his ignorance, glanced slyly and knowingly at one another, but not rudely. I gave the boys just one hasty glance of reproof. I quietly handed Moody my own book open at the right place, and took his." Moody said to himself he would "stick by the fellow who had stood by him and had done him a turn like that."

Samuel Socrates hinted darkly among the deacons that it was Betsey's fault—no family prayers or reading of the Scriptures. He was wrong. The weighty family Bible had been "about the only book we had in the house when father died, and out of that book she taught us." But it was not to be handled by grubby little Moodys, and Dwight had generally daydreamed during the readings. His first attendance at Mount Vernon church service was unpropitious, too. Moody took a place at the back of the gallery. Since he was tone-deaf, he could not enjoy the excellent new organ. During the long sermon of Pastor Kirk, whom years afterwards he described as "one of the most eloquent men I ever heard," Moody fell fast asleep.

Dr. Edward Norris Kirk was pastor of an unusual church, "gathered" only twelve years previously of Bostonians unsatisfied by the rigid doctrinal exclusiveness of Park Street, a few yards southwest, but rejecting the free-thinking charms of King's Chapel a few yards southeast. Kirk preached with intellectual wealth and a measure of fervor—not to make men orthodox, but to move their hearts. Here were no cold moral essays such as Everett had propounded from the Northfield pulpit with ethical exhortation. Kirk spoke much of a sinful and undone race, which could not attain its ideal if it wanted to. He spoke more of Jesus Christ, who, he said, had died for all mankind, risen from the dead (Everett would have winced), and lived to be the Friend of any who trusted Him. Kirk uttered fearful warnings to those who refused this great salvation and verbally lashed young men who dared not or cared not to take up the cross and be Christ's disciples.

In the next eleven months, Kimball's lessons and Kirk's preaching percolated Moody's consciousness as he hustled his way to the top of Holton's shoe-selling list ("I took as much as any one last Saturday . . . I am giting a long as fast as most of them") or swam, ran, tobogganed, or indulged in horseplay.

When first he began to grasp Kirk's drift he thrust the implications aside: "I thought I would wait till I died and then become a Christian. I thought if I had the consumption or some lingering disease, I would have plenty of time to become one, and in the meantime I would enjoy the best of the pleasures of the world." By early 1855, with Boston under hard snow and the Charles River frozen, Moody's colleagues saw the same jolly, willful, quick-tempered youth just eighteen; but scarcely recognized by himself at first, an inward struggle had developed.

Kirk stressed repeatedly that the spiritual issue was one of choice, of deliberate submission of will to Another, of a moment of faith leading to a life of service. Sensing that Kirk was right, Moody resisted. He could not mentally disentangle doctrines, but he recognized the issue and sought to avoid it. Forty years afterwards he said, "When I came to Jesus Christ, I had a terrible battle to surrender my will, and take God's will." In April the Mount Vernon Church held a revival, a term then used synonymously with "mission," as well as in the broader sense of a spontaneous spiritual movement.

In the midst of the revival, on Saturday morning, April 21, 1855, Edward Kimball walked out of his lodgings at America House, having

> decided to speak to Moody about Christ and about his soul. I started down town to Holton's shoe store. When I was nearly there I began to wonder whether I ought to go just then during business hours. And I thought maybe my mission might embarrass the boy, that when I went away the other clerks might ask who I was, and when they learned might taunt Moody and ask if I was trying to make a good boy out of him. While I was pondering over it all I passed the store without noticing it. Then, when I found I had gone by the door I determined to make a dash for it and have it over at once.

He found Moody in the back part wrapping up shoes in paper and stacking them on shelves. "I went up to him and put my hand on his shoulder, and as I leaned over I placed my foot upon a shoe box." Looking down into Moody's eyes he made what he thought afterwards a very weak plea. Neither could ever recall the exact words, but "[Kimball] asked him to come to Christ, who loved him and who wanted his love and should have it." There were tears in Kimball's eyes.

"It seemed," Kimball recorded, "that the young man was just ready for the light that broke upon him, for there, at once, in the back of that shoe store in Boston, [Moody] gave himself and his life to Christ."

Kimball slipped from the store a few minutes after he had entered.

The next morning, Sunday, as Moody came out of his room over the shut-up shop,

> I thought the old sun shone a good deal brighter than it ever had before—I thought that it was just smiling upon me; and as I walked out upon Boston Common and heard the birds singing in the trees, I thought they were all singing a song to me. Do you know, I fell in love

with the birds. I had never cared for them before. It seemed to me that
I was in love with all creation. I had not a bitter feeling against any
man, and I was ready to take all men to my heart.

Moody's first thought was for his family—his mother, brothers,
and sisters, and especially the young twin, Samuel, to whom he was
devoted. "Then and there I began to pray for them. I had never
prayed for them before."

He had sent home not only money but shoes, which he could buy
at trade prices, and much unsolicited advice on everything; and
now he wanted them to have this new, astonishing exhilaration and
peace. "I thought I could tell them what God has done for me. I
thought I had only to explain it to have them all see the light."

He was home for a few days quite soon (he helped in the potato
and watermelon planting at the end of May) and attempted to tell
them what had happened. They looked at him blankly—they could
not understand what he was getting at. Betsey murmured that she
would be a Unitarian till she died.

In Boston also he met rebuff. Mount Vernon as a Congregational
Church did not admit to full membership except on oral examination by pastor and deacons to test spiritual sincerity. Unwisely,
Kimball urged Moody to apply too soon, and he stood before the
committee, shaking with a nervousness that Kimball's presence
could not calm. "With utmost encouragement" they questioned
him: "Have you been awakened? Did you see yourself a sinner? Do
you feel dependent on Christ for forgiveness?"

Moody was tongue-tied. His sense of the Friendship that had
invaded his life was helplessly inarticulate. He grunted and
murmured, "Yes," "No," or, "Sure," which the clerk translated into
doctrinally correct statements, until at length the Chairman asked,
"Mr. Moody, what has Christ done for us all—for you—which
entitles Him to our love?"

"I don't know. I think Christ has done a good deal for us. But I
don't think of anything particular as I know of."

They deferred admission, and told two kindly deacons to teach
him. Moody wanted to be taught—he was upset when a fellow clerk
had worsted him with apparently watertight proofs that Christ had
never risen from the dead; but he resolved to keep away from that

committee: "You might as well try to get a man to go before a Justice of the Peace." It was not until the next year, in March 1856, that he appeared again and was accepted, although, in Kimball's words, "little more light appeared." Afterwards the worthies of Mount Vernon were sheepish about their attitude. Kimball defended them. Except that Moody no longer swore and that the Bible, which had been "the driest and darkest Book in the universe to [him]," was now his favorite reading, there had been nothing to hint that one day they would sit at his feet.

Moody at nineteen found Boston stifling. Its galaxy of talent, its old established business houses, its set ways, stiff manners, and rigid social levels combined to frustrate him.

As early as October 1855, he had written inquiringly to his uncle Calvin Holton, who had gone west to farm near Chicago. In the spring of 1856, his cousin Frank had joined the jostling crowd of Easterners and emigrants who answered the popular cry "Go west, young man, and grow up with the country."

In September Moody went.

3

Chicago Moneymaker

He·had not meant to go so soon.

Joined by his next older brother, Luther, Moody now managed the newly opened Holton store farther up Court Street. Moreover, his mother wept when he talked about the West, and he wanted time to win her around. Then came the quarrel with Uncle S. S.

The cause is obscure. To his mother Moody merely wrote, "Uncle S. S. objected to my goin," though adding in a second letter, "I was fairly drove out of Boston." To his younger brother Warren he was more frank. "I hope you will never have anyone to cross your path as they have mine and blast your hopes." Possibly Samuel Socrates had refused a raise. More probably he had demanded signed agreement that Moody would not go West, and on being refused had fired him; that would explain why Moody had money only for his fare to Chicago and for expenses until he should get a job, one reason against a farewell visit to Northfield. Whatever the cause, "I thought the quicker I went and got out of [S. S.'s] way the better . . . . I love Boston and have got some warm friends there, but as I was situated there it was not very pleasant."

He bought a through ticket on an immigrant train (five dollars from Boston to Chicago) and left from the Causeway Street depot of the Fitchburg Railroad at 4:00 P.M. on Monday, September 15, 1856.

The train drew into Keene, twenty miles from Northfield, after dark. Moody felt slightly guilty that his mother should go to bed ignorant that her Dwight was disappearing into the West. The train rattled northward, wood smoke from its enormous funnel swirling ash into the carriages to mix with the smelly whale oil of the swaying lamps, and crossed the Connecticut at Bellows Falls. At Rutland, Vermont, in the small hours of Tuesday, everyone got off the train; Moody sat through the night at the station.

The next day began with a morning run beside Lake Champlain, then westward all day to Ogdensburg on Lake Erie, to take the lake steamer through the second night and then a slow Canadian train to Windsor opposite Detroit, where the ferry timing prevented Moody's seeing his brother Isaiah, the prodigal who had returned after thirteen years, been forgiven, and now worked in Detroit.

The Michigan Central express ambled through the prairies until, at length, during the night of Thursday, September eighteenth, behind schedule, it rumbled across the long trestle bridge above Lake Michigan mud into what Chicagoans asserted was "the best depot in the country." Thus came Moody, excited but apprehensive, to "this far famed city of the west . . . my western home," a thousand miles away.

Two ladies who had been kind to him traveled onward. "Then I felt as if Christ was the only friend I had in Chicago," recalled Moody.

Jolly Uncle Calvin Holton of Des Plaines, a few miles out, promptly secured Moody a post at the Lake Street shoe store of Charles and Augustus Wiswall, both Massachusetts men.

The following Wednesday a lawyer named King was introduced at the prayer meeting of "Plymouth" Congregational Church to the newly arrived young man,

> one of the happiest looking I think I ever saw. His cheeks then were full, so red and rosy, and he possessed such a pleasant smile and look that he attracted much attention, and very soon became a general favorite, notwithstanding his very limited education—if he did come from Boston.

Moody was delighted. "As soon as I made myself known I had friends enough . . . After meeting they came to me and seemed to be as glad to see me as if I were their earthly brother."

He took to Chicago at once. "It is a very lively city, much more so than Boston." Into this hub of the West, by sail, steamer, and rail, poured emigrants and manufactures from the East, iron and timber down the Great Lakes, stock and grain from the prairies. Slaughterhouses and tanneries made Chicago stink, and foundries and factories filled it with smoke. Lake Michigan frequently coated it with mud. No one cared: the farther west the frontier pushed, the more Chicago grew.

"The streets are all lade out strate and broad," Moody wrote home. "You can stand and look as far as the eye can reach and try to walk out of the city but it is almost impossible for you to get out of the limits of the city." The land was not as closely built over as Boston was and this, since most of the houses were timber, was fortunate, for he lost count of the fires he saw or heard about.

The pace of life in Chicago was much to Moody's liking. He heard glowing tales of men who ten years back had arrived poor and had since become "worth from ten to fifty thousand dollars." But his New England soul was shocked by Chicago Sundays. He wrote home: "You don't know how anyone feels to be off in a city like this for it is so wicked   the stores are open on the sapath a grate many of them." And Moody never became urbanized; his heart remained loyal to the countryside. "You don't know how I like to get letters from friends being off in this far far city all alone   I think of sweet home and of my younger days often."

He was happy. He put on weight, had an enormous appetite, was the same irrepressible joker in that oafish style his generation thought funny. "The cobbler in Wiswall's store was a queer old character," Moody related with huge delight at the age of forty-six, "as most of these cobblers are, and although he thought a good deal of me and we were great friends I was always up to some trick with him." The naughtiest was to slit the leather seat of the cobbler's low stool and place underneath a full pail of water. While Moody watched out of the corner of his eye the cobbler returned, and jumped up with a cry; he wiped the seat, sat down again, and jumped, and so continued until he discovered the trick.

Moody flung himself into the craft of selling shoes to those who wanted or those who did not. "His ambition made him anxious to lay up money," Charles Wiswall records. "His personal habits made him exact and economical." He was a thruster and an enthusiast, and when Wiswall's started a jobbing department they let him meet the emigrant trains and bludgeon newcomers by blunt speech and boyish grins into buying boots. His aim, like that of all Chicago, was to get rich quick: "I used to pray God to give me one hundred thousand dollars."

"I can make money faster here thin I can in B," he wrote to his mother, adding, with Yankee hyperbole, "I hav me one of the best situations in the city. . . . I hav don the very best thing in coming hear."

Within a year he was showing the signs of a future millionaire, putting his savings into land, which he would sell at a profit, making loans at high rates, and thinking up this scheme and that to increase his income and capital. He rejoiced especially in one excellent aid to personal contentment and material progress: "I tell you," he wrote to his brother George, "hear is the place to make the money . . . and that is not all . . . I have enjoyed more Religion hear thean I have ever in my life . . . I find the better I live the more enjoyment I have."

Chicago already had a reputation for wildness, but religion lay close beneath its thick skin. Because of the many from strict Eastern homes, who had drifted in spirit and morals, disaster or perplexity could touch off religious fervor; it was not all self-centered or cynical.

On January 6, 1857, Moody wrote: "There is a great revival of Religion in this city   I go to meeting every night Ho, how I do enjoy it   seems as if God was here himself."

This preceded by nearly a year the similar and more lasting movement generated by the Wall Street financial panic, which led to the establishment of prayer meetings in many American cities, as well as the Revival of 1859 in Great Britain, and which caused Chicago's famous Democrat mayor "Long John" Wentworth to comment, "The effects of the present religious movement are to be felt in every phase of Society."

The revival of early 1857 tossed Moody out of his complacent view of religion as primarily an aid to fortune.

He rented four pews at Plymouth Church and filled them with young men from Wiswall's or nearby shops, or even passersby at service time. On Sunday afternoons he went slumming with a slightly older man, an architect named J. B. Stillson, who rated him "a young man of earnest purpose, plain habits and not very much education. We became co-workers in scattering religious reading among sailors in saloons, boarding houses and hundreds of poor families living in shanties."

Moody's attempts to contribute to the life of Plymouth Church by opening his mouth at prayer meeting made staid adults "squirm their shoulders when I got up." They told Moody he did not know enough grammar and asked Uncle Calvin to silence him. Moody took the hint. Meanwhile he had become an inveterate sermon taster, Sunday morning, noon, and night. He had his pews at Plymouth, could be found in the Methodist Episcopal, and sat under the outsize Presbyterian minister, Patterson. At the First Baptist he set eyes on a thirteen-year-old girl. He was not introduced, but he remembered the face. Her name was Emma, and her social standing clearly a cut above his.

There were plenty of other girls. To little sister Lizzie in Northfield he scribbled:

> When I went out to Uncle Cal's I see quite a number of fine looking young ladies here is the place for ladies . . . I always thought before I came out here there was hardley none but it is not so there is a nuft but they dont seem like the good old New england folks now I tell you I think befor I get married I shall hav to come home and let you pick me out a wife.

At the end of 1857, Moody left Wiswall for the post of traveling salesman and debt collector for the wholesale boot and shoe house of C. H. Henderson. His brother Luther, temporarily in Chicago, "thought it was very foolish in my leaving Wiswall but I have got me a situation that is worth five of that and if I have my health and my God is with me I shall sucksead better here in Chicago than I ever thought I should."

He enjoyed the new job "better than anything I have ever done it is nothing but excitement all the time." He hustled all over Illinois and, in late February 1858, was in the south of the state, where the scenery was pleasant, but he thought scorn of the inhabitants: "the people are more like heathen they all smok chew swere drink gamble and steel they are shifless losey ignorant miserable people a Yankey can do well here I think." Most of his customers lived on the railway.

Occasionally he had to hire a horse and trap to cross the prairies, and (or so he tried to persuade George) "I drove a horse into a slew the other day so nothing but his head stuck out I dint ever expect to see him out a gaine but I maid out to get him my hare stood rite up on I will send you a lock so you will see for yourself."

He grew "fat as a pig," a heavyweight at twenty-one who could look quite tall when he remembered to brace shoulders and lift his head, and had a short growth of beard to accentuate his chin and impress defaulting storekeepers. When the icy winter passed, Henderson sent him farther afield.

> I travel most all of the time it is very pleasant traveling at this time of the year in the country as you cross the prairies you can see the prairies wolf and deere chickens are as thick as grasshoppers in August I was down in Missouri not long ago and also in Iowa, Wisconsin Indiana I have not traveled much in Michigan but expect to have to go there before long and if I do I mean to call on Isaiah but since January I have not had time to turn around the folks I am now with do a very heavy business the largest business this side of N York so in the busy season we have to jump all hands of us as tite as we can jump.

At Wiswall's he had slept on the premises. He now lived in a superior boardnghouse on Michigan Avenue run by a Mrs. Hubert Phillips for the smart bachelors of Chicago. Among them was Levi Zeiter, who became a millionaire and the father-in-law of Lord Curzon, Viceroy of India and British Foreign Secretary. Moody used to say that he believed he could have beaten the lot except Marshall Field.

When pausing for breath in Chicago he searched for a Christian activity that could command his whole spare-time energy.

Mother Phillips, a member of the First Baptist Church, suggested trying their Wells Street mission Sunday school on the North Side, the poor part of the city. One Sunday morning Moody and another boarder crossed the river and walked up Wells Street to the corner of Chicago Avenue. Moody asked the superintendent for work, "but I don't think he asked for a class," Dr. Roy of Plymouth Church recalled. "He said in those days that he could not teach."

The superintendent, unaware whence his remark would lead, casually told Moody he might go out into the alleys and streets and bring in what boys he could.

4

"Go Fast or Burst"

A ragamuffin called Jimmy Sexton was playing in the streets with three or four other urchins on a Sunday morning.

> We were approached by a stalwart young man about twenty years of age. He was dressed in a checkered suit of gray clothes—close-cropped hair, a muscular frame, easy though awkward in manner, and might have been taken for a horse jockey or an all round sportsman.

"Boys, don't you want to go with me to Sunday school?" asked Moody in a "familiar and friendly way."
"Are you going to have a picnic?"
"Come along with me and we will find out."
They trooped behind as Moody hurried through courts and alleys until, sweaty and triumphant, he delivered to Wells Street no less than eighteen ragged boys, most of them barefoot. "That was the happiest Sunday I have ever known," Moody declared. "I had found out what my mission was." He had been two years "trying to find out what my work was before I succeeded. If I could not teach them I could take them where there were those who could."
The next week he hunted up the same gang and others. "We became at once close friends," Sexton recalled in a letter of 1892.

Notwithstanding his crude and somewhat uncouth appearance we found him to be a most agreeable companion, good humoured, ready and witty in speech, although awkward in the selection of his words, simple, unaffected, and kind, with a charm of manner and a personality so winning and interesting that we all immediately swore allegiance to our newfound stranger friend. His earnestness and sincerity gave us confidence in his loyalty, and soon made us feel that we stood upon an equality with a good fellow. Our boyish chaffing pleased rather than annoyed him.

"Drumming up scholars," as Moody described it, for the Baptists made this Congregationalist late for the Methodist Episcopal young men's class, which he had joined in disregard of the frowns of Plymouth deacons who set much store on sectarian exclusiveness. Another member of the class was one of the most successful and wealthy men in the city, John V. Farwell, who had first come to Chicago on a load of hay with less than four dollars in his pocket. Now, at only thirty-three, he controlled the leading big store. He was outranked later by his former partner, Marshall Field, but remained a prominent citizen for the rest of his long life.

Farwell despised the tardy youth until he discovered the cause, "and then my criticism turned towards home with tremendous force, and why wasn't I doing something for others as well as this young man?" The incident led to the start of a very great friendship.

One Sunday at Wells Street, Moody saw a new teacher for the girls, a young lady with good looks and elegance—and her face was the face he had never forgotten. He wangled an introduction. Almost before he knew it, he was paying a call on the Washington Street home of a shipbuilder, Fleming H. Revell, a comparatively recent emigrant from England. Emma Revell was only fifteen, and looked no older, yet she had a quiet maturity, a happy laugh, and, incredibly, did not seem to think a fellow crude, uncouth, or awkward.

When Henderson again sent Moody into the country, the ragamuffins drifted. "We boys did not like the school on Wells Street," where the lessons included much dreary learning by rote, "and as there was no immediate prospect of a picnic, we dropped out."

Moody was appalled by the endless back streets of the North Side. When first he had reached Chicago he could write glibly, "We

seldom ever see a poor person hear and very little stealing goin on."
He had since been embroiled in the stench and squalor of a great
city's backwash: a miserable medley of German and Irish emigrants
or American-born newcomers, who had dropped in the mad rush
westward to wealth, been plowed under by the violence of competition or the ravages of whiskey, and now crowded in the shanties and
tumbledown frame houses of an area known as "The Sands." The
original "Sands" had been a concretion of shacks on the Lake
Michigan foreshore, which "Long John" Wentworth had cleaned
away violently in 1857 ("an exhibition of barbarism in the name of
high morality").

The Sands were then the slums of the North Side. Their poverty,
and the fact that the churches did not touch the adults or Sunday
schools the children, startled Moody. As he rattled by train across
the prairies or drove pony and trap "into a slew" or battled to sell
Henderson's shoes at the best prices to hard-bitten storekeepers, he
thought constantly of Jimmy Sexton, Tom Stevens, and others
wilder than they—of their poverty and ignorance, their restlessness in the formality of Wells Street or its opposite number, the
North Star School.

Back in Chicago, early in autumn of 1858, Moody and his
architect friend Stillson appropriated an abandoned freight car on
North State Street. He sought out Jimmy Sexton and the gang.
Said Jimmy, he

> invited us to assist him in starting a mission Sunday school. We were to
> be co-partners, so to speak, or co-laborers, and, as one of the boys
> expressed it, "the whole thing." The idea that we were to boss
> somebody and to take part in the controlling of others was too
> captivating for our youthful ambition to withstand.

Stillson brought in another young businessman, Carter, who had
a fine voice and could sing and lead a rousing song and chorus like
the newly written "Stand Up, Stand Up for Jesus," though there
were few hymns extant that guttersnipes of the Sands could hope to
learn or remember.

The next Sunday afternoon anyone walking down that block of
North State Street heard extraordinary noises—shouts, whoops,
cheers, a moment of silence, a sacred song in a baritone voice swept
up into a shouted chorus. A man's voice (and it was not Moody's)
spoke for two or three minutes until murmurs and shuffling

indicated that another song alone could preserve peace.

After a few Sundays, with boys bringing pals to the new adventure until the sides of the old car bulged, Lawyer King heard about it. King thought Moody "should have a better location to teach the boys in, so I said to him I knew of an empty one-story-and-a-half frame house on Michigan Street," later renamed Illinois Street. It was a disused saloon called the Mansion House, one of the first to have been opened in Chicago, but now rotting and ratty. Moody was given the use of the large front room and a store at the back.

A Chicago minister, G. S. F. Savage, remembered how Moody "went out on the streets with candy and knickknacks and got the good will of the children," and by thus being a young, exuberant, rich uncle whose pockets trailed maple sugar, he made the school a draw. "All loved him," said King, "because he took such an interest in their welfare. No one forgets the pleasant smile and the cordial handshake, both of which were characteristic."

Sundays grew noisier by sheer numbers. On weeknights, while he was in Chicago, Moody sometimes collected smaller parties. That November, he invited Savage to attend a Thanksgiving Day service.

> There were no gas fixtures in the house and he was trying to light it with a half-dozen candles, but the darkness had rather the best of it. I found him with a candle in one hand and a Bible in the other, and a child on his knee who he was trying to teach. There were twenty-five or thirty children in all, and they were as sorry a lot of little ragamuffins as could have been found in Chicago.

Moody was hindered by continual absences, since Henderson paid for his return to Chicago only one Sunday a month, and he could not afford other weekends if operating very far away. He had now joined a church on the North Side, a "New England" congregation that worshiped in a small wooden building near the river and had attempted, unsuccessfully, to work up a Sunday school in The Sands. Church members noticed "a plump, active, keen-eyed young fellow come into our prayer meeting. Sometimes he had a word to say, very brief, and sometimes he prayed. His voice—how shall I describe it?—had electricity in it." One who noticed was Colonel Hammond, superintendent of the Chicago, Burlington and Quincy Railroad.

Much of the Henderson work lay along the C. B. & Q. line. Moody boldly asked Hammond for a free pass—the first recorded solicitation of the man who was to draw vast sums into Christian enterprise. Hammond sought the advice of another church member, a doctor called Blatchford, who urged him to agree. The next Sunday morning Blatchford was driving to an urgent case down Pine Street on the edge of The Sands.

> I thought I saw this man, Moody, and I stopped my horse. He was down, I guess, a block and a half from me. I saw him dart into a house, and in a little while he came out of that house with the children all about him, and the mother and father, perhaps, and then he would dart into another house . . . When I went to church that morning I said to Colonel Hammond, "Your pass will do good."

By early December 1858, as Chicago's temperature dropped toward zero, Moody's life seemed set in eternal spring. He relished his spare-time work for boys. His employer, Henderson, "the truest friend I have met since I left home," showed growing confidence, took "as much interest in my welfare as he would in the welfare of his own son," and hinted that Moody was being groomed to succeed him.

And there was Emma. Her small brother, Fleming H. Revell, Jr., then aged nine, would crouch behind the stove on those winter nights

> to listen to the conversation of this young man who came to the house to see one of my sisters—in a very democratic company, and a very democratic sort of courting, because I think I never remember his ever coming alone. Around that little sheet-iron stove there was always a circle of young men, and perhaps it was because there were three girls.

Emma Revell had been born in London on July 5, 1843. Her father, Fleming Hewitt Revell, was a French Huguenot who had gone to England, married an English girl, and built up a shipbuilding business until illness and financial troubles caused him to emigrate to Chicago in 1849 with his wife and his daughters Anna, Emma, and Sarah. A fourth daughter, baby Mary, had to be left with Mrs. Revell's sister, and their son was born in America.

Though Revell never made much, and young Emma earned her living as a teacher, the Washington Street home close to Moody's Michigan Avenue lodgings was cultured, hospitable, and rather English.

Emma Revell was a complete opposite to Moody. Moody, an extrovert, brimmed with health, strength, and energy. Emma, shy and retiring, suffered already from asthma and headaches. His humor was boisterous, hers deep and quietly playful. "No two people were ever more in contrast," their younger son, Paul, summed up, long after both were dead.

> He was impulsive, outspoken, dominant, informal, and with little education at the time they met. She was intensely conventional and conservative, far better educated, fond of reading, with a discriminate taste, and self-effacing to the last degree.

She took on Moody's education. But she never persuaded him to insert punctuation in his letters—he had no time. His large scrawl rushed across the page, leaving the reader to guess where a sentence closed, unless the first word of the next had a capital. His spelling was shaky to the end of his life, like that of many country-bred, self-educated millionaires, politicians, and generals of the period. Later, Moody could spell reasonably when he remembered, but in notes and letters to colleagues, family and intimates he spelled phonetically ("shure," "beleave," "clurk," "goin," and in a letter to his mother written in 1879 at the age of forty-two he spelled bed as if it were bread without the "r").

An English friend asked Moody in middle age why he did not write oftener in his own hand. "Spelling," Moody replied. "But Inglis, I'm getting over the difficulty. I am always sure of the first letter and the last, and anywhere between may be upstairs or downstairs." And that is what his letters look like.

They are vivid in the originals, but without punctuation would read tediously in print; and unless his speech also was reproduced in the phonetics of a New England accent his spelling would give a falsely illiterate air. I shall ease the reader's eye henceforth by generally (but not always) inserting essential punctuation and correcting the spelling.

The opening of Moody's mind, the slow polishing of his rough-hewn character, was largely Emma Revell's doing. Two years were to pass before they could be engaged when she was seventeen, two more to marriage. Paul wrote:

> My father's admiration for her was as boundless as his love. To the day of his death, I believe, he never ceased to wonder at two things—

the use God had made of him despite his handicaps, and the miracle of having won the love of a woman he considered completely his superior.

In the last week of 1858, Henderson died suddenly. He died intestate, and when the firm was reorganized under conditions that were annoying to the widow, Moody resigned in her support, 'although "it would have been for my interest to have stayed with the new house." He obtained a similar post with Buell, Hill, and Granger. A year later, Mrs. Henderson and her daughter begged him to help them unseat the incompetent administrator of the considerable personal estate, collect the debts, and wind it up. "I told them I was not old enough to take such an estate on my shoulders, but they insisted . . . I feel highly honored."

Business life slipped imperceptibly from first place in Moody's interest.

The Sunday school thrived. Numbers rose steadily, and, according to Farwell, noise and chaos kept pace. Lawyer King heard that the deserted saloon had become too small. "I became so greatly impressed with the great work, and [Moody's] earnestness and devotion to it convinced me that I in my humble way should do something in the same direction." King took Moody to see his close friend Long John Wentworth. Though Wentworth was no longer Mayor, his influence was enough to secure, rent-free, a hall built on the site of the old North Market.

It was upstairs—"a great grimy hall with blackened walls and ceiling, and as bare and uninviting as can be imagined." Underneath stood the local fire engine; sometimes in years to come, a school session would be madly distracted by the rush of firemen to harness the horses and gallop away, clanging the bell and stoking the engine boiler to get up steam to pump the hose.

The North Market Hall was used for the Saturday night dances of a German society, who threw all the school chairs, banners, and other paraphernalia into a heap, and left the floor a mess of cigar stubs, ashes, beer puddles, and paper. Moody would not employ labor on Sunday. Instead, he got up at six, however late he had arrived back from traveling, hurried to the hall, and alone—or with Jimmy Sexton, to whom he had assigned the task—spent hours rolling out beer kegs, sweeping sawdust, and scrubbing. Sexton recalled:

> This was as dirty, disagreeable, and unpleasant a chore as could be imagined. I have never done any work quite so filthy and disagreeable since, but then I was part of the machine and considered myself well paid for my labor if I received an approving word of encouragment from Mr. Moody.

Leaving Jimmy, Moody would rush out into the lanes "to drum up the scholars and new boys and girls." (Girls now came too; it is probable that a few had been admitted from the start.) If the parents of a boy or a girl were fractious, he had to persuade them; if he found them snoring off the previous night's booze, he actually washed and dressed their children.

At two o'clock the service began. For some months, the riot was beyond the wit of Moody and his more articulate helpers to break up into classes—the afternoon was one glorious improvisation of short talks, songs, and choruses. "The singing was a vent for their spirits," explained one of the early teachers, "and such singing I never heard before. The boys who sold papers in the street had an indescribable lung power, and the rest seemed not far behind."

When classes could be formed, Moody whipped up more of his friends to serve as teachers. To one he said, before the bell rang for the start, "I want you to take these lambs."

"*Lambs? Wolves,* I should say."

The school rose rapidly to some six hundred. Moody appointed a banker, Isaac Burch, as superintendent, and afterwards John Farwell, but he himself was the driving force. "I shall expect to have a good time next Sunday when I get home," he wrote to one of his brothers when on tour in July 1859, "for I have been away some time now, and the children are so glad to see me when I return. I think I have got the best school there is in the west, anyway it is the largest school there is this side of N York." He was wrong. John Wanamaker, founder of the great store in Philadelphia, had a bigger one.

Somebody said the school made him think "of those steamboats on the Mississippi that must either go fast or burst." That described Moody, too. "I am in a great hurry," he would scrawl in letters home, "I am in such a hurry tonight you must excuse me for not writing more this time I am in a hurry."

Moody had thought he could never speak in public until, wrote Emma, during those smaller evening children's meetings, "he found himself sometimes left without a speaker and would be obliged himself to say a little. Gradually he got so that he could talk to the audience." He had been intimidated by the polish and length of contemporary sermons.

To tell boys and girls a story or two about Bible characters, describing them as if they were living in the next block, proved easier, and, once Moody broke the silence, the dam burst; he could not thereafter resist the opportunity to release the love and gratitude to Christ that bubbled inside him, provided no minister was around, when Moody would start trembling and get tongue-tied.

On commercial tours he discovered place after place without Sunday schools. A small girl, a Miss Warner, went into the grocer's in the country town of Warren. Coming out, she saw two men, the larger one on a box preaching at the corner, and she stood with other children, entranced. "The railroad train was nearby, en route to Chicago. The other man got behind the speaker, pulled his coat-tail and urged him to hurry and catch the train. They did catch the rear car."

Moody would not preach to grown-ups, but there was something that he could do. He set about it in roaring Chicago fashion, Emma having scarcely begun to tame him.

Late in 1859 he announced that he really would visit Northfield. "You seame to think that there is some humbug about my coming home," he wrote to George in November, "but I think there is no dout but that I shall be to home next month with out fail if not in January shure." He came during January 1860, having given, in effect, a warning that Unitarian Northfield would soon learn "there is nothing like the religion of Jesus Christ."

Uncle Zebulon Allen, Betsey's brother-in-law, felt the force of it.

> My nephew Dwight is crazy crazy as a March hare. Came on from Chicago last week for a flying visit. I had not seen him, but he drove into my yard this morning. You know how cold it was and his face was as red as red flannel. Before I could say good morning he shouted, "Good morning Uncle Zebulon, What are you going to do for Christ today?" Of course I was startled and finally managed to say "Come in

Dwight and we will talk it over" "No I can't stop, but I want you to think about it" and he turned the sleigh around and went up the hill like a streak of lightning. I tell you, he is Crazy.

Another episode, back on the prairies in the spring of 1860, was less acrobatic.

William Reynolds, a banker of Peoria, Illinois, was in a train "when a stout cheery-looking stranger came in, and sat down in the seat beside me." The two men started talking, as American railway passengers will, and the stranger remarked on the pretty countryside they were running through. "Did you ever think what a good heavenly Father we have to give us such a pleasant world to live in?"

"Yes, indeed."

"Are you a Christian?"

"No."

Both knew what was meant; the American frontier in 1860 had a background of piety, family Bibles read at mothers' knees, and old camp meetings when an itinerant preacher would stir a place to repentance and faith, and then wander on to the next settlement.

"You are not a Christian? But you ought to be one at once. I get off at the next station. If you will kneel down right here I will pray to the Lord to make you a Christian."

They knelt. The stranger prayed. The train rattled to a stop and he hurried out, calling back, "Remember, my friend, now is the time to accept."

Reynolds, in a daze, ran onto the little platform of the carriage and shouted after him, "Tell me who you are!"

"My name is Moody."

Reynolds made inquiries, and one weeknight called at the old saloon, still used for smaller meetings, "and the first thing I saw was a man standing up, with a few tallow candles around him, holding a Negro boy, and trying to read to him the story of the Prodigal Son."

The banker became Moody's ardent admirer. To friends who were puzzled by this sudden conversion, Reynolds would tell of the talk in the train. He went to Chicago again, Moody explained, "to get me to go into the country & talk to the children. Well I went & had a good time. I will send you a peace cut from the paper."

Moody had leisure for the meetings in Peoria because he now served his firm on a part-time commission basis, confident that energy and astuteness would secure him almost as substantial a salary as if he were always on the road. He did not intend to abandon his trade. His future lay clear: to earn his bread as a quick-time businessman, amassing a fortune to pay for the philanthropic work next to his heart.

And so it might have proved, had not—on a June day of 1860—one of his North Market Hall teachers, a "pale, delicate young man," staggered up the stairs to Moody's office at Buell, Hill, and Granger, pushed open the door and "tottering and bloodless, [thrown] himself down on some boxes."

5

The Children's Friend

"What's the matter?" Moody said.

"I have been bleeding again at the lungs. The doctor says I cannot live on Lake Michigan, so I must go back to New York State. I suppose I am going to die."

He trembled and looked so upset that Moody asked, "What is the trouble? You are not afraid of death; you are ready to go?"

"No, sir. I am not afraid. But I am anxious for my class."

Moody knew that class, girls from twelve to sixteen, "the most frivolous set. They kept gadding around in the school room, and were laughing and carrying on all the while." He had once taken it in the man's absence, and "they laughed in my face. I felt like opening the door and telling them all to go out and never come back."

The teacher repeated, "I am anxious for my class. I've failed. Not one of them has been led to Jesus. And I haven't the strength to do it now. I believe I have done the girls more harm than good. Not one converted."

Moody was astounded. "I had never heard anyone talk like that before." His whole concentration in the school had been on numbers; he was elated at a full attendance—at hundreds of noisy children—and cast down when numbers dropped. He had not

49

supposed that any of the little savages could undergo a deep personal experience like a grown-up; he had not reckoned them as individuals.

After a pause, Moody said, "Suppose you go round and tell them how you feel. I will go with you in a carriage if you want to go."

He helped the man onto the street. They hired a carriage and drove into the slums. At the tenement home of one of the girls, the teacher called her and said faintly, "I have come just to ask you to come to the Savior."

The girl listened wide-eyed as he revealed that he must leave Chicago and would die, and as he explained why she should put her trust in Christ. And then, said Moody, "he prayed as I never heard before," and the girl, in tears, promised "to settle the question then and there."

The two men mounted the carriage again and rumbled off to another girl's home. The teacher struggled upstairs for a similar conversation. After three or four calls he was exhausted. Moody returned him to his lodgings.

At the end of ten days, recalled Moody, "he came to the store with his face literally shining: 'The last one of my class has yielded herself to Christ. The great vital question of their lives is settled. They have accepted my Savior. My work is done, and I am going home.'"

"You are not going today. Wait till tomorrow and get the whole class together. Bring them all to tea tonight."

Moody said afterwards that if he had known what that meeting would do to him he might have stayed away. All of the girls came, and the teacher spoke and read to them. They tried to sing a parting hymn. Then they knelt to pray. The man begged God to deepen the girls' newfound faith. Moody prayed. "I was just rising from my knees when one of the class began to pray for her dying teacher."

Astonished, Moody listened to the faltering prayer of a slum girl whom he had known as an empty-headed scoffer. A second besought her God for power to win others to Himself. One after another, the girls stumbled into prayer. As Moody heard those genuine, fervent thanksgivings, those earnest petitions, the hundred thousand gold dollars of his dreams turned to tinsel, the ambition to build a commercial empire showed up tawdry and transient. Better to spend his years as this dying teacher had spent ten days, he decided.

The next evening, "as the sun was going down over the Western prairies," Moody hurried to the Michigan Southern to see his friend off. Without any prearrangement, every one of the girls was on the platform. They sang a hymn, and "as the cars rolled out of the depot we could see his pale hand pointing towards the heaven where he wished to meet them."

Many of the girls became Moody's ardent helpers in the Sunday school. In the early 1920s, after Will Moody told that story at a service in California, "a middle-aged lady came up and said, 'Mr. Moody, I want to meet you. My mother was one of those girls.'"

As for D. L. Moody, that "beautiful night in June" left him with a problem that took three months to solve. Like Matthew of old, he had heard a call to leave business. He did not want to leave his trade. "I fought against it. It was a terrible battle. But oh! how many times I have thanked God's will."

To lose the prestige of wealth, in a city that knew no other criterion of fame; to postpone marriage and then have a mere pittance to offer Emma; and to abandon the excitement of commercial warfare, the race to be first millionaire of his set, and the power that money brought—all this was the cost that took three months to count.

A day came in the autumn of 1860 when J. V. Farwell discovered that Moody had left Buell, Hill, and Granger, had left Mrs. Phillips's select boardinghouse, and was bedding on a settee in one of the rooms used by the YMCA in the Methodist Church block. He ate in cheap restaurants or made do on cheese and crackers, determined to stretch his savings and to spend freely on his school. "I said to myself, 'I'll live on what I've saved. When that is gone and there is no means of support I'll take it as a call to return to business.'"

The next year, when Moody was appointed an official of the YMCA, the clerk who inserted the Resolution of the Board of Managers wrote " . . . for the coming year at a salary of $_____." But the blank never was filled in. Farwell said, "I urged him to take a salary, which he refused," because it would shackle his freedom. There would come an even greater renunciation, but this one of 1860 was a decision of genius, giving Moody a moral right to beg hard for mission causes.

"No!" confirmed Fleming H. Revell in a letter of 1917. "Mr. Moody never accepted a salary after he gave up a business I have always understood yielded him $5,000. His first year after, his income was $150. A test of real faith."

A close friend, J. H. Harwood, summed it up: "That a young man full to overflowing of animal spirits and interest in everyday life, should be able for Christ's sake to put the world completely under his feet and ask for nothing that this world had to give is not to be accounted for on any natural principle."

Moody now poured himself, recklessly spending the resources of his nearly full-grown mighty physique, into the mission Sunday school. The North Market Hall could hold twelve hundred; it must be filled.

His pockets, as always, were full of toothsome delights. He would offer a prize such as a squirrel in its cage to the scholar bringing the most recruits in a given time. He never failed to keep the children to their promise of attendance. One of the girls remembered,

> If for some reason I broke my promise, I would sneak along the streets, in the hope of avoiding Mr. Moody and a reprimand. When I had almost reached home, he would stand before me with his hand outstretched and a sad look, and would greet me with, "Why, Jennie, where have you been? I missed you at Sabbath school. I hope you were not ill? Your folks are well? You will not disappoint me this coming Sabbath will you? It will make me very sad indeed if you fail me."

He mobilized his friends in systematic slum visiting. "We used to carry with us bread tickets," wrote J. B. Stillson, "and a little money to relieve the sick, widows, and orphans, and [we] had an arrangement with several physicians to visit the poor and sick without charge, also to furnish night watches."

Moody was most persistent. In an upper flat above a store on North Clark Street lived six children who were, in the memory of the people below,

> noisy and ill-bred, and the father (a giant in size) was habitually drunk and violently abusive to his tiny wife, who supported the family as best she could by washing and scrubbing. Mr. Moody went again and again to try to convert the drunken father. Almost every day they would receive baskets of groceries, fruit, coal or cordwood.

On whiskey he waged a ceaseless war that Betsey would have approved. However, she might have sighed over Dwight's evangelical fervor. At one slum house, where the father was absent, Moody found, in Farwell's words, "not only children but a jug of whiskey.

He took both out of the house, the children to his school, and the jug of whiskey to sprinkle the streets with." On his next visit the irate father roared at him, "Did you pour away my whiskey?" Taking off his coat and rolling up his sleeves, the man bellowed, "I'll thrash you!"

"I broke the jug for the good of yourself and family. If I am to be thrashed, let me pray for you all before you do it."

Moody's heartfelt prayer on the tenement floor was different from the whining cant the man expected from preachers. Shamefacedly he mumbled, "You had better just take the kids, not a whipping."

Moody was as prodigal in time as in energy. A small girl—the story was all over Chicago—promised she would take Moody home to get her mother's consent to her joining the school; first, said the girl, she must do an errand, if the kind gentleman would wait on the street corner.

The kind gentleman waited no less than three hours, in vain. A few days later he caught sight of her. She fled. He chased. She flew along the raised plank sidewalks—Moody after her—clattering up and down the steps where the levels varied, dodging the horse-drawn tram, scattering dogs and old ladies, until she darted through an alley—Moody after her—into a saloon and up the stairs to a bedroom—Moody after her—and under the bed. Moody, breathless and perspiring, coaxed her out. "And when," as one of his friends said, "he drew that little girl from under the bed, he drew a whole family into heaven."

This daily extravagance of stamina on indifferent diet brought Moody such frequent shadows under the eyes that John Farwell gave his twenty-three-year-old friend a little piebald Indian pony. Thereafter a mounted Moody clopped by on his rounds, with a basket of oranges behind or small boys riding pillion, and a trail of older boys scraping through the mud on their homemade wooden handslides taking a tow, and the risk that Moody with a burst of laughter might drop somebody's rope. He was on the pony when D. W. Whittle, fresh in from the Connecticut Valley and afterwards one of his closest associates and dearest friends, first saw him. "As I was passing up Clark Street someone on the sidewalk said, 'There goes Crazy Moody.' I turned, looked down the street, and saw a young man riding a small pony, his trousers in his bootlegs, a cap on his head."

The pony was a powerful aid to recruitment. Seventeen years later Moody could claim, "Some of the most active men in Chicago were little barefooted boys once picked up in the lanes and the byways." The same element of shameless bribery with best intentions pervaded the North Market Hall. Clara Goldy remembered how "the children would always find a bag of peanuts, popcorn, apples, and candies, topped with an orange, awaiting them at the foot of the stairs, and it was quite an inducement. A wash basket full of these bags was always in reserve."

Sparks flew too. There was a boy who made his teacher's life a misery and disrupted neighboring classes. At length Moody told Farwell, "I am going to take that boy into the police office below and whip him, and when you see me start for him have the school rise and sing the loudest hymn in the book until I return." Farwell did so, "and when Mr. Moody returned, his face was very red from this religious exercise. In a month's time the boy became a Christian and a great help to his teacher," and many years later, an active supporter of Moody's Chicago Campaign of 1876.

Stories soon clustered round this self-appointed children's missionary: how, when Irish boys broke the Hall windows and beat up scholars in the streets, Moody called on the Roman Catholic bishop, the famous James Duggan, and actually had him praying with a Protestant; and how, when drunken fathers rushed at him with shillelaghs, he took to his heels, not trusting his quick temper and hefty fists to remain lamblike under the blows.

A boy whom he had been asked to secure for the school proved to be son of a saloonkeeper. I "had never been in a saloon in my life," recounted Moody. "I walked by the door about a dozen times. I said, 'I can't go there, people will think that I have come to get a drink.'" He looked left and right, saw no prying deacon, and went in.

> The old father was behind the bar, and when I told him what I came for, he said, "We won't have any canting hypocrites here," and I went out quicker than I came in. I went in a second time, and again he drove me out. I went back the third time, and the old man wasn't quite so drunk or quite so cross, but he said he would rather have his sons drunkards and his daughters harlots than Christians.

Having discovered that the fellow edited a cheap rationalist rag,

Moody waded through Tom Paine's *The Age of Reason* in return for the man's promise to read the New Testament.

One Sunday morning Moody said to him: "I wish you would go to church with me."

"I haven't been to church for eighteen years." He gave a vigorous rub to the gin glass he was polishing. "No, I won't go. But you may have a church here if you want to."

Moody was shocked. "A *church in a saloon?*" It was the only way to the man's heart. Afraid of deacons' disapproval, Moody set the hour at a time when they would all be in a proper church. The saloonkeeper said: "I want you to understand, young man, that you are not going to do all the preaching."

"What do you mean?"

"I may want to say something, and my friends may want to say a word. We won't let you preach all the time. We may want to answer back."

The atheists were allotted forty-five minutes, Moody fifteen ("The fact was, I didn't think I could preach for more than fifteen minutes"), and the press of infidels itching to mince him made it necessary to move to a larger room down the street. In support he had brought one of his best boys, very small for his age; but, even so, Moody felt "a scared man. I shook from head to foot."

"They began to poke questions at me, but I said, 'No sir. You have got to preach forty-five minutes.'" They did so, until Moody was "sick and tired of infidelity." Then he said, "Let us pray."

They protested. He knelt. They jeered and sneered as he prayed aloud. He called up his reinforcement, and Moody's instinct was right: the small boy created a sensation when "with a pleading voice [he] prayed God to forgive these men for talking so against his dear Son." It was a saccharine scene, but the atheists, silenced, began to steal away. The old saloonkeeper said, "If that is what you teach your children, you may have mine."

So the school grew. Moody had felt when in business that he "got the children for one hour in the week and the devil had them all the rest." The balance was righted. "I have been holding meetings in my school every night this winter," he wrote home. "It has taken all of my time."

As, from the platform, his eye roved over grateful if dirty parishioners, or as he greeted a thousand ragged scholars jostling into the hall, mounted his pony to ride the back streets, or accosted a recalcitrant parent, Moody had no doubt that he had found his life's work—the years would be devoured in the confined sphere of the Chicago slums, serving generations of children.

6

Drums in Tennessee

Abraham Lincoln, President-elect, spent Sunday November 25, 1860, in Chicago. At the invitation of Farwell, who on a brief excursion into politics had been prominent for Lincoln, he agreed to visit Moody's school, provided they expected no speech. He attended morning service at St. James Episcopal Church and left a luncheon early when Farwell called for him.

Cheered to the echo, Lincoln sat through the opening hymns and prayers. He rose to go. Moody then naughtily announced, "Mr. Lincoln has come to see the school, on condition that he *be not asked to speak*. But if he wishes to say a word before leaving, we all have our ears open."

Lincoln strode slowly to the center of the meeting hall. He stopped, looked around, and said: "I was once as poor as any boy in the school, but I am now President of the United States, and if you attend to what is taught you here, some one of you may yet be President of the United States."

After that, being from Boston and living in the city of which Lincoln affirmed, "After Boston, Chicago has been the chief instrument of bringing this war on the country," Moody found that there could be no two opinions about it: he was strong for Union and Abolition; he rated Southerners nothing but slaveholding rebels, and the Civil War plain conflict between good and evil. In fact, between 1861 and 1865, Moody would probably have snorted at reports of the winds of deep spiritual life that swept the Southern ranks.

When Lincoln called for volunteers after Fort Sumter, seventy-five members of Moody's school joined the colors. Jimmy Sexton rose to be a colonel. Moody stayed behind, primarily because he would not abandon his mission, and also because he had a somewhat nebulous sense of personal pacifism ("I felt that I could not take a gun and shoot down a fellow being. In this respect I am a Quaker"), which did not dampen zeal in recruiting.

At the outbreak of war, a military city was thrown together—tents, barrack huts, parade grounds, and guardrooms—to mobilize and train the citizen army flocking in from the Northwest. Camp Douglas was located a few miles south of Chicago, near the site of the future Illinois Institute of Technology. Moody and Benjamin Franklin Jacobs, the young real estate agent who was his opposite number in the North Star Sunday School, were deputed to provide religious ministrations in the camp by the committee of a small, new struggling organization, the name of which had little significance as yet in Chicago: the Young Men's Christian Association.

The YMCA's principal activity had been a prayer meeting held daily at noon in the Association rooms at the Methodist Episcopal church block. When in May 1861, Moody put his activities under its wing and was appointed "Librarian, with the understanding that he shall act as Agent for the Association, and City Missionary," the grandiloquent titles covered the fact that he was "all there was to it officially."

At Camp Douglas, Moody and his friends began regular services and reaped the harvest of which they had dreamed. The soil was fertile. The war brought out qualities and defects dormant in the American character. Sheltered lads from farm or forge were thrown into the rough barrack life, where excitement, puzzlement, and all the temptations they had been warned against by pious mothers in frame houses or log cabins swirled around them in a heady atmosphere of manly toughness and boyish simplicity.

"From the commencement the interest in these meetings was

very great," runs the dry account in the YMCA Report.

> To supply an immediate demand for hymnbooks, an edition of 3,500 was printed from plates of the Sabbath School Union. The work enlarging, an Association Army Committee was appointed . . . The meetings at the camp continued to increase in interest until as many as eight or ten were held each evening, and hundreds were led to seek Christ.

Every night Moody would return with packs of surrendered playing cards, which, rather oddly, he stored away carefully in a corner of the YMCA rooms.

"I am all taken up with this," he wrote in June to his mother. She had complained of desultory correspondence. "Oh no, Mother," he had responded, "I think of you as often as I ever did but if I could see you and tell you how the Lord is blessing me in my labors I think you would say God bless you, go forward . . . I am drove more now than ever in my life." He had Sunday school conventions and his own school to occupy him, in addition to his YMCA responsibilities.

Camp Douglas—especially when casualty lists began to appear and the war ceased to resemble a picnic—burned into Moody the sacredness of the individual. Each one mattered; each of these cheery boys might be soon a sprawling corpse in some Southern wood or wheat field, and each needed the gift and assurance of eternal life.

It faced him too with a personal problem: He could not rely solely on Jacobs or others who knew how to preach. As Emma wrote, "When he was called to meet the soldiers he felt that he must tell them, at every opportunity, of the power of Christ to save." Moody had to conquer his shyness in addressing men of his age or older; he could not stifle the desire to "talk with [them] about my Saviour that seems so near me— Oh what would life be without Christ?"

Never had Moody felt more aware of his poor attainments. Daniel McWilliams, a young accountant and a Presbyterian, was present at a small dinner given in the summer of 1861 by Reynolds of Peoria to enable ministers and laymen to meet his friend of the railway carriage. Their dominant impressions, wrote McWilliams, were Moody's

> earnestness in seeking to lead persons to the Saviour, and his intense thirst for the knowledge of the Bible; for the entire dinner hour was

taken by Mr. Moody in quoting verses and in asking the ministers to tell him "What does this verse mean?"

Farwell said of Camp Douglas that it was Moody's "kindergarten of training." He received quick promotion. In the autumn, the chaplain of an Illinois regiment that masked its city origins with the glorious title of Zouaves, invited him to visit their camp at Elizabethtown, Kentucky, near Lincoln's birthplace. The regimental newspaper reported that "the active missionary of the YMCA of Chicago . . . has labored unceasingly both day and night in distributing books, papers, tracts, hymnbooks" and added, with more truth than grammar, "His advice and example convinces and converts." In the improvisations of the Civil War, an unordained chaplain was not improbable; but Emma records that Moody's "friends in Chicago begged him not to join the army as chaplain as some of the soldiers urged, feeling that he could do more for the soldiers by being free rather than confining himself to one regiment."

Chicago, sobered by this strange sad war of brothers' blood, and pregnant with fear for sons and lovers, where crepe hung on doors and maimed ex-soldiers searched miserably for work, where livelihoods had been blasted yet profiteers fattened, awarded Moody, for the present, a broad measure of respect and admiration.

He was ceaseless in city and camp. He wrote to his favorite brother, Samuel, on a bitter January day in 1862:

> I have some 500 or 800 people that are dependent on me for their daily food & new ones coming all of the time. I keep a sadall horse to ride around with to hunt up the poore people with & then I keepe another horse & man to carry around the things with & then I have a man to waite on the folks as thay come to my office. I make my headquarters at the roomes of the Young Mens Christian Association & then I have just raised money enough to erect a chapell for the soldiers at the camp 3 miles from the city. I hold a meetig down thare evry day & 2 in the city so you see I have 3 meetigs to atend to every day be side calling on the sick & that is not all. I have to go into the countrey about every week to buy wood & provisions for the poore also coal wheet meal & corn.

For his preaching:

> I do not get 5 minuets a day to study so I have to talk just as it happens . . . I do not answer one letter out of 10 that I get—I cannot get time—it is 11 to 12 every night when I retire & am up in the

morning at light . . . I wish you could come in some time about 1 to 3 o'clock my office hours and see the people waiting to see me.

Allowing a discount for Moody's purpose in writing—to show why Northfield letters went unanswered—this discloses the man a few weeks before his twenty-fifth birthday: not slothful in business, fervent in spirit, but with a dangerous assumption, nearly to wreck him a few years later, that godliness must be measured primarily in terms of ceaseless action: "Go to church all you can, as many prayer meetings as you can." None, however, would quarrel with his motto: "Do all you can to make the world better than you found it. Do all you can for Christ and then you will make others happy."

Haphazard voluntary services for relief, welfare, and religion in the Federal armies were at length coordinated by formation of the United States Christian Commission, a private organization with official sanction, somewhat a mixture of Red Cross, Navy, Army, and Air Force Institutes and auxiliary chaplains' department. Farwell became President of the Northwestern Branch. Moody, inevitably, served frequently as one of the delegates to the front (they received expenses but no pay).

In February 1862, when the unknown Grant rose to fame by capturing Fort Donelson on the Cumberland in Tennessee and coining the term "unconditional surrender," Moody was down from Chicago among the casualties. "I tell you, you do not know how roughley the poore fellows are treated. I was on the battlefield before they had buried the dead. It was awful to see the dead laying around without being anyone to burrey them." On return home he was sent back immediately with further supplies for the wounded.

The following month Grant fought the ghastly Battle of Shiloh, or Pittsburgh Landing, a partial defeat, though inducing Confederate withdrawal. An emergency call to Chicago brought a trainload of extra doctors, nurses, and medical students, organized by the YMCA for the Christian Commission. "In the forward end of the car was Mr. Moody conducting a prayer meeting," noted a medical student as he settled for the night; "in the rear end was a company of men playing cards."

Shattered limbs, gangrene, amputations often without chloroform, and deaths that might have been avoided, had medical science and hygiene advanced a little further, sharpened Moody's acute sensitivity to human want in all its forms. He became certain that his urgent message could make an immediate difference to a man's eternity and anxious to get an honest answer to his constant question in the presence of death, "Are you a Christian?"

"Coming down the Tennessee River we had four hundred and fifty wounded men on board. A good many of them were mortally wounded." Moody and his companions "made up our minds we would not let a man die on the boat without telling him of Christ and heaven—we would tell them of Christ as we gave them a cup of cold water." Moody came upon a youth dying from shock and loss of blood. He gave the boy brandy and water in the hope that he would briefly recover consciousness.

The casualty next on the deck said they were buddies from the same company, the same town, had enlisted together, and that the dying boy was the only son of a widow. Moody knew that the mother "would be anxious to get some message from her boy and I asked if she was a Christian. He said, 'Yes, she is a godly woman.'"

At intervals Moody called the lad's name, and at length his eyes opened. Moody gave him another sip of brandy and water.

"William, do you know where you are?"

"Oh, yes," he murmured, "I am on my way home to Mother."

"The doctor told me you cannot live. Have you any message to send to your mother?"

"Tell my mother—that—I died trusting in Christ."

Moody's heart leaped—"It seemed as if I was at the very gate of Heaven." He asked the boy: "Is there anything else?"

The boy's eyes closed. "Yes, tell my mother and sisters—to be sure and meet me—in heaven."

It was the authentic voice of the old American frontier, deep in simple piety and love of home, speaking to the man who, unknown to himself, was being bred to proclaim the old, sure foundations to the garish age being born.

Emma Revell, who had fallen in love with a prosperous shoe salesman, become engaged to a children's missioner, and was now about to marry a six-horse Jehu, wondered where it would end.

They were married in Chicago on Thursday, August 28, 1862, and went "away on my weding tower," as Moody described it.

In June he had been back to Northfield where his heart so often strayed. "I am homesick" had been a constant theme; "Tell Mother she does not know how good a letter would seem if it was penned with her own hand . . . As she never was away from her mother she cannot tell how good it seems to get a letter from a mother."

He was always generous to the family, beyond his means, and concerned for their affairs. He yearned to "see my mother and all my brothers and sisters converted to God." The "very pleasant time" in Northfield, supposed to be a holiday, he transformed into a mission that created enough stir for some twenty-five townsfolk to come and see him off at the station. Two of his brothers started a prayer meeting, but Betsey's prejudice deepened because Dwight was about to marry a girl who was English-born and a Baptist.

They settled in a tiny house on the North Side (Chicago divided itself into the then fashionable South Side, south of the Chicago River, and the slummy North Side) where Emma continued at short range the long slow task of taming Moody, to make him the man she saw he could be. She was "before everything else practical and orderly." She threw away those patent shirts he was so proud of that did not, he claimed, need washing for weeks on end. She failed, for the time, to make him eat regular or ample meals. She remained unflustered by the cascade of improbable events.

Her achievement may be gauged by the change she wrought, so gently and imperceptibly that he could say at the end of his life, "She was the only one who never tried to hold me back from anything I wanted to do and was always in sympathy with every new venture."

Samuel Moody, the ailing lovable twin with political and intellectual interests, who merely smiled when Moody talked of religion, had come to stay in the autumn of 1862, with a view to finding work in Chicago. "Dwight is run from morning to night," he wrote:

> He hardly gets time to eat. Camp Douglas is situated here (there is about 17,000), he holds meetings down there most every night—it is a treat to go down there and hear the soldiers sing, which is about 300 or 400 gathered as they come from most every state. The Rebel prisoners are among them.

These were Fort Donelson men. Moody was quite hurt when they refused to sing out of hymnbooks decorated with stars and stripes. And Farwell had "never seen him so excited" as at the discovery of the famous conspiracy to break out and burn Chicago.

Emma said that Moody went to the front nine times. He was under fire in January 1863 and among the wounded at the bloody battle of Murfreesboro, or Stone River, as Rosecrans pushed for Nashville. He watched the dying find peace as he ministered, until the certainty drilled into his consciousness that a man may know immediate, assured salvation. Moody was reaping a well-sown field, for few of the generation that fought the Civil War lacked background of basic Christian teaching—not that he was under illusions about the "evil ways" of men calloused by battle and barrack.

"Chaplain, help me to die," whispered a casualty of Murfreesboro, in the small hours. "I've been fighting Christ all of my life. I had a praying mother and I disregarded her prayers always."

Moody, Bible in hand, repeated promise after Scripture promise, "but he could not see them, and I got nearly discouraged." Moody started to read the story of Nicodemus from John's gospel. "As I read on, his eyes became rivetted upon me, and he seemed to drink in every syllable."

The comforting Yankee accents cut into the thick atmosphere of the ward. "'And as Moses lifted up the serpent in the wilderness, even so must the Son of man be lifted up: that whosoever believeth in Him should not perish, but have eternal life.'"

The soldier feebly put up a hand. "*What's* that? Is that true? I want you just to read that again . . . That's good! Won't you read it *again?*"

As Moody read the third time, the dim candlelight showed that the man's "troubled expression had given way to a peaceful smile." The orderly next morning, standing by the empty cot, said the man had died restfully, murmuring the words of promise.

Moody, a quick learner where his heart was engaged, was seen to move and speak in the wards "as though the special study of his life had been the wants of sick men." Nor was it thus in hospitals only, or distributing magazines and games among convalescents. The diffident amateur of 1861 had become, by the fourth year of the war, a practiced if homespun preacher.

"I was bringing together my Fourth Army Corps," wrote Major General Oliver Otis Howard of those spring days of 1864 in

Tennessee when Sherman mobilized for the Atlanta campaign and the March to the Sea.

> Two divisions had already arrived and were encamped in and near Cleveland. Our soldiers were just about to set out on what we all felt promised to be a hard and bloody campaign, and I think we were especially desirous of strong preaching. Crowds and crowds turned out to hear Moody. He showed them how a soldier could give his heart to God. His preaching was direct and effective, and multitudes responded with a promise to follow Christ.

An infantryman of the 96th Illinois described his experience:

> [I] went to the meetings one night and was much impressed with his earnestness. I wasn't at the time a Christian, though the thought had come to me that it would be well to begin the Atlanta campaign a soldier of Christ as well as a soldier of my country. The next morning, or soon after, I went to my dog tent, opened a little copy of the New Testament, which some men of the Christian Commission had given to me, and then and there began to read and pray my way into the kingdom of Christ. The joy of salvation came to me after a few days. I have always looked on Mr. Moody as my spiritual father.

Moody did not march through Georgia, nor see Corse's men hold the fort at Altoona, although that event was to inspire the most famous of the "Moody and Sankey" songs.

Great matters were stirring in Chicago.

7

The Rescue Shop

In autumn of 1862 the North Market Hall had been partly burned, in spite of the fire engines below. For about a year Moody transferred his Sunday school to the more dilapidated Kinzie Hall. Numbers dropped. The school had to be nursed back to strength.

Moody never ceased to conjure up new tricks to win recruits. He picked a dozen or fifteen of the raggedest boys he could find— their names eloquent of their condition: Smikes, Madden the Butcher, Darby the Cobbler, Jackey Candles, Black Stove Pipe— and promised a new suit to each one who attended every Sunday until Christmas. He formed them into a class under Farwell. All but two of them won their suits, and Farwell called this uniformed set "Moody's Bodyguard." Moody had the group photographed before and after the issue of suits and circulated the pictures, the first captioned, "Does It Pay?" and the second, "It Does Pay." In at least one case it did pay: thirteen years later a colleague of Moody was told by a railway office manager to go and "pick out the worst-looking one in the lot, and you will see your humble servant, now a church member and a Sunday school worker."

But Moody began to doubt bribery: his City Relief Society was fooled too often. "I came to the conclusion that a loaf of bread in one hand and the Gospel in the other was wrong." Succor of the sick and destitute continued to absorb much of his time as a Christian ministry in itself; Moody had no patience with those who preached bliss in heaven while doing nought about misery on earth.

His Sunday school's famous picnics were more an outflow of his own exuberance than a deliberate attraction. He "loved contests and games of skill," his sons used to say; Farwell went only once, because he claimed that the "physical exercise to keep up with Mr. Moody in a race was too much for me."

"Few at the picnics were his equal in racing, jumping or other sports," another helper remembered, and Moody liked to show it. He seized a heavy barrel of apples and ran ahead of the horde, tipping out a trail of apples which the smaller boys picked up while the older chased him to try for the lot; he kept ahead until a naughty bystander tripped him.

To play a practical joke on Moody was to pay him his own coin. The teachers once wanted a swim in the lake, nicely secluded, but reached only by wading through a bog. A young dandy shirked the mud.

> Finally, Mr. Moody, with a mischievous twinkle, said, "Mr. C., you get on my back and I will carry you across." All went well until the middle of the swamp, when Mr. C., with white vest and lavender pants, was unhorsed and had to help himself to terra firma.

A joke with a streak of cruelty was sport to Moody right to the end of his life. As Paul Moody wrote: "While the tenderest-hearted man in the world, he would enjoy laughing at something the victim did not consider so excruciatingly funny." And when young Paul (at a time when Moody must have been in his late fifties) had a fracas with infuriated bees, "worse than the stings of the bees was the sight of my father actually rolling on the ground with laughter, but at a safe distance." There was a grain of truth in the family proverb "No Moody ever laughs at anything unless blood is drawn."

On December 26, 1863, Emma wrote to Sam:

> The building for the Sunday School is almost completed, the plastering is being done now, and we hope to get in the building in a few weeks. We need it badly for the hall gets worse every Sunday. We expect to have good meetings when it is finished as several prominent

clergymen from different cities have promised to come and preach for us.

This new building, the first to be owned by the Mission School, was erected on Illinois Street, between La Salle and Wells, two blocks from Kinzie, at a cost of $24,000, subscribed by Farwell and many others, with pittances from parents and scholars. It was opened in the early months of 1864, "a queer-looking brick building," with some resemblance to a church. "Houses crowd it in on either side so as to scarcely leave room for it to stand upon. It looks almost as if pains had been taken to make it as plain as possible so that no one, however poor, might be driven away by any outward display."

On the right of the entrance stood a gilt sign: EVER WELCOME TO THIS HOUSE OF GOD ARE STRANGERS AND THE POOR, and a notice: THE SEATS ARE FREE. The interior was decked with texts "neatly done in scroll and panel," and the wall behind the platform proclaimed "God is Love." On entering,

> you faced the classes, which were chairs in a circle, the teacher's chair being designated by a silken banner bearing the number of the class and also a Scripture verse. These banners were in different colors, their poles being fastened to the chair-back so they would stand upright. With the sun shining in the room, these banners of many bright colors and the rosy, happy faces of the children surrounding them, made a most beautiful picture.

It is doubtful that the slum children's faces were rosy.

Flanking the doorway, two Bible classrooms—one for each sex— had glass partitions that could be thrown back to enlarge the hall. Above, another glass partition made an area for an infants' class or for a reception room where guests could watch proceedings below while the superintendent (as Moody was in name now, as in fact) extolled his system and pointed out his teachers. He had a small library upstairs, too, where he could interview.

On either side ran a gallery. Charley Morton, a discharged soldier in his twenties, who had lost his right arm at Williamsburg and drank heavily to deaden the pain, was idling with two or three pals one Sunday afternoon when they happened to pass the building. "People seemed to be going in, men, women and children, as though they belonged there, and we turned in, too, to

see what it was." The usher said, "The gallery for young men."
They found themselves under an assistant whose

> hair was very long, his trousers very short, and he was nervous. He
> talked very loud in teaching the lesson, and I saw very soon that he
> didn't know very much about the lesson himself. The boys wanted to
> leave, but I said, "Let's see this out."

Charley Morton never forgot the impact of the whole school
singing "Do You Know Any Little Barefoot Boy?" and its doggerel
chorus, which evoked the very atmosphere of Moody's mission:

> Go bring him in, there is room to spare,
> Here are food and shelter and pity;
> And we'll not shut the door
> 'Gainst one of Christ's poor
> Though you bring every child in the city.

Morton looked down as they sang,

> and I noticed most of the boys and girls were poor-looking, some
> barefoot, and most of the teachers seemed to be well dressed and
> altogether different from the scholars, and I said to myself, "Well,
> there isn't much looking after money here. They won't get much pay
> for looking after those boys and girls," and I made up my mind I
> would come again, and I did. And it was not long after before I put my
> hand in Jesus Christ's hand, where it has been ever since.

Farwell once asked a small boy why he walked three miles every
week to Illinois Street, when there was a school near his home. He
replied: "They love a fellow over here."

When Moody went South in the spring of 1864, before Sherman's Atlanta campaign, his mission in Chicago not only had a new
home but was developing alarming possibilities.

During the North Market Hall days, adults had attended
weekday evening meetings at the old saloon, and there, in Emma's
words, "many souls were born of God." Moody exhorted converts to
join city churches, but "some of the poorer ones felt strangely in the
more beautiful church buildings." When the mission secured a
permanent home and held meetings every night, they wanted to
make that their church. The "gathering" of a new church was

neither unusual nor difficult under Congregational custom.

Moody hesitated. His mission was not Congregationalist but united, its one formal link being to the YMCA. Constantly he would say: "If I thought I had one drop of sectarian blood in my constitution, I would open a vein and let it out."

The converts pressed. For them it must be Illinois Street, or they would be sheep scattered and unfed.

Moody yielded. It would seem that Sunday evening services were held that summer. At the end of 1864, on December 20, "a meeting of the most interested in the movement was held." So runs the official *Manual of Illinois Street Church*, printed in 1867,

> and the opinion was unanimous that a church should be formed. All were agreed that it must be independent of all denominational connection, since those already gathered in the work represented nearly every evangelical denomination. It was therefore voted that the church be an Independent Church.

A half-hearted scheme to entrust the oversight of the church to some Council of Chicago Churches came to nought. Moody and two friends drew up a simple doctrinal statement and articles of organization based on Congregationalist custom. At Emma's behest, a baptistry as well as a font allowed both adult and infant baptism.

Moody invited students from the Chicago Theological Seminary (Congregational) to fill the pulpit until, as Farwell remembered, "one of them failed to appear, when I suggested that it was providential, and that he must take the pulpit himself. He finally consented, and from that time he was wanted every Sunday." Thereafter, students preached in the mornings, and Moody in the evenings. He found delivering a formal sermon alarmingly different from talking extemporaneously to troops or children.

"It was hard work for him to preach in those early days," a Chicago minister remembered. "One day I found him in his room trying to get up a sermon. He had thrown off his coat and was struggling with his Bible and a concordance, while the sweat ran down his face." (This may have been back in July 1864, when Moody himself wrote, "I have gained 20 lbs. since last summer—I am so fat that I have to sweat a good deal for it this hot weather.")

The seminary desired to regularize the ecclesiastical position by having Moody ordained at once as a Congregationalist minister, bad grammar and all. He could then administer the sacraments himself.

"What do you think about my being ordained?" he asked his ministerial friend G. S. F. Savage.

"Don't," replied Savage. "If you are ordained you will be on the level with the rest of us. Now you are a preaching layman, and that gives you an advantage. You are on the right road, keep to it."

Moody declined the Congregationalists' offer. In 1865 he enrolled as a student in the newly formed Baptist Theological Seminary. How many lectures he attended is obscure; he did not proceed, so he was never ordained. Had he become a minister of one denomination, he would not, in that generation, have attracted the broad support from ministers of other denominations, wherein lay much of his secret. As Farwell commented, "He had more power as a layman, and as such he was more welcome in union meetings, which were his ambition and delight." Certainly neither the Church of Scotland nor the Church of England would have cooperated. He would not have become a national influence in Britain or in America, but remained unknown to history.

He remained as lay pastor until 1866, when a young man was ordained to the pastorate, and Moody retained the title of superintendent—and effective control.

The making of the Illinois Street Independent Church symbolized that Moody's mission no longer was a Sunday school with extensions, but an all-age rescue shop within a yard of hell. Ecclesiastically, however, it could have formed the basis of the new denomination which Moody in years to come was urged to found, and refused, or it might have sidetracked him into a "No Church" movement like the Plymouth Brethren. It did neither. Instead, it was a useful proving ground for methods later to be used among the tens of thousands drawn to meetings in London, Philadelphia, and New York, which to Moody were Illinois Street writ large.

There is no evidence that Moody ever sported a clergyman's white neckerchief, but he worked himself somewhat into the image—his sermons clerical, his tone strident, and his theme smacking of brimstone to an extent that made even Emma admit that she "cringed" as he painted terrors of divine judgment. While a children's missionary, Moody had not been face to face with degradation in those he sought to save; it formed their background only. As a missionary to all ages, he was inescapably confronted with human nature at its worst, and he reacted in the manner traditional for mission preachers of his day. "[Moody] preached that God hated sinners; that he was standing behind sinners with a double-edged sword, ready to cut off the heads of sinners."

A dichotomy appeared in D. L. Moody. From the pulpit he stressed stridently the wrath of God, in the tradition of the old camp meetings. In personality he remained genial and buoyant, bubbling with love and merriment. Watts de Golyer, a deacon at Illinois Street, said that, in the Moody home,

> it was not an infrequent occurrence to hear peals of laughter over some joke administered mainly by the host, or somebody trying to get even with him. I well remember a rule adopted and passed by himself that hereafter any person failing to hang up his hat or coat on the rack would find it in the yard, and the result was, shortly afterwards that I was busily employed finding and separating my belongings in the yard. I would not have you think that the sole and only topic discussed or thought of in the minds of those composing it was that of religion, but it was as much the absorbing theme and desire, as to temper and sweeten everything else.

Meanwhile, on October 24, 1864, Moody's first child had been born, and named Emma Reynolds. "Both of her little fingers are as crooked as mine," he told his mother in December. "They all say she looks like me, but I must say I cannot see any resemblance." Emma could. The resemblance grew. When the child was two, they said, "She is so full of mischief. You would certainly think she was a second edition of D. L. Moody in his childhood."

Before the baby was six months old, Emma left her temporarily in the care of Mrs. Revell and accompanied Moody to Grant's army for the climax of the Civil War. They were at the great base of City Point near Hampton as casualties flowed from the last battles in Virginia. Moody claimed to be among the first to enter fallen Richmond, ministering to the freed slaves, the wounded of both sides, and the Federals liberated from the horrors of Libby Prison.

8

"Brutally Ridiculed"

Discharged soldiers streamed into Chicago. The city leaped to seize fortunes out of Reconstruction. Moody flung himself more deeply into the work of the YMCA, long one of the apples of his eye.

At the noon meeting he was a familiar figure except for his whiskers, which he had altered three or four times, as if to ape the latest war hero, until he settled on a smart, short, rounded beard, lengthened in the early seventies to the dark wavy forest that Great Britain came to know. "A stocky, bustling Simon Peter sort of man standing at the door and shaking hands with all who entered," a student described him. A country boy attending commercial school said,

> [I was] miserable, lonesome and homesick in the great city amid its great throngs who passed me by in restless haste and left me alone. Even in my boardinghouse no attention was paid to me. In my desperate loneliness I dropped into the noonday meetings. I can never forget that Mr. Moody was first to grasp my hand and inquire all about me.

They sang. They had brief Scripture reading. They prayed extemporaneously, "no long speeches or prayers tolerated"—a breath of fresh air which Moody was to blow upon wider fields of American and British religion. Requests poured in from city and countryside to be read out by Jacobs, Moody, Major Whittle, or whoever was leader for the day. At an affecting plea from some mother whose son had succumbed to city temptations, Moody would weep unashamedly; in him lay always something of the impressionable child—never far from tears, never far from laughter.

> Mr. D. L. Moody is so earnest, aggressive and regardless of all namby-pamby notions of propriety in his work that he occasionally shocks the exceedingly proper people. At other times he is known to betray them into a laugh, a veritable guffaw right in prayer meeting.

Moody and his friends of the YMCA were not pietists; they sent the state legislature a petition for the establishment of a Board of Health, and they set up a committee to investigate flouting of Sunday liquor laws. But the introduction of so much as a chess set had to await the next decade. Activities were centered on bringing their constituency to face the issues of heaven and hell, belief and unbelief. And to urge action. "I want a faith's got legs 'n' c'n run around," Moody would say. The Chicago YMCA published and distributed tracts and a four-page paper, administered charity, and helped in a cholera epidemic; Moody risked his life again and again. And he ran an informal bureau to trace prodigal sons lurking in the Chicago underworld.

In 1866 the presidency of the Chicago Association was offered to a prominent businessman, who was an energetic and able supporter. He refused: "We have been talking about a building," he said. "We need a man who has the time, the holy purpose, and the faith in God to make this project a success. I nominate Dwight L. Moody for President and John V. Farwell for Vice-President."

Some members said, "Many of our church people count Moody as too radical." But, at twenty-nine, he became president. Without delay, "Moody was on the warpath securing subscriptions"—thus they described the energy with which Moody badgered the worthy and wealthy of the city; he reveled in turning the dollars of the rich into an institution that should, in a favorite phrase, "do good." Each subscriber was to receive stock and be repaid over ten years, it was hoped, from rents received by the YMCA for offices to be rented in this magnificent new building. Subsequent profits were to go to city charities. Cyrus Hall McCormick, a Presbyterian, inventor of the combine harvester, which revolutionized prairie farming and brought him great fortune, promised no less than $10,000, and within a month the full sum of $199,000 had been pledged.

Farwell, McCormick, and George Armour, the meat king, were among the trustees. McCormick regarded 1866 as the year when he "became sure of Mr. Moody's great worth." The Moodys were invited frequently to the millionaire's mansion. A contemporary describes "points of similarity in the characters of these two men. Both had great earnestness and great sincerity, and both hewed out their career by hard strokes . . . Both of them were bright and cheery."

Once in the late sixties (the year is uncertain) Moody rushed into the study of a Chicago minister named Harsha, with a sealed envelope. "Open that!" he cried. "Open it! There is a check for two thousand dollars in there."

"How do you know? Have you seen it?"

"No. But I asked the Lord for it, and I know it's there! I came all the way across Chicago that you might prove my faith in prayer."

Young W. T. Harsha "stood by [his] father's side as he tore open the envelope. Truly enough, there was a two thousand dollar check within, payable to the order of Mr. Moody and signed by Cyrus H. McCormick."

Moody bubbled out his story. He had gone to the millionaire: "Mr. McCormick, the mission school is in dreadful straits!"

"Why, you are striking me rather hard of late. I gave you something not long ago."

"I want a thousand."

"A thousand! Why, surely you don't mean that, after all I've given you of late?" But he went upstairs to write the check. "And then," continued Moody,

> I thought to myself, what a fool I was not to ask for two thousand! And I fell on my knees there in the parlor, and asked for two thousand. Mr. McCormick came downstairs with this sealed envelope. I thanked him, and rushed over to you. Isn't my faith confirmed?

Old Mr. Harsha was so bemused that he asked McCormick, "Can you recall the inducements or influences acting on your mind leading you to make the check for twice the amount asked for?"

> Well, as I remember, I went upstairs to my desk and took out my checkbook. I wrote in "D. L. Moody," and then I began to think of the

noble work he is doing in our city, and what a splendid fellow he is. Finally I concluded to make the check for the amount I did.

Long afterwards at Northfield the younger Harsha asked Moody about the incident. Moody replied,

> God gave me the money that day because I needed it. And He has always given me money when I needed it. But often I have asked Him when I thought I needed it, and He has said: "No, Moody, you just shin along the best way you can. It'll do you good to be hard up awhile."

Whatever McCormick thought of him, Chicago's wartime respect for Moody had dissolved. "He was often most brutally ridiculed and buffeted and persecuted," recalled de Golyer. "His language, his looks, his methods of work were made objects of ridicule and burlesque, and the most cruel remarks were passed from mouth to mouth about him."

Frederick Francis Cook, then a journalist with the *Chicago Tribune*, deploring Moody's "early excrescences of manner," wrote:

> The established pulpit, especially in its higher or formal ranges, contended that he lowered religion. While the man about town judged him from the standpoint of ordinary social intercourse, and resented his intrusions . . . Aye, what a hustler he was in early days! . . . Always on the go, except when he might halt a stranger anywhere to interrogate him on the state of his soul; and even when his amazed or abashed victim was gathering his wits to frame an answer suited to the astonishing occasion, off he would be to startle somebody else into "fits of salvation."

"'Are you a Christian?' became an arrow point directed to every man, woman or child in Chicago," wrote Farwell's daughter Abby, then just out of the schoolroom and, like her father, Moody's devoted slave. "He shouted it from the platform, he whispered it in the narrow passageway, seated at your side at the dinner table, as he joined you on the sidewalk, in fact, everywhere."

He kept a vow in those years not to pass a day without speaking to someone about Christ. "Seeing a man leaning up against a lamppost, I went up to him and said, 'Are you a Christian?' He damned me and cursed me and told me to mind my own business." The man later told a mutual friend that he had never been so insulted.

Three months later, sometime after midnight, Moody heard a knock on his door, "and there stood this stranger I had made so mad at the lamppost," to confess that he had known no peace since their encounter. "Oh, tell me what to do to be saved," he implored.

Moody would not be intimidated. A Presbyterian called Potwin happened to walk north up Wells Street "just behind a big powerful fellow, when Mr. Moody, coming from the north, stopped him with the question 'Are you a Christian?' The stranger was enraged, drew back, and would have hit him a powerful blow had I not caught his arm." The *Tribune* shorthand clerks were interrupted (Moody had come to insert a YMCA notice) with the abrupt question "Is Christ among you?" In the startled silence a middle-aged Scot slowly removed his pipe and answered. "Na, Maister Moody. He was here a bit ago, but he's stepped oot to see a friend round the corner. He'll be sorry to miss ye. Will ye wait?"

Moody never laughed on such occasions. Nor would he betray that he was sensitive to mockery: "The most banal sallies left him wholly unscathed." William Reynolds remarked to Whittle some years later "how he used to be alone with Moody and often Moody would cry at the abuse heaped upon him by those who misunderstood and opposed him," but he had "made up [his] mind to keep sweet . . . You cannot do any good unless you keep sweet."

Farwell was urged, even by his wife, "Why don't you tell him he does more harm than good by shouting at people at every turn?" When Farwell did so, Moody replied, "You are not my boss. God is my boss."

Moody was heckled in the stockyards, and ridiculed and subjected to catcalls outside the courthouse. At the back of the crowd, a young doctor, impressed by the preacher's "dauntless manner," asked who he was. A bystander "glanced at the speaker with a contemptuous smile and then said, 'Why, that's Moody!'"

Moody drove his frame to its limits. "I wish you would learn to eat your meals regularly," Mrs. Farwell would scold. "You will undermine your health." Emma must have said the same. He would not listen—then. Afterwards he admitted, "I was an older man before thirty than I have been since." In his frenzy to carry the city for Christ, he was redeemed by humility—a willingness to listen, to learn, and to experiment; by basic common sense, although not always obeying its dictates; and by Emma. But Moody was wrapped in the one ambition "that every soul be saved." He did not mind much what happened further, except that the saved be put to save others. "I lived in Chicago knowing but *one* truth and thinking it the only necessary one, ignoring all related truths till I built up a wall of prejudice all around me."

It would have been hard to imagine that Crazy Moody in a few years would hold the respect of Gladstone and President Grant, the affection of the Lord Chancellor of England, the gratitude of the Princess of Wales, and the attention of millions of all sorts and conditions in Britain and the United States.

9

The Little
Lancashire Lad

Had it not been for Emma's asthma, Moody would have been a proof of Shakespeare's dictum "Violent fires soon burn out themselves . . . He tires betimes that spurs too fast betimes."

In occasional pauses on his breakneck gallop, Moody had brooded on visiting England. Conscious of spiritual and mental lack, he knew that in Chicago he never could detach himself from ceaseless scramble. There were three in England he yearned to meet: George Williams, the London wholesale draper who founded the YMCA; George Muller of Bristol, the elderly German who prayed and—without capital, or asking a soul for a penny—maintained a large orphanage and numerous overseas missionaries (and lived to be ninety-three); Charles Haddon Spurgeon, Moody's senior by three years only, yet a preacher of fame and like himself a rustic, virtually self-taught, jovial, and rather stout. Echoes of Spurgeon's sermons at the Metropolitan Tabernacle, his Baptist church in South London, fluttered all over the world; their homely language, fund of anecdote, humor, and grasp of Scripture made Moody greedy: "Everything that I could get hold of in print that he ever said, I read."

Nothing would have come of Moody's hankerings for England, had not asthma so pained Emma during the early winter of

1866-1867 that the doctor advised a sea voyage. Somehow Moody found the money. Mrs. Revell promised to keep little Emma. On February 24, 1867, D. L. Moody, just thirty, and his twenty-four-year-old wife steamed out of New York on the *City of Washington,* "which is considered a very fine boat."

Emma loved the trip, but, as she wrote to her brother-in-law, "Mr. Moody was sick more or less from the time we started till the time we landed at Liverpool, which was two weeks." She was the sole lady among sixteen cabin-class passengers and had "plenty of attention," even if "rather a gay crowd" had "no scruples about drinking champagne and wine and playing cards and even gambling for money, at which I was much surprised and shocked."

On reaching England, the woebegone Moody, affirming "one trip across the water is enough for me," perpetrated one of the most exploded prophecies of the nineteenth century: "I do not expect to visit this country again."

They landed on a Sunday. Moody sermon-tasted. Emma contented herself with a Sunday school, "which [she] thought rather a dull formal one and the room was very gloomy and dark." The next day they speeded from Liverpool to London by rail, "much faster than in America, at the rate of from 40 to 50 miles an hour, and the cars do not stop to get water but scoop it up from a sort of ditch as they rush by without stopping."

From Euston they took a "growler" (four-wheeled cab) "a very long distance" through the city and the East End slums—where they saw barefoot boys in streets more grim than Chicago—to Poplar. Emma's uncle was postmaster and lived at No. 3 Pennyfields, near the West India dock, and here Emma and her younger sister Mary met, after eighteen years.

The Moodys' first English surroundings were scarcely choice, and it rained or snowed most of that week. Early impressions made them both sniff and forget that Emma was a Londoner. Moody wrote to his mother, "I do not like the old country as well as our one, I must tell you how glad I am I was born and brought up in America." He missed the informality, thought England must be a "horrible place to live in." Emma considered the city as sooty as Pittsburgh, the Bank of England timeworn. Of St. Paul's Cathedral, she said, "A very grand building but seemed to me more appropriate for any other kind of performance than for church service."

The next Sunday they went to the Metropolitan Tabernacle.

They had no tickets but bluffed their way up to the gallery. Moody marveled at the congregation of nearly five thousand, and as Spurgeon "walked down to the platform, my eyes just feasted upon him, and my heart's desire for years was at last accomplished."

"His manner is very simple," Emma said, describing the sermon, "and he is a very plain-looking man but had the undivided attention of his whole audience . . . And then the singing . . . So many voices mingled together in such harmony and good time seemed perfectly grand." Moody longed to preach like that, and to see singing led like that.

Moody duly visited Bristol to imbibe a heady draught of Müller's faith. In London he met George Williams and was invited to the annual breakfast of the original YMCA on Aldersgate Street; he prodded the participants into beginning a daily noon prayer meeting on the Chicago pattern, which was maintained unbroken until the First World War.

Through Frederick Hartley, Secretary of the Sunday School Union, who had visited Illinois Street, the Moodys received several social invitations. They were taken to a House of Commons debate by an M.P.: Emma saw Newgate Prison and the Bank. London seemed prettier in the spring, "in some parts most beautiful— especially the parks and square gardens."

By early May, Emma "liked the English better than when I first came. I do not think them as reserved as I expected them, but do not think them as free and open as Americans." Moody enjoyed the sensation of being appreciated. Episcopalians in Chicago had passed by on the other side of the street, or had called him names, but Church of England clergy and laymen whom he met were kind. Evangelicals, Anglican and nonconformist, took to him. His expansive geniality, his sincerity and drive caused a religious newspaper to remark how with an unknown name he had swiftly won his way "deeply into the affections of a multitude of Christian brethren."

The month of May, in the Victorian age, was sacred to "May meetings," that sober succession of anniversaries for every mission and charity. Moody wanted, American-tourist style, to "do" as many as possible, and even hurried Emma across to Dublin and north to Edinburgh, where—on this first brief visit to the city that would, surprisingly, become so familiar—she thought the street stairs and old stone houses "quaint." In London he addressed the

May meeting of the Sunday School Union, at that Mecca of evangelicals, Exeter Hall in the Strand. He was allotted the moving of thanks to the chairman, the great philanthropist Lord Shaftesbury. At the appropriate moment, the vice-chairman announced: "We are very glad to welcome our American cousin, the Reverend Mr. Moody of Chicago."

Moody rose. He looked at the serried ranks of the godly, the ladies' bonnets and crinolines, and the whiskers and formal black of the men; all sleepy and surfeited with speeches on a warm May afternoon and thinking an American a sort of colonial who was not quite English and had a vulgar accent.

Moody said: "The vice-chairman has made two mistakes." The audience sat up.

> To begin with, I'm not "the Reverend Mr. Moody" at all. I'm plain Dwight L. Moody, a Sabbath school worker. And then I'm not your American cousin. By the grace of God I'm your brother, who is interested, with you, in our Father's work for His children. And now about this vote of thanks to the "noble Earl." I don't see why we should thank him any more than he should thank us.

The audience gasped. Lord Shaftesbury, who had great sense of humor and no pomposity, was delighted. Emma made a mental note to scold Moody—it is certain that five years later he never would have committed such a solecism.

The stuffy atmosphere had been too much. And he had cleared it. A young customs clerk, Tom Bond Bishop, soon to help found the Children's Special Service Mission, "heard Mr. Moody for the first time . . . [he would] remember how it thrilled the audience," as he urged them to have done with colorless catechisms and tedious verse-learning, and to act on the belief that children could trust in Christ as a Friend.

Both Moodys had strange experiences in Britain. Emma, traveling alone by train, entered what she supposed was an empty compartment in which someone had left a bundle of old clothes. The train started. Out of the bundle a man's voice said, "Do you know what I would have done with my wives if I had been Henry the Eighth?" He slid across to her side, leering. No trains had corridors in the 1860s. The next stop lay twenty minutes on.

Emma, unrattled always, merely said, "No, do tell me." The maniac recited blood-curdling details, with strong hints that he intended to test his theories on her. When he paused to enjoy the effect of his words, she briskly said she knew better ways of execution, and each time he suggested a horror she capped it, keeping him still and absorbed until the train stopped and she escaped.

Moody's experience was less macabre. Henry Varley, a wholesale butcher in West London, who was about Moody's age, had become an evangelist and a Plymouth Brother, preaching at a mission hall with such force that his assembly numbered several hundred. Recalled Moody,

> I visited that man to find the secret of his success. At home he prayed for the meeting. After supper we took a [carriage], and as we were rattling along the rough stone streets of London he said, "Now, brother, let us have prayer for that meeting."

He knelt on the swaying floor of the carriage, among the wisps of straw. Moody had never tried praying aloud on the floor of a carriage: "Rattling through the streets wasn't exactly a comfortable place in which to pray." After the service he watched (or so he embroidered the tale in America afterwards) "seventy butchers with tears streaming down their faces gathered round that man of God," and knew that prayer was Varley's secret.

Through Varley he was invited to speak at other Brethren halls. And it was in Dublin, at the close of a service, that he heard a voice at the level of his shoulder: "Ah'm 'Arry Moorhouse. Ah'll coom and preach for you in Chicago."

Moody turned and saw an insignificant, beardless little man. "He had a boyish appearance, did not seem to be more than seventeen years old." Quite unaware that this was one of the significant confrontations of his life, Moody hid his disdain under a kind smile. "Ah'm 'Arry Moorhouse," the fellow repeated. "Ah'll preach for you in America. When d'you go 'ome?" Moody told him he didn't know and told himself he would not have revealed it if he had known.

He had heard of Harry Moorhouse, a Lancashire lad, out of the gutter, a converted pickpocket, the Boy Preacher. Moody did not believe such a stripling could preach. Moody soon forgot him.

After spending ten days in France in June to see the Exposition (and start a little daily prayer meeting at La Salle Evangelique), the Moodys returned to England for a farewell dinner. Emma's asthma had left her. They were now pining for America and little Emma. Moody said he had to jump "to keep from getting homesick, and whistle to keep up his courage." The fortnight's seasickness on a gentle summer ocean was not a high price to pay.

Back in Chicago the first excitement was the gift house. "Mr. Farwell is building me a house to live in," Moody had written from London to his brother George. "It is about three blocks from where I used to live. I don't know if it will be brick or stone—I have not heard." Farwell, developing land as an investment, had decided to put the Moodys into one of the houses rent-free, inviting mutual friends to help him furnish it. When the travelers returned they were taken to this pleasant home on State Street; and in a prominent place hung their two portraits, the one of Moody having been done without fee by the most famous American portrait painter of the day, G. P. A. Healy, a Roman Catholic Chicago resident.

The next excitement was the opening of the new YMCA hall on Madison Street, in the heart of the business center, testimony to the power of organization and fund-raising. It had been designed by a member, W. W. Boyington, architect of Crosby's Opera House, the Sherman and the Grand Pacific hotels, city churches, and the new waterworks. It could justly be claimed as the first building in the world to be erected by a YMCA, and the scale was magnificent: five stories high, a marble facade, the largest auditorium in Chicago on the first floor, five shops for lease at street level, a library, a reading room, lecture rooms, a gymnasium, a dormitory for forty-two, and—ironically, in view of its swiftly striking fate—the spare office space was rented by the fire, police, and health departments.

The YMCA intended to name it Moody Hall. At the grand dedication, on September 29, 1867, Moody carried by acclamation his motion that the place be called Farwell Hall—"The only mistake," said Farwell gallantly, "Mr. Moody ever made in connection with this enterprise."

The opening of Farwell Hall appeared to crown Moody's achievement in Chicago. He was a leading, if much abused citizen. A description in a religious newspaper of November 1867 shows that by now he appeared shorter than he actually was, and not, to Chicago at least, ill-educated:

Mr. Moody is rather below the medium height, and inclined to fleshiness, not corpulence. As he goes to the platform with a quick, nervous step that means business, you notice that he has a round, ruddy and good humored but earnest face but back of it a busy brain . . . When Moody speaks, everybody listens, even those who do not like him. His remarks are short, pithy and practical, and his exhortations impressive and sometimes touching even to tears. He is aggressive and his remarks always have a martial ring.

Unexpected irritant, came a letter from Harry Moorhouse that he had arrived in New York and would preach in Chicago if Moody wished. Moody wrote him a note: "If you come West, call on me," and "thought [he] should hear no more about him."

Harry Moorhouse, who was twenty-seven, had served time in jail before he was twenty-one, and afterwards stumbling on a back-street mission had heard an ex-prize fighter and coal miner preach on the Prodigal Son. Moorhouse was transformed, slowly: he had to wear thick gloves for a while to keep from picking pockets. He became a respectable auctioneer, married a childhood friend, and then moved to a tiny cottage on the outskirts of Manchester to give his whole time to preaching—preaching with a difference.

A whimsical, gentle, self-effacing creature, whose burning sense of mission was balanced by a strong sense of humor and an ability to prick any bubble of pretension or cant, he had Moody much in mind during the Atlantic crossing. His first reaction to New York was absurdly like that of the Moodys to London. He thought it a horrible place. "Everybody seems to think he is better than everybody else and it is hard to get a civil word from anybody." It was also most expensive: "Ten shillings for a coach to bring my luggage to the hotel, five minutes' journey; fifty cents, or two shillings, for hair-cutting . . . " Soon he was taken into the home of a rich Quaker, William Kimber, who wrote, "I spent many hours with him over Murray's grammar etc. that he might correct the grammatical errors which at first marred somewhat the public delivery of his wonderful gospel messages."

Moody knew nothing of that. He thought, by New Year, that he had heard the last of this peculiar character. He soon had something else to try him.

On January 7, 1868, shortly before midday, fire broke out in

Farwell Hall, still shining with new paint. No police, health, or fire department on the premises could save it in the city of strong winds. Members, bystanders, and firemen rescued furniture, all the records, and five hundred books. A young boarder, David Borrell, subsequently a famous preacher, had reached the doorway with his trunk on his shoulder, smoke filling the street, flames crackling, fire bells clanging, when he heard a voice, "Put it down." He saw Moody. "Borrell, throw it away and help me. We want to have a prayer meeting in the Methodist Church."

The noonday meeting took place. "Scores wept as though their own home burned," the minutes recorded. That afternoon secretary and committee "ran about among the merchants in the city for subscriptions: "Our hall is burning, sir. There is no hope. We shall want a new one. Let us have money enough to begin at once." Thousands of dollars were subscribed before the rubble cooled. Insurance had been incomplete; three months later McCormick had an appeal from Moody, "struggling to raise the balance of the funds necessary to rebuild our hall."

Some weeks after the fire, Moody, to his annoyance, heard again from Moorhouse that he was coming soon to Chicago and would like to preach.

Moody scribbled a note to him. "If you happen to come West, drop in on me," and thought that would settle him. Moorhouse's reply gave the date and time of arrival.

Reading it, Moody blew an impatient puff. Surely the man could not preach, and on that day Moody was supposed to be in St. Louis for the Missouri Christian Convention. He asked Emma to put Moorhouse up, told the deacons, "Try him—and if he fails I will take him off your hands when I come back," and boarded the train for St. Louis.

He had been in demand in the Northwest for conventions designed to draw together ministers and lay people of differing denominations or of opposing sympathies in the war. Men who had served on the Christian Commission and now sought to continue the amity bred in wartime knew Moody of Chicago as a man to stir sluggish saints, differences forgotten, into united assault on the unbelief, apostasy, and indifference fast gaining ground in a nation absorbed in material advance. In Missouri he was nominated as chairman and made a strong speech. "We can carry this state and hold it for Christ," he said, using a political simile in a presidential election year. "The power lies buried in the church, and the question is, how to get it developed."

It was easy for him to forget Moorhouse.

Seventeen-year-old Fleming Revell, boarding with his sister and brother-in-law, was the first to see him. Revell had expected

> some long-bearded, stately, dignified, man—I went to the door and saw a little stripling standing there, an insignificant-looking little Englishman, he was.
> He said, "I am 'Arry Moorhouse."
> "What, sir?"
> "I am 'Arry Moorhouse. This is Mr. Moody's 'ouse, isn't it?"
> We asked him in and the little fellow toddled in.

With much misgiving, that Thursday night they set him a trial run at a small meeting in the Illinois Street Church basement.

> We didn't quite know what to make of it. He talked differently from anybody we had ever heard. He seemed to have a different message from anything we had ever heard, and the deacons got their heads together just at the close of the meeting, and while the hymn was being sung, and agreed that we would announce that 'Arry Moorhouse, as he called himself, would speak the next night.

Returning on Saturday, Moody asked Emma about Moorhouse.

"They liked him very much," she replied. "He preaches a little different from you. He preaches that God *loves* sinners."

Moody puffed impatiently, having "concluded that if he preached different from me I would not like him. My prejudice was up."

"He is wrong," said Moody.

Emma said: "I think you will agree with him when you hear him, because he backs up everything he says with the Bible."

At Illinois Street on Sunday morning, Moody noticed that the members of his congregation were all carrying Bibles. He had never told them that persons in pews should bring Bibles. "It was something strange to see the people coming in with Bibles, and listen to the flutter of the leaves."

Moorhouse announced his text: "John 3:16: 'God so loved the world that he gave his only begotten son, that whosoever believeth in him should not perish but have everlasting life.'" Instead of dividing the text into firstly, secondly, and thirdly, in ministerial manner, Moorhouse, as Moody noted, "went from Genesis to Revelation giving proof that God loves the sinner, and before he got through, two or three of my sermons were spoiled." Moody's teaching, that God hates the sinner as well as the sin, lay shattered at his feet. "I never knew up to that time that God loved us so much. This heart of mine began to thaw out; I could not keep back the tears."

Fleming Revell remembered all his long life the sight of Moody drinking it in on that Sunday morning, February 8, 1868, and how "on Sunday night little Harry Moorhouse stood swaying from one foot to another in his seeming awkwardness but you forgot all about it as you heard the message coming from his lips." The text was the same, "God so loved the world . . . " unfolded once again from Genesis to Revelation, by a different route, his address not a sermon so much as a string of related texts or passages, briefly commented upon to form what came to be known, rather oddly, as a "Bible reading."

At the end, Moody jumped up. "Mr. Moorhouse will speak every night this week. Everybody come. Tell your friends to come."

Night after night, Moorhouse announced, "God so loved the world . . . " and drew his hearers by a fresh line through the Bible: "My friends, for a whole week I have been trying to tell you how much God loves you, but I cannot do it with this poor stammering tongue."

Outside, in the sharp February air, Chicago life rolled on unawares. Merchants wined and dined; the poor huddled half-frozen round smoking stoves; and sailors from iced-up ships lechered or boozed or brawled. At Illinois Street—amid that crowd of humble citizens, a few new immigrants, and a sprinkle of the rich—the spirit of love ran unfettered. And D. L. Moody turned in his path to become from that time forth an apostle of the love of God, his dichotomy resolved.

Day by day, too, in the State Street house—presided over by the Healy portrait—where Moorhouse had become a firm favorite, with his little ways and comic sayings and Lancashire accent, Moody was learning a lesson as compelling as the lesson of love. Moorhouse taught him how to read and study the Bible.

Moody had always looked on the Bible as textbook and weapon. He was unaware as yet, and for years to come, of critical problems and disputes that had scarcely penetrated even the theological world of Chicago. To him it was the Word of God. But he had regarded it as an armory of well-worn texts on which to peg talks and sermons, or to throw at individuals. He was curiously ignorant of much that the Bible taught. Moorhouse told him he didn't know his Bible, showed him how to treat it as entity and to trace the unfolding themes of Scripture, made him see that "it is God's Word, not our comment upon it, that saves souls," and warned him he should take time to receive more than he gave out. Moody began to rise before the household was astir (being a man who needed little sleep), light and trim the oil lamp in the study, and pore for an hour or more over his big Bible, scribbling notes in the margin.

Harry Moorhouse was of the Plymouth Brethren. Moody never denied their influence, and he eagerly bought their commentaries. His common sense kept him from selling out to theories or speculative allegories that marred their attempts to allow Scripture to interpret Scripture, and he had no truck with the separatist or fissiparous tendencies of some of them, "eating their gingerbread all by themselves in a corner," as he expressed it. In his relations with the Brethren, Moody showed his knack of drawing strength from a movement without becoming its slave.

Fleming Revell wrote: "D. L. Moody had great power before, but nothing like what he had after dear Harry Moorhouse came into our lives and changed the character of the teaching and preaching in the chapel." John Milton Hitchcock, who became one of Moody's closest assistants, first heard him soon after, in the summer of 1868. It was of then that he wrote: "The most impassioned, powerful, incisive, pathetic and effective appeals I ever knew him to make were before he had acquired a reputation beyond the shadow of his own chimney."

And Moody, addressing the Illinois State Sunday School Convention at Du Quoin that same summer said: "Be kind—conquer by love. If a man has his heart full of love and a little common sense, he will succeed."

10

Sankey on a Soapbox

The years 1870-1871 were decisive. They brought Sankey, put Moody on the right path of several he was attempting to travel at once, and gave him unlooked-for strength to fulfill his commission, bringing down the curtain on "Crazy Moody."

Moody had long been conscious of the power of song. He himself, as his later associate singer George Stebbins wrote, had "no more idea of tune or time than a child. He was one of those unfortunate people who have no sense of pitch or harmony, and hence are unable to recognize one tune from another or to sing in unison or harmony." That did not prevent him from making a noise like "one of the notes of the organ, sounding when it ought to be silent."

He could be powerfully impressed by a hymn. It is true, as his daughter-in-law discovered, that if he asked for "Rock of Ages" and she played "Yankee-Doodle" slowly with soulful chords, he would wipe tears from his eyes. But a sacred solo or the sweep of a congregation caught up in a chorus of praise could move him profoundly, not only by the impact of the words. He saw too that singing created a mood of worship and response, especially among the semi-illiterate poor, and whereas, like others cradled in Puritanism, he suspected oratorio and counted opera devilish, he wielded hymn singing as a weapon. "You sing over there!" he would cry. "Now you sing. Now you sing down there. And now everybody sing."

"Why do you want them to sing that way?" Robert Weidensall, a YMCA leader, once asked him.

Moody replied: "Weidensall, they will forget what I say, but if they learn 'Jesus, Lover of My Soul,' and will sing it to themselves, they will get it in their mouths at least, and they will get the Gospel along with it."

During the sixties, Moody was somewhat vaguely searching for a song leader. He worked occasionally with Philip Phillips, an older man, known as "the pilgrim singer," but Phillips did not live in Chicago. In the summer of 1869, Moody met Philip Paul Bliss, a Pennsylvanian of nearly his own age, who, according to their mutual friend, Major D. W. Whittle, "crystallized" Moody's senses "of the power of singing in Gospel work."

By all expectation, Bliss, already a fertile composer and versifier, as well as a spirited singer, should have been Moody's Sankey. He had been based in Chicago since 1865, traveling for a musical publisher to give concerts and teaching in northwestern cities, but he and Moody had not met. "To think," said Moody in 1869 in a hurt tone, "that such a singer as Bliss should have been around here for the last four years and we not known him." Bliss was a cheerful and lovable man, with beautiful manners and many "curious conceits so piquant and varied." And he could write hymns that children and the semi-illiterate picked up easily.

Bliss helped Moody on Sunday evenings when he was in Chicago. In May 1870, having heard Major Whittle describe the defense of Altoona during the Atlanta campaign, when Sherman signaled his famous message "Hold the fort: I am coming," Bliss wrote the words and music of the hymn that would sweep Britain and America. Then, in July he became choirmaster of First Congregational Church and was lost to Illinois Street.

That same July, Moody attended the YMCA International Convention (held in Canada and the United States in alternate years), at Indianapolis, Indiana.[1] There he met a twenty-nine-year-

[1] Moody intended at Indianapolis to change the whole character of the North American YMCA, having got into his head that it would be a good idea to merge YM and YW into one glorious and most un-Victorian Youth Association. The international chairman made short work of him. "Mr. Moody got thoroughly whipped by Mr. Brainerd, for Brainerd just wiped that away, and he did not take very much time to do it, because the boys were schooled on that question." (Robert Weidensall)

old delegate from Pennsylvania named Ira David Sankey.

Moody was announced to lead an early prayer meeting at seven. Sankey, a fastidious dresser, arrived late, every hair of his handsome mutton-chop whiskers in place, and sat near the door. A windy delegate was praying. Sankey's neighbor, a Presbyterian minister from his own county, whispered, "The singing here has been abominable. I wish you would start up something when that man stops praying, if he ever does."

When the wind ceased, Sankey began "There Is a Fountain Filled with Blood." The congregation joined in, and the meeting thereafter proceeded with pace.

The Presbyterian introduced Sankey to Moody. Moody, as his manner was, sized him up in a second.

"Where are you from? Are you married? What is your business?"

"New Castle, Pennsylvania. I am married, two children. In Government service, Revenue."

"You will have to give that up."

Sankey recorded: "I stood amazed, at a loss to understand why the man told me that I would have to give up a good position. 'What for?' I exclaimed."

"To come to Chicago to help me in my work."

To Sankey's protest that he could not abandon his business, Moody retorted: "You must. I have been looking for you for the last eight years."

Sankey obliged Moody by joining him briefly in the vestry to pray, "but as yet I had no thought of giving up my position." He was, however, aware that only a day or two earlier, the singing of another delegate had been

> a revelation to me of the marvelous power there was in a simple Gospel hymn when the singer put his whole heart and soul into it. I shall never forget how the great gathering was thrilled by the wonderful pathos of the singer's voice. It was an entirely different style of singing from that which I had so often heard in many churches where I attended. Every word could be distinctly heard in the remotest part of the building.

Under the influence of that hymn there had arisen "a great desire in my own heart that I might some day be able to use my voice in like manner." Sankey had not expected his desire to be fulfilled so quickly or so literally.

The next afternoon Sankey received a crisp note, commanding his attendance at a street corner. As factory crowds streamed homeward, Moody told Sankey to get on a soapbox, an undignified posture for a smart young man. Sankey smoothed his whiskers, straightened his bow tie, and somewhat gingerly mounted. He sang a martial solo. Moody watched as Sankey's voice drew a crowd; this swelled to a mass when Moody began to talk, and Sankey saw how "the people stood spellbound as the words fell from Moody's lips with wonderful force and rapidity."

After twenty-five minutes, Moody said they would continue in the Opera House rented by the Convention. Sankey and his friends led the way,

> singing, as we marched down the street, "Shall We Gather at the River." The men with dinner pails followed closely on our heels instead of going home. The Opera House was packed to the doors. Moody first saw that all the workingmen were seated. His second address was as captivating as the one delivered on the street corner.

Sankey left Indianapolis undecided. "I presume I prayed one way and he prayed another. However, it took him only six months to pray me out of business."

Ira David Sankey had been born on August 28, 1840, at the village of Edinburg in western Pennsylvania and had lived since 1857 nearby, in New Castle—a curious foreshadowing, since international reputation was to come at Edinburgh in Scotland, and Newcastle-upon-Tyne was to be the birthplace of the Moody and Sankey hymnbook. Son of a bank president and state senator, Sankey always had about him a faint air of colonnaded bank and senate plush, "rather given to frock coats and silk hats," Paul Moody writes, "thus presenting a good deal of a contrast to my father's more informal appearance." Sankey was "a very jovial man," of the sort that delighted in puns and elaborate comic stories; he could skylark under Moody's influence, but whereas Moody even in old age frolicked with the abandon of a schoolboy, Sankey would be distinctly avuncular. Sankey lived on the verge of being pompous, while Moody could not have been pompous had he tried.

Sankey was a Methodist. He had been Sunday school superintendent, had helped to found the local YMCA, and was choirmaster of his church. Having served briefly in the Civil War, he is said to have owed his life to his voice: he had been on sentry duty one night when he began to sing a favorite hymn. A Confederate sniper who had him in his sights was so moved by the singing that he lowered his rifle. Sankey's baritone never received professional training; he sang in church, at Sunday school conventions, and in local churches in western Pennsylvania and eastern Ohio.

Back in New Castle, after meeting Moody at Indianapolis, Sankey discussed the future with his wife, Fanny. The daughter of another state senator, she had been a member of Sankey's choir, when he married young in 1863. She was as lovely as her husband was handsome—shy, too, and retiring like Emma Moody. It was much to ask Fanny Sankey to accept the extinction of her husband's career in the Civil Service that he might assist a missioner based in the slums of Chicago with occasional flings to other cities.

Sankey consented early in 1871 to a trial week with Moody. At the end of the week, he resigned from the Revenue, but reserved an option, in that he did not bring Fanny, but set up bachelor quarters in the rebuilt Farwell Hall. "Thus we commenced work together, visiting poor and needy ones of Mr. Moody's little flock, singing and praying with the sick, speaking and singing at the daily noon prayer meetings."

Sankey's advent was unheralded. "A comparatively obscure man," John Hitchcock noted. "His presence amongst us was not regarded in musical circles as a great acquisition to their forces."

11

Fire

The Moody that Sankey joined was Moody in a quandary.

After his encounter with Moorhouse, Moody had become an apostle of love in public speech as in private life, and he knew how to draw waters of wisdom from the well of Holy Writ. But he stood uncertain at the crossways. While postwar America dragged its moral anchor, worshiping money in the North, resentment in the South; while Britain lay half-bogged by smugness laced with hypocrisy, half-stirred by spiritual quickenings and missionary adventures that needed to be knit together; the man of the hour dithered.

He might remain primarily a Sunday school worker. Moody, J. H. Vincent the future bishop, and B. F. Jacobs the businessman—all three still in their thirties and living in Chicago—formed a triumvirate that led the Northwest, and the Northwest led American Sunday schools. Moody was President for 1869 of the Illinois Convention, at Bloomington. His mission school was famous, and he held the reins:

> He is a man that does a great deal of hard work himself and surpasses all men in finding something for others to do. Sluggards don't like him and he doesn't like them . . . . Much of his success is due to the *personality* of his efforts.

He might remain primarily a city missionary, an American William Booth. It was as a successful slummer that he had held the attention of the great national convention at the Marble Church in New York in 1868. Some of the elders had protested: "The idea of putting Mr. Moody on with Dr. John Hall and Henry Ward Beecher!" Moody spoke at the end of the day.

> He claimed attention at once, and I believe you could have heard a pin drop all through that hour. Why, it seemed to me that he just grew larger and larger . . . Mr. Moody was a revelation to us on "How to reach the masses." He told his simple, straight story of how he had done the work.

The YMCA claimed as much of him. He gloried in being an Association man in days of rapid expansion.

There lay another opening: to Congress. In 1868, an election year, he had led a Christian convention at Leavenworth, then the capital of the young state of Kansas. A group of politicians called on him.

"See here, Mr. Moody, you come out here and run for Congress."

"I have got a higher service than that!"

They left him in disgust. One politician exclaimed, "I think that is one of the strangest of men. Just think of it! He could just as well go to Congress, and I believe we could make him Governor." And, if Governor, it is not beyond bounds that, with the powers he developed of administration, command, and speech, D. L. Moody eventually could have run for President.

Sunday school, city mission, and YMCA—in each he evangelized. He was not, nor intended to be, a full-time itinerant evangelist. He loved a dash to some city of Illinois, Michigan, Wisconsin, or farther afield for a revival in a church or YMCA, but he belonged to Chicago. The rest were secondary. Chicago held his home, doubly dear since March 25, 1869, birthday of William Revell Moody. Here he could romp. Here was little Emma's enormous rocking horse crafted in gratitude by a man Moody had helped. Here was that latest idea, a bathroom, where Moody could take his cold bath winter and summer in the built-in tub.

A delicate, home-loving wife and two small children were no background for a peripatetic preacher.

This dithering yet dynamic jack-of-all-trades had one major defect of character. Certainly he was not introspective. Nor was he gloomy; indeed, a journalist who rode with him in a train wrote of "D. L. Moody who with all his real piety is sometimes unbearably funny." He had compassion, kindness, and (under Emma's gentle pressure) a growing courtesy, though formalities of handing ladies to their seats, of "please," "thank you," and "you're welcome" generally were crowded out. Despite his quick temper (with his intimates he could be brusque, or even snappish), he flared rarely under deliberate provocation, scurrilities, baitings, or misrepresentations. "I suppose if Jesus Christ could eat the Last Supper with a Judas Iscariot I ought to shake hands with you," he said one time when a persistent heckler offered him his hand. Once Moody knocked down the steps at Illinois Street a man who had vilely insulted him—or probably had made some filthy insinuation about Emma. Within five minutes, Moody had made a public apology, with never a word of the insult.

Moody's grave defect was another violence, a vehemence that sought to carve a kingdom for Christ in Chicago by sheer expenditure of energy, as in the two hundred calls he made on a New Year's Day, remembered by Hitchcock, who was with him and the church officers as they trotted briskly from State Street in a hired omnibus immediately after breakfast.

> On reaching a family belonging to his congregation, he would spring out of the bus, lead up the stairways, rush into the room, and pay his respects: "You know me: I am Moody; this is Deacon De Golyer, this is Deacon Thane, this is Brother Hitchcock. Are you all well? Do you all come to church and Sunday school? Have you all the coal you need for the winter? Let us pray." And down we would all go upon our knees, while Mr. Moody offered from fifteen to twenty words of earnest, tender, sympathetic supplication that God would bless the man, his wife, and each one of the children. Then, springing to his feet, he would dash on his hat, dart through the doorway and down the stairs throwing a hearty good-bye behind him, leap into the bus, and off to the next place on his list; the entire exercise occupying about one minute and a half.
>
> Before long the horses were tired out, for Moody insisted on their going at a run so the omnibus was abandoned and the party proceeded on foot. One after another his companions became exhausted with running upstairs and downstairs and across the streets and kneeling on bare floors and getting up in a hurry; until the tireless pastor was left to make the last of the two hundred calls alone; after which feat he returned home in the highest spirits, and with no sense

of fatigue, to laugh at his exhausted companions for deserting him.

This violence was a symptom of inner tension. Another was his passion for crowds. Every Sunday evening, rather to the distaste of the regular ministry, Moody preached in the rebuilt Farwell Hall—under its two hundred gas jets and its biblical frescoes—and could boast, "I have an audience of about 1,200 to 1,800," mostly young men. If the hall was nearly full, he would "be lifted up at the sight of so many people before me." If numbers dropped, his morale dropped. Another symptom, mixed with a general sense of adventure, was the restlessness that took him with Vincent and Philip Phillips that spring of 1871 by the new Pacific railway to visit California, through Wild West lands where the train dared Indian attack, through desert and mountain, to hold a Sunday school convention on the rough-and-tumble coast where, Moody observed, gold, fast horses, tobacco, and rum held high carnival.

At the other end of the scale lay a moment of stark discouragement, if the unsupported evidence of B. F. Jacobs' brother, Will, be accepted. Will Jacobs claimed (in 1911) to remember Moody's coming to their office on a "cold, cold day in that winter of 1870-1871" without an overcoat, his jacket nearly threadbare.

> I stood listening, and this is what Mr. Moody said. "Jacobs, I do not know but I will have to give it up after all . . . I left my wife and children this winter morning without a mouthful of food at home, and without a dollar to purchase any. Jacobs, I would not care for myself . . . But, oh"—and the great form shook with agitation—"it is hard for a man to leave his wife and children without a morsel of food."

Moody never remembered, or never revealed, such a moment of destitution; and during that winter Fleming Revell still boarded and lodged with the Moodys, earning good pay at a printer's. Did he go without breakfast?

There is no disputing that Moody was empty in his soul, and refused to admit it.

He was dissatisfied with the multiplicity of his administrative duties. The YMCA had become a hive of activity, with Moody as queen bee. There was also the tract campaign: "what I am trying to do for the people who do not attend church," scattering a million pages a week, "and I can't tell you how much good they are doing." He was busy with fund-raising, badgering McCormick for $2,000 toward an organ for Farwell Hall ("the singing is horrible without it"), as well as organizing the "Yokefellows," who would frequent saloons, boardinghouses, and street corners to herd people in for the Farwell Hall services. Every week, Moody claimed, 1,500 different young men came to the YMCA rooms, and over 5,000 had been found employment in a year—but Moody's figures generally suffered from his countrymen's complaint of hyperbole. It all meant office work. "I was on some ten or twelve committees. My hands were full. If a man came to me to talk about his soul I would say: 'I haven't time: got a committee to attend.'"

Moody knew that he had to choose, once for all, whether to be a social-religious organizer or an evangelist. What is more, by early 1871 he perceived, but pretended he did not, that "God was calling me into higher service, to go out and preach the Gospel all over the land instead of staying in Chicago. I fought against it."

He was therefore becoming as sounding brass (certainly not a tinkling cymbal), but not because he had not charity; nor, since Moorhouse, because he lacked wealth of Bible lore. But his inner tension, his half-recognized rebellion, tangle of objectives, and utter lack of integration ensured that his speech and his preaching were not any longer like Paul's, "in demonstration of the Spirit and of power."

Two women in his congregation noticed this.

Sarah Anne Cooke was a recent emigrant from England— hence, English influence again on the one so to influence England—a Buckinghamshire woman only ten years older than Moody, but generally known as Auntie: Moody always thought of her as elderly. Her husband worked in meat-packing, and she was a Free Methodist, a woman of intense earnestness, "continually going to every kind of religious gathering within her reach," who could speak only in the language of Zion, probably lacked a sense of humor, was full of good works, and buttonholed the unwary to exhort them to flee from the wrath to come.

At a camp meeting in June 1871, "a burden came on me for Mr. Moody that the Lord would give him the baptism of the Holy Ghost and of fire." With her friend, a widow named Mrs. Hawxhurst, Auntie Cooke settled in the front row, and while Moody preached they prayed in an obvious manner.

"We have been praying for you," they said afterwards.

This nettled him. "Why don't you pray for the people?"

"Because you need the power of the Spirit."

"I need the power?" Moody puffed.

He had not a chance. "No opportunity was lost after that in urging upon him his great need." They pursued him like the Hound of Heaven; in the mist of tears he hid from them, and under running laughter. They found "little conviction of his need" at first, but their unhurrying chase

> set me thinking. I asked them to come and talk with me, and they poured out their hearts in prayer that I might receive the filling of the Holy Spirit. There came a great hunger into my soul. I did not know what it was. I began to cry out as I never did before. I really felt that I did not want to live if I could not have this power for service.

It would not come. He refused to admit to himself that he was called "to go out all over the land."

In September he invited Auntie Cooke and Mrs. Hawxhurst to pray with him every Friday afternoon in his room at Farwell Hall. They each prayed aloud in turn. On Friday, October 6, "Mr. Moody's agony was so great that he rolled on the floor and in the midst of many tears and groans cried to God to be baptized with the Holy Ghost and with fire." Rolling on the floor in prayer would have been un-Moodylike enough to render suspect Auntie's evidence (put in a letter to S. B. Shaw twenty-eight years later), were it not for D. W. Whittle, reliable observer and Moody's close friend, who mentioned in his private diary only five years afterwards that Moody at that time had been "continually burdened and crying to God for more power. He was always wanting to get a few praying ones together for half a day of prayer and would groan and weep before God for the baptism of the Spirit."

The heavens remained brassy as the sky throughout that memorable Indian summer. Day after day had passed in drought and high wind. Prairie and city were dry as tinder, dry as Moody's heart. Moody leaped and cried like a prophet of Baal, but there was no voice nor any that answered. For Moody would not place himself on the altar; he would not yield in his determination to stay in Chicago. How could he desert the thriving mission building on Illinois Street? Who else could hold sway in that fine monument to his organizing zeal, Farwell Hall—with its two hundred gas jets, its monster reflectors, its seats for 2,500, and its splendid organ? Nothing should move him from those two dear buildings. The still, small voice that kept saying, "Go out and preach the gospel all over the land," could not be from heaven, he had decided.

On that Friday, October sixth, Moody "cried to God to be baptized with fire."

On Sunday evening, October eighth, the doors of Farwell Hall closed on a capacity crowd. Moody spoke superbly. Sankey at his little organ began a final solo, "Today the Savior Calls." He reached the closing words of the third verse: "and death is nigh," when

> my voice was drowned by the loud noise of the fire engines rushing past the hall and the tolling of bells, among which we could hear the deep sullen tones of the great city bell, in the steeple of the old courthouse close at hand, ringing out a general alarm. Tremendous confusion was heard in the street, and Mr. Moody decided to close the meeting at once, for the audience was becoming restless and alarmed.

Moody and Sankey went out at the back and saw an angry red smudge to the southwest, upwind from the main part of the city. They separated, Sankey to help at the scene, Moody to cross the river for home to reassure Emma and the children. As he walked, the southwest wind rose almost to hurricane force, and the sky became a fireworks display, as sparks blew and house after house caught fire. Moody's first words to Emma were: "The city's doomed."

By midnight, much of Chicago had become a holocaust of roaring flames, crashing buildings, wild neighing of terrified horses, and the shouts of firefighters and refugees. Sankey hurried back to Farwell Hall—"several times I had to shake from my coat the falling embers"—and rescued a few belongings before the pride of the YMCA went up in flames. He made for the lakeside.

In the neighborhood where the Moodys lived, a temporary sense of security was shattered during the small hours of the night, as the police woke up those families who had gone to bed, and urged flight. Moody may have gone to Illinois Street; his secretary, Katherine Abbott, helped to move valuables from his office. He was back at home before the flames engulfed the mission church and its whole street. Emma had awakened the children. "If you will not scream or cry," she told them, "I'll show you a sight you will never forget." She dressed them in two of everything and took them to the

French windows in the first-floor drawing room.

While the Moodys hastily threw their things together, little Emma wandered to the front door. The ragged street people were running wild for loot. A filthy old woman saw the well-dressed little girl and beckoned to her. Emma, bewitched, started to run out, but her dress caught in the door; had it not, she might have been lost.

The flames consumed a neighboring block. Moody arranged for a neighbor who owned a horse and buggy to take the children with his own through the panic-mad streets to safety with friends in a northern suburb. Then he pushed Bibles and a few valuables into a pram. Emma begged him to save the Healy portrait. "Take my own picture?" He laughed.

> That would be a joke. Suppose I meet some friends in the same trouble as ourselves and they say, "Hullo Moody, glad you have escaped. What's that you've saved and cling to so affectionately?" Wouldn't it sound well to reply, "Oh, I've got my own portrait!"

He would not touch it. Looters had entered. One of them politely cut the portrait out of the frame and handed it to Emma.

The Moodys, after abandoning State Street, did what they could. "Mr. Moody, please save my doll!" cried one little girl from a window or door of a house lapped by fire. He carried the girl to safety. At last, exhausted, they reached Emma's sister Sarah Holden and her attorney husband in their safe western suburb.

The fire raged throughout the next day. Homeless thousands streamed out of the city. Thieves looted; martial law was proclaimed; and buildings were blown up to make a fire break. For twenty-four hours Moody and Emma did not know whether their own children had been trapped or saved: Emma's hair began to turn gray. And they had no idea whether Sankey had been burned to death.

But Sankey had spent the night by the lakeside, with his precious bundle of belongings, and much of Monday in a boat by himself out on the lake. In the evening, "[he] went back into the burnt district. Farwell Hall was gone, and every building in that part of the city had disappeared. The paved streets [were] covered with hot bricks and long coils of burnt and twisted telegraph wire." He found a railway station still functioning and boarded the train for Pennsylvania. "As we left the city it seemed as though the whole country was on fire; in all directions we could see huge banks of flame sweeping across the prairies, and the air was filled to suffocation with smoke."

By Wednesday the fire had burned out. Chicago lay prostrate. Relief, badly organized, flowed from neighboring states.

A fortnight afterwards Moody drove the family, as young Emma records, "to the ruins of our house. Father went over everything in the ruins with a cane. The only thing of value he found was a toy iron stove of mine in perfect condition."

New York, November 24th, 1871.

My dear Sir, you know something of the sad state of things in Chicago so far as the spiritual work is concerned. Fifty churches and missions are in ashes and the thousands of men, women, and children are without any Sabbath home. The temporal wants of the people are well supplied, but there is no money to rebuild the churches and missions. The churches in the part of the city that was spared can do nothing. Their moneyed men are either bankrupt or as badly crippled as to prevent them from helping outside enterprises. My mission school and Free Church, on the North Side, went with the rest. One thousand children and their parents are looking to me for another building. I have no earthly possessions and apply to those in sympathy with God's work who have the means of helping. My plan is to raise $50,000 and put up a Tabernacle to accommodate seven or eight burnt out missions. It is for this purpose I have come to New York on a hurried visit. In a very short time there will be 50,000 Mechanics and others back to the North Side. The grog shops are already rebuilding and some are doing business. The theaters are helping the theaters . . . Will you help us? . . .

Yours respectfully,
D. L. Moody.

He met generous response in Philadelphia from George H. Stuart and John Wanamaker; in a Massachusetts coastal city a man took him around to rich neighbors. In New York—Moody hated it—"My heart was not in the work of begging. I could not appeal. I was crying all the time that God would fill me with His Holy Spirit."

His prayer remained unanswered because he fought the will of God. Farwell Hall and Illinois Street were in ashes, and the ten or dozen committees had scattered like dying embers. Moody could not face the weariness of reorganization. Had God, then, burned him out so that he should "go all over the country," or perhaps the world? Moody said no. The chains that bound him to Chicago had snapped—all but one, his own will.

Yet he craved power. He began to pace the New York streets at night, wrestling within, and panting for a Pentecost.

In broad daylight he walked down one of the busiest streets, Broadway or Fifth Avenue—he scarcely remembered which—while crowds thrust by, with the clop-clink of cabs and carriages and the shouting of newsboys in his ears. The last chain snapped. Quietly, without a struggle, he surrendered. Immediately an overpowering sense of the presence of God flooded his soul. "God Almighty seemed to come very near. I felt I must be alone." He hurried to the house of a friend nearby, sent up his card, and brushed aside an invitation to "come and have some food." "I want to be alone. Let me have a room where I can lock myself in."

His host thought it best to humor him. Moody locked the door and sat on the sofa. The room seemed ablaze with God. Moody dropped to the floor and lay bathing his soul in the Divine. Of this communion, this mount of transfiguration, he later would comment, "I can only say that God revealed Himself to me, and I had such an experience of His love that I had to ask Him to stay His hand." Turmoil of mind glided into peace, and conflict of character snapped into integration. That masterful strength which had hammered at the gates of hell and charged full tilt at the world, the flesh, and the devil was melted and remolded, leaving him gentle as a babe and utterly dependent on a power beyond his own.

Not for him to see and choose his path, nor pride to rule his will, he decided. God must lead, and God supply. Moody need never thirst again. The dead, dry days were gone. "I was all the time tugging and carrying water. But now I have a river that carries me."

The clock of a nearby church chimed the quarter, the half, three quarters, the hour, the hour again.

Crazy Moody became Moody the man of God.

PART TWO

The Man from the West, 1872-1875

12

The Unanswered Letter

London on a Sunday in the summer of 1872. A butler off duty walked, as fast as dignity allowed, by Westminster Abbey and the Houses of Parliament, and up almost deserted Whitehall until he reached Downing Street. He did not turn left to the house of the Prime Minister, Mr. Gladstone, but continued along Richmond Terrace toward the river, as yet without embankment.

The butler hurried down the area steps of No. 5 into the basement, took off his billycock hat, changed his clothes, and waited impatiently until he heard his young master and mistress, Mr. and Mrs. Quintin Hogg, return from church. He walked upstairs, coughed politely, and said, "Excuse me, sir, but there was a wonderful American gentleman preached at Chelsea Chapel. Real powerful, he was. He would do our lads a power of good, sir."

"What was his name, Edwards?"

"Mr. Moody of Chicago, as I heard, sir."

"Moody? The man whose Sunday school I visited on our honeymoon last year, before that awful fire?"

"It must be him, sir. He preaches again tonight, if you would please to give me leave, sir."

Quintin Hogg went too. An Old Etonian of twenty-seven, son of a baronet, partner in a sugar firm, athlete, he spent much time among rough slum boys in the alleys and tenements of Charing Cross where he had started a Ragged School and a home for destitutes, assisted by his butler, his coachman, and a couple of Old Etonian friends. It grew into the London Polytechnic. Hogg was the British counterpart of the man Moody might have been, had he remained in business. He had much in common with Moody—a love for poor boys, a complete absence—rare in the England of the seventies—of any sense of social barrier, so that he brought ragamuffins into his house by the front door, and a partiality to fun and practical jokes.

He listened to Moody that night with delight. "He spoke with much power," Hogg wrote to a co-worker in the Ragged School, the Honourable Tom Pelham,

> and I was glad to find that he was going to a hotel, which enabled me to secure him as a guest. On the Monday following we closed school, and I invited the home boys and your class to come to tea here on Tuesday and then go to hear Moody at Chelsea Chapel. They did so, and every single boy there was broken down more or less. Eleven professed to find peace that night. The following night I asked any who liked to come again and fifty boys came to the chapel and we had a special service in the schoolroom for them. I went around after the gas went out and prayed with each alone.

It was odd that Moody was preaching at all. "I went to London in 1872 just to have a few months of rest and study the English Christians. I was determined not to get into work if I could help it."

The previous winter Moody had returned to Chicago in November 1871, with a modest $3,000 to construct a less ambitious "tabernacle" of pine boards, the first building in the devastated section. He had sent for Sankey, opened the building on Christmas Eve as a center of relief and evangelism, and slept there with his assistants (they had to place their boots over the cracks to keep out icy draughts), while Emma and the children lodged with her sister.

A young man who slipped into the watch night service on Sunday, December 31, recorded his impression:

> Consider the desolation all about. The midnight, the midwinter stillness, the yawning cellars and gaunt walls, one had to pass walking southward for 45 minutes before reaching buildings and inhabited

houses again. Ten below zero, a clear sky, a full moon overhead and absolute quiet. At last I came to Moody's Tabernacle just built among the ruins. It seated 1,400 and I found it nearly full. Mr. Moody was just finishing an address. Another preacher followed whose uproariousness made no impression except in contrast to Moody's quiet ways. Then Mr. Sankey followed with his organ and extremely sweet voice singing some of his hymns. Mr. Moody was last and ended with saying that it was a few minutes of twelve. He called for silent prayer. Presently the complete silence was broken by his wishing us a Happy New Year.

Moody had accepted that he should undertake his mission again but would not entangle himself in committees. Chicago no longer held him. He must be an evangelist, and presumably would discover where to begin. He went east again in January. In Brooklyn, a casual remark led to a series of meetings in the new mission chapel of a famous church, after which a wealthy layman, Morris K. Jessup, wanted him permanently in New York.

Jessup wrote to Farwell on January 17, 1872.

The more I see of Moody the more I like him. I believe God is making him the instrument of a great work among the people. Moody and I had quite a talk about getting hold of the masses in this city, and he quite cheered me up . . . . Moody is the man to come here . . . . I should be willing to take the expense on my shoulders.

But Moody did not intend to cast off from Chicago merely to anchor in New York.

The Moodys had gone on to Northfield. And the best portrait of D. L. Moody in those months of pause on the verge of fame comes through the eyes of a Northfield child, Eva Stebbins Callender, on a Sunday morning in the Trinitarian Congregational Church:

After the service had begun there was ushered into the first pew a stout pleasant-faced man and a lady. Mother whispered they were Mr. and Mrs. Dwight Moody of Chicago. I had heard of the Chicago Fire and wondered if they too were burnt out. Probably had been— because Mrs. Moody wore a very pretty bonnet, a flat three-cornered affair trimmed with quite small black feathers and black velvet ribbons, but made of straw, white straw, which was not the usual material for bonnets in wintertime, so perhaps her real winter bonnet was burned. Our old minister came down from the pulpit and cordially greeted Mr. Moody while the choir were singing the second hymn. Then Mr. Moody briskly arose and followed up the three steps into the pulpit, taking off his overcoat as he did so and threw it carelessly on the long shelf behind the desk. Quickly turning he said, "If the ushers will open the windows we will sing again, Number—" He seemed to have entirely forgotten they had just sung the second hymn of the morning, and now another—surely he was different.

The sermon usually bored Eva, though she was forbidden to fidget.

> As soon as Mr. Moody began to talk I found to my surprise that I could understand him and I liked it. He told stories—and it was Sunday too—stories when he knew people could not help but laugh, and then it might be a story when the grown-ups would cry. I would have cried too but was too busy watching this very enthusiastic preacher who talked with his hands and feet as well as his mouth, as he paced up and down the narrow platform. No, he didn't preach, he only talked using the simplest language, sometimes with a loud voice, as he denounced wrongdoing, but always holding the attention of the hearers. I distinctly remember in one part that, to give emphasis to his remarks he brought both hands down in no gentle manner on the cushion on the pulpit desk. A cloud of dust immediately arose, and it also seemed as though a small feather flew into the air.

In summer, with Chicago fast nursing from its ashes, and the Tabernacle mission working well, Moody left Emma to go to the British Isles.[1]

He attended conventions and conferences, occasionally being prevailed upon to speak, and always stuffing the roomy pockets of his Scotch tweed suit with notes and pumping his British friends for sermon illustrations. Near Dublin a wealthy Plymouth Brother opened his mansion for a "Believers' Meeting," and there Moody met "Butcher" Varley again. Together, with some twenty of like fervor, they spent one entire night in prayer.

Next morning, as the two, sleepy but elated, rambled in Bewley's well-tended shady grounds, Varley let slip a remark that flashed an inspiration to Moody. It was an unpremeditated, casual remark—Varley forgot it instantly, until he was reminded about it, more than a year afterwards.

---

[1] A curious transposition in W. R. Moody's *D. L. Moody* (1930) has given rise to the belief that Moody was in Britain in 1870. The incidents noted therein belong to 1872.

Varley said, "Moody, the world has yet to see what God will do with a man fully consecrated to Him."

The phrase startled Moody. He made no comment at the time, but devoured Varley's words, sucked at them, digested them, and regurgitated them for days and weeks:

> "The world has yet to see what God can do with and for and through a man who is fully and wholly consecrated to Him." . . . A man! Varley meant *any* man. Varley didn't say he had to be educated, or brilliant, or anything else. Just a *man*. Well, by the Holy Spirit in me I'll be that man.

Back in London, in the gallery of the Metropolitan Tabernacle, Varley's remark and Spurgeon's preaching focused Moody's attention on "something I had never realized before. It was not Spurgeon who was doing that work: it was God. And if God could use Spurgeon, why should He not use me?"

It was then that the visit to Britain got out of hand.

A Congregationalist minister persuaded Moody to preach at Arundel Square near Pentonville Prison, in a lower middle-class district. And Sunday morning's smug, stolid drowsiness made him rue his irresolution in accepting.

Unknown to him, a woman hurried back to her younger sister, a mere slip of a girl but permanently bedridden, named Marianne Adlard, and broke the news that Mr. Moody of America had preached. Marianne exclaimed: "I know what that means! God has heard my prayers!" She drew from under her pillow a crinkled and faded newspaper cutting, and together they looked again at the account of this unknown American's activities in the slums of Chicago, which had caused Marianne, day after day, to pray, "O Lord, send this man to our church."

That evening, from the moment Moody mounted the pulpit, the congregation listened, hushed and alert. His every word seemed charged as with electricity. At the close, he asked any who wanted their "lives changed by the power of God through faith in Jesus Christ as a personal Savior," and wanted "to become Christians," to rise, that he might pray for them. People rose all over the chapel.

Surprised, Moody thought that either he or they had made a

mistake and told them to sit. He repeated what he meant by "becoming a Christian" and asked that those who wished should withdraw to the adjoining hall or schoolroom. He watched, astonished, as scores of men, women, and older children made their way quietly to the connecting door. The schoolroom had been prepared as an Inquiry Room by placing out one or two dozen chairs. Many more had to be sent for.

Moody addressed this second meeting with the utmost care, enlarging on repentance and faith. The whole room rose when he put his question the third time. He told them to meet their minister, who was as dazed as he was, the next night. Moody had to leave London in the morning. He was telegraphed for on Tuesday because more people had come to the minister's Monday night meeting than had been in the room on Sunday. He returned and spoke nightly all that week and the next. "Four hundred were taken into membership of that church," James Sprunt, a Baptist minister in Somerset, wrote fifty-three years later, "and by the grace of God I was one of that number."

After that experience Moody could not refuse to hold a short mission for the Anglican incumbent of Chelsea Chapel where Quintin Hogg's butler had heard him. Hogg even postponed his holiday in Scotland, sending ahead his wife and baby, the future Lord Chancellor Hailsham, while he made the most of Moody's influence on wild street arabs and urchins.

A few days later Moody called at a hotel where his friend the noted Presbyterian preacher Cuyler of Brooklyn was staying. "They wish me to come over here and preach in England," Moody said.

"Do. These English people are the best people to preach to in all the world."

"I will go home, secure somebody to sing, and come over and make the experiment."

Henry Bewley had evidently said at Dublin that he would help with expenses, so Moody understood. Cuthbert Bainbridge, a rich, elderly Methodist layman of Newcastle-upon-Tyne was explicit in his promise of funds. The invitation of predominant importance came after Moody's return to America, from William Pennefather, the outstanding evangelical Anglican of those not yet on the bench of bishops, a man of saintly character, authority, insight, and drive, whose parish of St. Jude's, Mildmay, had an influence far beyond

London. Pennefather had his finger on the pulse of British religion and, according to his close friend and biographer, "was strongly impressed with the conviction that Mr. Moody was one for whom God had prepared a great work." Pennefather, though only fifty-seven, was a sick man. From the Black Forest, during a tour abroad for his health, in the third week of August 1872, he wrote "a letter of invitation to Mr. Moody, telling him of the wide door open for evangelistic effort in London and elsewhere, promising him a warm welcome if he would come over and help."

Moody, American-fashion, sent no reply.

There followed the most extraordinary behavior by the man who was afterwards to be not only an evangelist, but an efficient, decisive administrator as well. Because of Moody's uncharacteristic inaction, Britain's greatest religious revival since Wesley would begin so haphazardly as to exhaust human explanation for its success.

Moody made plain to Chicago during the winter and spring of 1872-1873 that he was leaving. "I did all I could," Farwell wrote, "to persuade him to stay and help build up from the ruins of the fire along religious lines, but to no effect." He backed the fund for the third Farwell Hall, launched an appeal for a permanent replacement to the Tabernacle, and secured the site at the corner of LaSalle Street and Chicago Avenue—a location that has been linked with his name ever since—and set builders to work. That was all. His heart was across the sea.

"I want," he told a great meeting at the Second Presbyterian Church in the spring of 1873, "to dream great things for God. To get back to Great Britain and win ten thousand souls!"

"Are you going to preach to the miserable poor?" Auntie Cooke asked.

"Yes, and to the miserable rich, too!" Moody replied.

No word came from the United Kingdom. Moody seemed to have imagined that three men of different denominations living in widely separated parts, who probably were unacquainted—Bewley, Bainbridge, and Pennefather (to whom he had not bothered to reply)—were organizing an evangelistic tour. He may have been reluctant to push himself. He was certainly true to his countrymen's belief that plans may fructify in a vacuum of unanswered correspondence.

A letter came from a young druggist in the cathedral city of York, George Bennett, founder-secretary of the local YMCA. They had met at a breakfast in Leeds, and he wrote to say that if Moody were over again, would he please speak at York? Moody sent no reply and continued to prepare for his visit to Britain.

Sankey, who had brought his family to Chicago, and J. H. Harwood, the official pastor, were ordered to look after the Tabernacle for the six months, during which Moody expected to be abroad. The then famous, now forgotten, Philip Phillips was invited to be singer for the tour, as he knew Britain well. He had recently performed a hundred nights of sacred song there. Phillips refused; he was arranging a tour of the Pacific Coast. Indeed, Phillips made Sankey "a very enticing offer, including a large salary and all expenses, if [he] would go and assist him." Sankey, to whom money meant much, was tempted; but decided to stay with Moody's Tabernacle at the price, it seemed, of certain fortune and possible fame.

Moody turned to Bliss. Bliss regretfully declined because he could not afford, with a young family, to abandon his professional engagements. There was no alternative but Sankey the amateur. Moody gave Sankey a personal guarantee of one hundred dollars a month.

No word came from Britain except another letter from young Bennett of York. Moody had occasion to write to Morgan and Scott, religious publishers in London. Through them he sent Bennett a noncommittal message. Bennett wrote again in late spring, to receive a cautious reply direct from Moody, "saying he thought of coming and as I seemed earnest about it, he might commence at York and would bring someone to lead the singing." Moody's thoughts were on more influential sponsors than a tradesman of York; no doubt these were being carefully prepared. On the strength of such expectation, he booked steamship passage for himself, Emma, little Emma (aged eight and a half), and Willie (just four), and for Sankey and Fanny, who would leave their two children with grandparents.

Still no money or letter came from England, nor was that a wonder.

On the afternoon of farewell from Chicago, John Farwell brought a gift of five hundred dollars. Moody kept fifty and asked him to invest the rest, as all expenses were to be paid from the moment of leaving America. The fifty dollars took them to the coast. *The City of Paris* was due to sail on June 7. From New York, Moody had to wire Farwell, who released the four hundred fifty dollars, not knowing that without them the party would have been stranded on the quay. The last English mail brought nothing. A letter from the persistent Bennett, promising to make arrangements in York, if Moody would state his wishes, "and when he would be likely to be here," missed the Moodys and was sent in pursuit.[2]

Crossing the Atlantic, Moody was seasick, as usual. From New York he had alerted Moorhouse, who on June 17 came on board at Liverpool to tell them that Pennefather had died in April and Bainbridge in March. And Bewley must have forgotten about his coming. There were no arrangements, no committee, and no funds.

The Americans were stranded, three thousand miles from home. Moody turned to Sankey. "God seems to have closed the doors. We'll not open any ourselves. If He opens the door we'll go in. If He don't we'll return to America."

They went to the North Western Hotel. Putting the children to bed, the Moodys rejoined the Sankeys and Moorhouse in the lounge to mill their problem, and there Moody recalled the York invitation that he had treated so airily. "This door is only ajar," he said.

Next morning, Wednesday, the eighteenth of June 1873, George Bennett, who in view of Moody's vague answer and subsequent silence had told no one except the doctor at the lunatic asylum, was horrified to receive a telegram from the secretary of the Liverpool YMCA: MOODY HERE ARE YOU READY FOR HIM.

---

[2] This disposes of the oft-repeated legend that Moody found Bennett's letter, unopened in his pocket, after arriving at Liverpool. Bennett gave a full statement of the whole affair to W. R. Moody in a letter of March 12, 1900, after reading the inaccurate account in the hurriedly produced *Life of Dwight L. Moody*. Extracts from that letter have never before been published.

13

White Elephants

"I have no doubt that if I had known when I reached England of what was before me I would have been frightened," remarked Moody, two years later.

He waited in Liverpool throughout Wednesday, June 18, 1873, for a reply from York. Richard Houghton, a shipowner interested in the YMCA, took the Moodys to his mansion for the night, while Moorhouse carried off the Sankeys to the Manchester cottage. The Moodys left for London and then Leytonstone-in-Essex, the home of sister Mary, now Mrs. Alfred Sharpe. On Friday morning a telegram arrived from Bennett, forwarded from Liverpool: PLEASE FIX DATE WHEN YOU CAN COME TO YORK.

Moody tossed his head at such dilatory planning. He wired back: I WILL BE IN YORK TONIGHT TEN O'CLOCK STOP MAKE NO ARRANGEMENTS TILL I COME.

He traveled north alone. On stepping from the train, he asked Bennett: "How far is it to Manchester? I might have meetings there first before York."

"Sixty or seventy miles. But you can't go now. You must come with me for supper and the night anyhow, and then we can talk it over."

Bennett, to Moody's amusement, appeared dazed as they walked the short distance beside the city walls, through Micklegate Bar to the drugstore in New Bridge Street. Over supper Moody made up his mind:

"Every man has to make his own way, so I propose we make arrangements tomorrow, Saturday, to commence meetings Sunday. You telegraph Mr. Moorhouse to have Sankey here sometime tomorrow."

Bennett's account described their plans:

> We mapped out there and then matters for posters to be printed and posted next day, and knowing he was tired I showed him to his bedroom. I apologized for the bedcurtains being covered up—we had not had time to put them in apple pie order. Mr. Moody replied "I don't think the Lord Jesus had any curtains to His bed. What did for Him will do for me."

On Saturday afternoon, Sankey found Moody alone and in high spirits. "I say, Sankey, here we are, a couple of white elephants! Bennett is away all over the city now, to see if he can get us a place. He's like a man who's got a white elephant and doesn't know what to do with it."

Bennett returned discouraged. Ministers were suspicious: "*Americans?*" "Why do they want to come to *York?*" "What's the YMCA up to?" "Whoever heard of a mission in midsummer?"

He had booked the large and ugly Corn Exchange for the afternoon, and the Congregationalist deacons had grudgingly promised the morning pulpit at Salem Chapel, because their new minister was away. Young men were scouting the city to inform likely persons that this would be a meeting for "Christian workers"; detailed posters were being printed.

That first Sunday morning Moody cut little ice with the staid dissenting congregation of tradesmen—all clad in sober black— their ample wives, numerous children, a footman or two from the Deanery and the Canons' houses, a few soldiers from the barracks, and a sprinkling of washerwomen and railwaymen up from back-to-back streets beyond the station. In the afternoon, as the Americans walked with Bennett toward the Corn Exchange, Moody stopped at the YMCA and filled his arms with Bibles.

"Now, Sankey, you bring a pile of Bibles."

Bennett said: "What do you want to do?"

"Oh, I shall have your hair standing straight on your head before I have finished in York!"

Some eight hundred people waited in the Corn Exchange, which could hold more. Moody briskly distributed Bibles here and there, in each copy a slip with a number and a reference, and ordered, "Read the text out when I call your number." The resulting "somewhat novel but very profitable Bible lecture on 'God is love,' as the *Yorkshire Gazette* called it—in a brief paragraph on "Mission Work," set between notices of a banquet and of a court case over a local Dotheboys Hall—caused interest.

All week at evening meetings in chapels "the spiritual atmosphere seemed at zero and little result was effected." So thought Bennett. Beneath the surface, however, in the hearts of men and women for whom chapel-going was essentially an emblem of respectability, something stirred. Sankey could make them sing new, rousing songs utterly unlike the dirges thought proper to divine service; even the strait-laced as they went about their daily business found it hard to resist humming "Hold the Fort." When this charming American sat at the little harmonium, his solos, every word distinct, lifted hearers to worlds unknown and faced them with Christian teaching that had been blurred in a haze of tacit, impersonal acceptance. If tears were inclined to run too easily, this was a lachrymose age.

Moody's informal preaching shocked, then intrigued. His hearers noted that he did not seek to score by denigrating the regular ministry; indeed, he let it be known unequivocally that he "prefers preaching in chapels, and so strengthening existing causes, to commencing a new work in public halls, etc." In their cage of convention they were warmed by his emphasis that religion was a friendship: "'To as many as received Him,' he would quote, 'to them gave He power to become the sons of God'—*Him*, mark you! Not a dogma, not a creed, not a myth, but a *Person*." They noticed the blend of reverence and affection with which he would speak of *"the Lord Jesus."*

Behind the scenes Moody had started a noon prayer meeting in the YMCA's "small ill-lit room" in Feasegate. "I can see Mr. Moody standing there to lead it," wrote one of Bennett's friends in old age, "little realizing that it was seed-germ of a mighty harvest."

On the second Wednesday, July 2, the movement broke surface. Moody spoke at the Wesleyan chapel in the heart of the walled city on "Redeemed with the Precious Blood of Christ." Bennett wrote: "The Holy Spirit's power was mightily manifested and anxious souls were all over the building, in the body as well as in the gallery. The aged superintendent of the Chapel seemed paralyzed by astonishment, he could do nothing but weep for joy."

That night had been the last of their invitation to the Wesleyan chapel, and they moved south of the Ouse to Priory Street just within the walls, to the new Baptist chapel, its dark brown varnish still glossy, and its imitation Early Decorated exterior bright and clean.

Moody had preached there the previous Sunday morning, his second in York. The starchy young minister, Frederick Brotherton Meyer, consulted by Bennett on Moody's telegram, was puzzled as to what an evangelist did that he could not do himself, being correct in doctrine, painstaking in preaching, a most worthy young man, but with only the slightest curl of his classical nose had invited Moody to his pulpit. He listened unmoved to the story of that dying Sunday school teacher in Chicago. But the woman who taught the senior girls' class had been so gripped that she missed her midday dinner to pray. At teachers' tea Meyer asked casually, "Well, Miss Lines, how have you got on this afternoon?"

"Oh, I told that story again and I believe every one of my girls has given her heart to God!"

That had shaken Meyer, who now watched his moderate-sized chapel, night after night, its "vestries, lobbies and pulpit-stairs crowded!" And in the minister's parlor at the close of each evening he saw subdued citizens of York seek the way of release.

Toward the end of his life, the leading nonconformist in London—past president of the National Free Church Council, social reformer, preacher, and author of seventy books of which, according to the *Dictionary of National Biography*, 5 million copies were circulated—F. B. Meyer, declared of that mission in York:

> For me it was the birthday of new conceptions of ministry, new methods of work, new inspirations and hopes . . . I had been brought up in a holy home. I had been in business for a little, then took my degree at college, but I didn't know anything about conversion, or anything about the gathering of sinners around Christ, and I owe everything, everything in my life, I think, to that parlor room where for the first time I found people brokenhearted about sin. I learned the psychology of the soul. I learned how to point men to God.

The revival remained parochial, scattered, the churches not united, the stirrings limited to a "parcel of dissenters." One or two clergymen of the Established Church offered Moody and Sankey verbal encouragement, but the canon-in-residence as he robed for the daily services in the minster, remained unaware of their existence. Had good Archbishop Thomson, "the People's Archbishop," been told at Bishopsthorpe that in less than two years his brother primate of Canterbury, would write a long earnest letter about them to the Lord Chancellor, he would have been amused.

Mrs. Sankey had already joined her husband. Emma and the children arrived on July 4, the day before her thirtieth birthday, guests of Dr. Hitchings of the Friends' Retreat, a private lunatic asylum. He let the children play with harmless inmates, rather to Emma's disquiet; once when the Moodys were roused in the middle of a night by a scream from Willie and found his bed empty, there followed frantic searching of house and asylum until he was discovered beneath his own bed, having fallen out, screamed, rolled over, and gone fast asleep out of sight.

The Moodys and the Sankeys were homesick. Moody implored Farwell to send full details of the YMCA and Mission in Chicago. Sankey complained that the sun would not go to bed at a civilized hour: nor would it, for a man from a place on the latitude of Rome who worked in midsummer on the latitude of Edmonton or parts of Labrador.

Sankey was agitated by a summons to Sunderland. An ex-sailor called Arthur Rees, who was a Baptist minister, wanted the evangelists, but doubted that an unknown soloist of sacred song would prove acceptable to the northern shipbuilding town, whose nonconformists had an almost Scottish suspicion of music in worship. Sankey was dispatched by train in a state of nerves. He and Rees were at once taken to the back parlor of a butcher's shop, where the butcher's wife proudly displayed a dilapidated harmonium, which had been played by the great Philip Phillips six years earlier. The instrument was out of tune, and a stench of meat and blood percolated from the shop. But Sankey sang, and Rees sat entranced.

Sankey returned to York, the evangelists moved on July 19 and found that Rees had neatly dodged local prejudice by announcing that Mr. Moody would preach, and "Mr. Sankey will sing the Gospel." The Sunderland campaign (Moody carried forward the terminology of the Civil War just as Billy Graham seventy years later adopted Eisenhower's word *crusade*) was a disappointment. At

the end of its five weeks, the Moodys—Emma noted in her diary—
"had a feeling that one minister had done much to hinder blessing
among others."

The Methodists, however, had persuaded Newcastle-upon-
Tyne, a dozen miles northwest, to offer a hearing to the Americans.
When Moody entered the great coal seaport on August 25, he
determined to stick there until prejudice died.

At the end of September, John Cairns, a Scottish minister of the
United Presbyterians in Berwick-on-Tweed, and a brilliant theologian in his fifties who held a part-time professorship in Edinburgh,
passed through Newcastle.

He wrote to his sister:

> There was a great crowd at Mr. Leitch's church. At the meeting,
> which was opened by Mr. Leitch and myself, the chief peculiarity was
> the singing by a Mr. Sankey with harmonium accompaniment, under
> the direction of a Mr. Moody, an American gentleman who has been
> laboring in Newcastle for five weeks. The singing was very impressive,
> the congregation striking in at the choruses with thrilling effect. The
> address by Mr. Moody, though thoroughly Yankee, was deeply earnest
> and produced a great impression. It was on the grace of God, and had
> many happy strokes though here and there grotesque. The audience
> was fairly carried away at times by this mingled impulse of singing and
> appeal and at the close a good many persons, impressed for the first
> time waited to be spoken with.

He added that the movement had spread all round Newcastle and
into the countryside, and that he had discussed it with many
acquaintances, "who all speak warmly of its results."

From the obscurity of York, Moody and Sankey had become the
talk of the greatest city in the north of England.

The Newcastle campaign started among the well-churched
middle classes. It spread slowly upward and downward. Rich
merchants, shipbuilders, and coal-mine owners began to attend
the meetings, encouraged by a vigorous commendation from a
local Member of Parliament. His *Newcastle Chronicle* praised the
"wonderful religious phenomenon," its lack of sectarianism,
Moody's singlemindedness, and especially that "the jingle of money
is never heard at these meetings." The "Geordies," sallow and

stunted from overlong hours underground on scanty diet, the people of the slums who lived in a lifelong atmosphere of coal dust, and the "masses" whom Moody longed to reach held aloof—until he tried a mothers' meeting. A baby-in-arms had yelled until the irritation of the audience drove to tears its working-class mother, at which Moody, in contrast to an early twentieth-century evangelist who refused to continue until a noisy baby was removed, charmingly announced on the spur of the moment a women's meeting at which no one would be admitted unless carrying a baby. His supporters' delicate ladies (there was sharp distinction in the seventies between "women" and "ladies") went, Emma recorded,

> to the poorest meanest streets and told the women to come and bring their babies with them. Such a squealing! . . . But the poor women listened while the tears ran down their faces and Mr. Sankey and Mr. Moody were both able to continue their talks remarkably well.

Enlarging attendances brought a demand for copies of the hymns Sankey sang, especially of "Jesus of Nazareth Passeth By," an affecting ballad on the healing of blind Bartimaeus, written by an American in New Jersey ten years before, which struck home to hearers left unmoved by Moody's preaching. Bliss's happy, stirring, or sentimental hymns likewise were the rage. As Sankey said, it was then "that we began to realize the wonderful power there was in these Gospel songs." Families wanted to sing them as they gathered round pianos in parlors, but the only copies in England were in Sankey's personal scrapbook.

He wrote to the English publishers of Philip Phillips's collection, used at the meetings, offering his own selection without charge if they would print it as a supplement. They refused, and threw away a fortune. Moody promised another publisher, Richard Cope Morgan of Morgan and Scott, whose weekly *Christian* had been the evangelists' warm friend, to guarantee an edition of a sixteen-page pamphlet of Sankey's selection.

On September 16, *Sacred Songs and Solos*, in its first short form, at sixpence a copy, or a penny for words only to be used in alliance with Phillips's book, was for sale.

Moody and Sankey had brought a warm breeze into the fusty religion of nonconformist churches in the northeast corner of

England, though churchmen remained aloof from lay and unac-
credited preachers. But other American visitors sponsored by
nonconformist chapels had come in years past and had flown
forgotten as a dream. Would Moody and Sankey be different?
They planned to move to Darlington for nine days in mid-October;
they had accepted a week in Bishop Auckland, where lay the
Bishop of Durham's palace. After that, they would give one or two
days to several small towns on Tees or Tyne. Two-thirds of the six
months that Moody had allotted to Britain would be gone, and
despite numerous invitations to scattered parts of the country the
mission seemed in danger of fizzling out.

One autumn day changed the prospect.

In the Newcastle suburb of Walker, where the leaves were falling
already, Moody, as he dealt with inquirers in a chapel vestry, noticed
a clergyman who introduced himself as "the Reverend John
Kelman, minister of the Free Church of Scotland, at Leith, the port
of Edinburgh."

Kelman made him a startling proposition. Come to Edinburgh,
he said, and I and my friends of the Free and Established Churches
will form a committee. We will prepare the ground, and I believe
that every presbytery will support you. Win Edinburgh, and you
will win Scotland. Scotland needs you.

Moody was aghast. Edinburgh, the Athens of the North where his
lack of formal education must appear an impertinence? Able Presbyterian theologians and dry scholars of intense earnestness—grave,
discriminating, and rigid—would be on the platform. His racy torrent
of anecdote and informal Bible teaching might shock or irritate them.
As for Sankey, most Scotsmen considered offensive the singing of
"human" hymns (those other than metrical versions of the psalms).
Moody lamely suggested accepting a prior invitation to Dundee.

But Kelman was emphatic. "Edinburgh *first*. Then you will reach
the nation."

Moody did not give him an immediate answer. This was a
decisive moment, his first opportunity to work in a capital city
prepared by a representative committee. Edinburgh's leading men
of religion, Kelman asserted, would rally behind him. That, Moody
reflected, was only an opinion.

If he accepted, it would be at the risk of being laughed out of
Britain, never to return.

14

Surprise in the North

Moody and Sankey slipped into Edinburgh, which Emma considered the most beautiful city in the world, on a dismal storm-swept Saturday night, November 22, 1873, and from Waverley Station took cabs for hotels, until run to earth by the committee. The Sankeys were carried off to the manse of the veteran hymn writer Horatius Bonar, while the Moodys stayed with the elderly Professor William Blaikie, the friend of Livingstone. "D. L. very hoarse," noted Emma in her diary. "Prof. Simpson sent for." He diagnosed acute tonsilitis.

Prominent Presbyterians, mostly of the Free Kirk, had risked good repute to sponsor unknown, unordained Americans and had held six weeks of preparatory meetings. "I've just had a letter from one of the most eminent ministers there," a Scotsman had told Emma early in November, "and they are most enthusiastic over Mr. Moody coming."

On the opening day, November 23, despite the rarity of evening services in the Scotland of 1873, the Sabbath calm of Princes Street was broken by the tramp of countless feet and the rumble of a few carriages, defying the current interpretation of the Fourth Commandment, to say nothing of folk who had come in by train paying the double fare by which the railways quieted their Sabbath conscience.

The committee tended to hazard wild guesses at attendance figures, but on this first night Sankey could see the city's largest hall "densely packed to its utmost corners; even the lobbies, stairs, and entrance were crowded with people, while more than two thousand were turned away." Sankey felt nervous. He had overheard carpings about his use of "human" hymns, even more against the "kist o' whustles," as they were pleased to dub the little American organ, and moreover the chairman's first words, greeted with gasps of disappointment, announced that Moody was too unwell to attend.

Sankey had the sense to begin by inviting the congregation to unite in a familiar "praise," the "Old Hundredth." When he sang "Jesus of Nazareth Passeth By,"

> the intense silence that pervaded that great audience at once assured [him] that even "human hymns," sung in a prayerful spirit, were indeed likely to be used of God to arrest attention and convey Gospel truth to the hearts of men in bonny Scotland, even as they had in other places.

The address was given by James Hood Wilson of the Barclay Free Church, whom Moody had honored at once as a man of love, vigor, and military precision. Sankey wound up with "Hold the Fort," and to his delight the congregation joined in the chorus lustily.

Moody spent the day spraying his throat from the latest invention, since Professor (Sir) Alexander Simpson "had taken a handspray with me, for medicine had just entered on the microbial era."

Professor Blaikie had initiated him into the mysteries of a land that wore an impressive cloak of piety and conduct, but in which love lay expunged by law; joy and religion were divorced; and most men believed it blasphemy to claim certainty of heaven, saying that, though Christ had died for all, none knew whether he or she were predestined to salvation. In this severe, chilling Calvinism, the "Guid Book" had less authority than the Westminster Confession. Industrial areas, moreover, held a widening circle of the "lapsed mass" who never attended kirk; university and divinity schools were lapped by ripples of "Doubt," and the nation was weakened by schism. The Disruption of thirty years before had left a legacy of competition, mistrust, and disputation. Movements toward reunion, either of the Established Church with the Free, or the Free with the older Secession church, the United Presbyterians, had bred merely an unhappier atmosphere.

Then Blaikie spoke of those who, like himself, Hood Wilson, Kelman, and Professor Charteris, sighed for a divine wind. The Revival of 1859 from Ulster and the United States had blown little beyond Scottish country districts, yet with all its extravagances had been a sign to those who could discern. And now, fourteen years later, an aged saint, R. S. Candlish, shortly before dying that very autumn, had prophesied a great blessing, which should not be despised though it came strangely.

The newfangled throat spray enabled Moody to attend the second night of the mission, held in the Barclay Church, where the evangelists arrived to find the "kist o' whustles" left in the concert hall. A committeeman jumped into a cab and galloped into the night. Twenty minutes later, came a cry from outside and a crash. The cabbie had rounded the corner too fast and spilled the committeeman and the "kist" onto the cobbled street. Sankey shook his head sadly. The repairs would take a day, and he would not sing without his "kist." Moody heard one Scotsman say to another that it "all had a gr-r-and tendency to break up any scheme the evangelists might have in their working together." From the third evening on, the mission could run its course.

"The church was crowded in every part," wrote Hood Wilson, within a week

> every spot of standing ground was occupied. A number have come to peace in believing—some of them the most unlikely. Night after night ... all sorts of people from all parts of the city. Many have come in from the country, ministers and others. I have felt much stirred up and hope to get a blessing. We have a busy time before us.

Moody, thirty-six years old, swept from obscurity to fame.

Surprise was the keynote of those fantastic seven weeks. Moody marveled that staid Scots should listen to the torrent of his "profuse diction which stops neither for colons or commas" (Simpson said that Moody could pronounce "Jerusalem" in two syllables), tolerate his Yankee accent, and forgive him for sometimes deliberately making them laugh in church. His audiences were surprised by joy. No sudden break, as at York, but a steady brightening like some spring sunrise dispelling the chill November murk, as men and women grasped the astonishing fact that God loves sinners; they had believed He loved only saints.

"A young man," they heard Moody say,

> told me last night that he was too great a sinner to be saved. Why, they
> are the very men Christ came after! "This man receiveth sinners, and
> eateth with them." The only charge they could bring against Christ
> down here was that He was receiving bad men. They are the very kind
> of men He is willing to receive. All you have got to do is to prove that
> you are a sinner and I will prove that you have got a Saviour. And the
> greater the sinner, the greater the need of a Saviour. You say your heart
> is hard. Well, then, of course you want Christ to soften it. You cannot
> do it yourself. The harder your heart, the more need you have of
> Christ. The blacker you are, the more need you have of a Saviour. If
> your sins rise up before you like a dark mountain, bear in mind that
> the blood of Jesus Christ cleanses from all sin. There's no sin so big or
> so black or so corrupt and vile but the blood of Christ can cover it. So I
> preach the old Gospel again: "The Son of man is come to seek and to
> save that which was lost." It was Adam's fall, his *loss* that brought out
> God's love. It was his fall, his sin, that brought it out. A friend of mine
> from Manchester was in Chicago a few years . . .

and Moody was off on another anecdote.

His hearers could hardly believe their ears. It sounded so simple.
"Scotch preaching," wrote a layman, signing himself "Onlooker,"
in the correspondence column of the *Scotsman*, "has for fifty years
been little else but a reiteration of doctrines which, to me, at least,
are an unintelligible puzzle. The whole ingenuity of our preachers
has been to convince us that we are the subject of God's wrath," who
could gain forgiveness only by believing in "a complex theological
puzzle." "Onlooker" begged the clergy learn a lesson from the two
strangers who had come to "sing and recite the declaration of God's
goodness and forgiveness . . . Throw aside that complex system."

Moody's addresses seemed brief to an age of sermons an hour or
more long, and he often interspersed them with silent prayer or a
song from Sankey. He made "no attempt to awaken excitement or
sensation," an Edinburgh divinity professor noted with satisfaction; provoked "no articulate wailings, no prostrations, no sudden
outbursts of rapture which we have heard in former revivals." But
he preached for decision. He would not trim his message to suit
Calvinistic hesitancy, which feared lest appeal for a definite step of
faith overrode Predestination, a word Moody could not pronounce; "I preach the Gospel to *every* creature," he contended.

Moody, said Blaikie, placed his emphasis "upon the doctrine that Christianity is not mere feeling, but a surrender of the *whole* nature to a personal, living Christ." And thus, as at Chicago, the inquiry room after-meeting was the very hinge of the campaign. The idea was not new to Edinburgh. Indeed, the secretary of the Carubber's Close Mission, which did for Edinburgh slums what Illinois Street did for Chicago's, asserted that Moody had picked up the idea during his visit of 1867, but few had seen such a meeting, and ministers suspected the Inquiry Room to be an emotional forcing-house or complete surrender to an unbalanced doctrine of free will, or even a dark imitation of the Roman Catholic confessional.

Fears were soon quieted. The *Daily News* reported ministers "finding their difficulties melting away by personal contact with the work," until Moody noticed pews or benches, in church or parish hall used for after-meetings, dotted with black-coated, white-neckerchiefed bewhiskered figures, Bibles open, talking earnestly to inquirers. Moody urged upon his "personal workers," as he called them, "*patient* and *thorough* dealing with each case, no hurrying from one to another. Wait patiently, and ply them with God's word, and think, oh! think, what it is to win a soul for Christ, and don't grudge the time spent on one person." He had come far from his breakneck Chicago days.

The inquiry room drew a cross-section of Edinburgh, young men especially: medical students from the university and sons of generals or lawyers from spacious Georgian squares, and rough fellows from huddled alleys of the old city, who stood out by their shabby homespun. To work among all of them Moody conscripted theological students of the Free Church's New College. Thus he met Henry Drummond.

Moody and Drummond were a contrast. The twenty-two-year-old Drummond, future author of *Natural Law in the Spiritual World*, had a supple, incisive mind, powerfully educated in natural science and theology; he was cultured, refined, a little of a dandy, a fine sportsman, and quiet, with what one fellow student called "a perilous sense of humor." The soul of Drummond knit with the soul of Moody, who recognized in him a high quality of leadership, and knew him at once as a "humble, unselfish and cheerful friend." Night after night, men noticed Drummond walking back through the gas-lit streets in swirling mist, a green and black tartan plaid thrown over his head and shoulders, and his arm linked through the arm of some youth he had helped.

By mid-December, all Edinburgh was awake, amazed. "If," said Professor Charteris, "anyone had told us that our decorous city would be stirred to the depths by two strangers, we could not have believed the tale."

Moody and Sankey had put a match to the well-laid dry sticks of Scottish religion. They had done more. Charteris continued:

> If anyone had said that the sectarian divisions which are so visible not only in ecclesiastical concerns but in social life and in private friendships, would disappear in presence of two evangelists who came among us with no such ecclesiastical credentials as we are accustomed to value most highly, the idea would have seemed absolutely absurd.

It was this "most blessed and precious result" that at once gave Moody a place in Scottish history. Dimly, after weary years of wrangle, Scotland perceived that the road to unity lay through service, and that what discussion failed to promote, mutual devotion to Christian mission would produce almost unawares. It would be twenty-six years to the first major reunion and fifty-five to the great reunion of 1929, after which only a small section of the Free Church remained apart. But already Blaikie could comment, "We all seemed to be lifted above our usual sectarian limits." A year later, an Edinburgh man told his London brethren: "We have rather a character of being theological porcupines, but a vast number of the quills have been drawn and there has been a warmth and kindness between the various ministers and denominations such as I have never witnessed before."

Nor was that all. Stiff, conservative Edinburgh took from Moody and Sankey what they would not from their own kin. Thus, the Committee had started a noon prayer meeting before the mission. Moody sat through a few prayers, long, scriptural, doctrinal, obliquely controversial, comprehensive and quite indefinite, and banged his fist on the table. "I tell you, friends, some people's prayers need to be cut at both ends and set fire to in the middle." As a Scotsman declared, "Only he, at that date, could have done it and lived!"

Sankey's personal conquest was even more extraordinary. In

early days he could almost smell disapproval of his "kist," and, one night in the Free Assembly Hall, he was startled in the midst of a solo by a shrill female from the gallery: "Let me oot! Let me oot! What would John Knox think of the like of you?" At the end of the solo he crossed to the overflow meeting in the Tolbooth Church. "I had just begun to sing when the same voice was again heard, "Let me oot!'"

By December 22, Blaikie could write, "It is almost amusing to observe how entirely the latent distrust of Mr. Sankey's 'kist o' whustles' has disappeared." None rejoiced more than the veteran Horatius Bonar, whose hymns "Fill Thou My Life," "I Heard the Voice of Jesus Say," "Go Labor on," and many others, were banned by the elders of his own parish kirk. The Church of Scotland's hymnbook of the previous decade had little use. Scottish conscience had jibbed at Bonar and refused the immortal organ music of Bach and Handel except as secular entertainment. Astonishingly, it surrendered to the "kist o' whistles" and Sankey's "touching pathos." The hymns he popularized (he himself had written only one, to words of Bonar, since arrival in Edinburgh, "the first Gospel song I had ever composed") were now heard everywhere.

By the new year, 1874, word of happenings in Edinburgh had sped across Scotland like some latter-day fiery cross.

An Appeal for Prayer, signed by leading Edinburgh ministers and laymen, went to every minister of every denomination in Scotland. A specially raised fund of two thousand pounds provided a weekly copy of the *Christian* for each minister throughout the British Isles, carrying special reports. Eyewitnesses hastened to highland glens and lowland burghs and villages.

In a village on the Firth of Clyde, Inverkip, lived a young railway employee called John McNeill.

Quiet little village; quiet little Free Kirk; worship of the quiet stereotyped sort. No frills, certainly not. When suddenly there's a stir! Our minister has been to Edinburgh; he has heard a preacher, an American called Moody, and a singer called Sankey, and according to him Edinburgh's on fire! There's a revival on—whatever that may mean. The sough of it is on our minister's breath, his prayers and his preaching. We young folks begin to talk to each other, quietly, about the deepest things; we begin to seek, and we find.

The minister called a "testimony meeting, on a Sunday night; unheard of thing in our wee quiet village. Folks mightily stirred; gathered round the doors." McNeill and two other lads got up in turn. "They hammer and they stammer, but they're out with it. They have taken Christ to be their Saviour, and mean henceforth to live for Him." All three remained sturdy Christians, McNeill a spectacular evangelist.

Inverkip was one of dozens of parishes and towns set spiritually ablaze. Invitations poured in to Moody and Sankey. They were able to make a day trip on January 12 to Benwick-on-Tweed where, a fortnight later, John Cairns was still

occupied from morning till night in seeking out persons who either come to our inquiry meetings, or whom I expect to find anxious or willing to be conversed with on personal religion. The Corn Exchange is filled, and sometimes crowded every night . . . Our noonday prayer meeting is attended by from one hundred and fifty to two hundred . . . It has been hard work but I never came anything so near the souls of men. If the half hold, it will be the most wonderful experience by far I have ever passed through.

15

Glasgow Conquered

Sudden fame made Sankey a little heady, his step more jaunty. His wife remained her retiring self, "very pleasant and friendly," looking forward to the arrival of her two children from America and—though this, of course, in hushed tones with no stranger near—to a little arrival of a different sort.

Emma scarcely noticed fame, and Moody, consciously the mere instrument of a higher power, was too aware of the worth of the men around him to have a swollen head. And too occupied. He barely had a moment to scrawl a letter to Illinois Street: "I am lonesome often when I think of you all but I shall soon be with you for the weeks go like days when I am busy."

After three weeks in Dundee they came to Glasgow, on February 7, 1874. A special United Evangelistic Committee had prepared assiduously; massed choirs had practiced, prayer meetings drew hundreds daily; and tickets to hear Moody were distributed through parish ministers to prevent unsafe overcrowding. The great industrial city and neighboring burghs were agog, fed by reports of nightly services in Edinburgh, continuing unabated since the evangelists' departure.

And instead of a white elephant in the half-prepared bedroom of an obscure druggist, Moody, with his family, was the honored guest of a leading minister, Andrew Bonar, Horatius's younger brother, a superb Bible teacher, who entered at the exact moment when Moody, after six months' preaching, with an indefinite stay in Britain ahead, was in danger of drying up. Moody sucked out the rich reserves of Bible knowledge and insight. "Come and join us," he would cry if a friend dropped in to Lynedoch Place, "we are having a dig in the Rock." To an American afterwards he said that, in all of Britain, Bonar was one of the two men who helped him most.

It was a happy house, with a nursery for the children, the one defect being that, as in similar British homes, there was no built-in bath. A hip-bath by the fire, filled by steaming cans lugged up steep stairs by the housemaid was all very well for Emma, but not much good for a fellow who wanted a cold dip (in February), especially when he was almost the same diameter as the tub!

The campaign opened at nine on "Sabbath" morning, February 8, in the City Hall, before three thousand Sabbath school teachers.

One of them, David Russell, recalled in old age how, after the "Old Hundredth" and Andrew Bonar's prayer, Sankey announced that he would sing "I Am So Glad That Jesus Loves Me," a Sunday school ditty by Bliss in peculiar measure, with chorus—to Russell as to most, unknown. Sankey enraptured him.

> I had never heard such magnificent singing. The great consecrated voice, the glad face of the singer and the almost childish simplicity of the words overcame me, and I found tears streaming down my face. I felt ashamed lest anyone should see my weakness, but ere long I noticed tears on other faces. Mr. Moody needed no introduction . . . On the platform beside him were many of the leading ministers and laymen of the city. Mr. Moody's manner of holding his Bible in his right hand was significant of his hold on it and its hold on him. For a few minutes I thought I would not like him. The American accent, and what to me at first appeared to be a lack of reverence and dignity, jarred upon my sensitive Scotch nature, but a pathetic story told in his inimitable way caught me and bound my soul to him. It was a great, inspiring meeting, and I believe that there that morning Mr. Moody conquered Glasgow.

Moody did not have to "make his way." He was borne on a surge. Week after week, through bleak winter into spring, the meetings continued in churches, the City Hall, and at last in the Kibble

Palace, an enormous glass exhibition building generally called the Crystal Palace. On foot, by horse-tram, by train, in trim carriages and creaking cabs, the people came; from shipyards and mills and grimy tenements of the Gorbals, where the air was heavy with soot and bitter winds swept cheerless streets; from sumptuous houses nearby in Hillhead; and very many from middle-class homes, where *Sacred Songs and Solos* lay on every cottage piano.

"People were thoroughly roused, either to opposition or sympathy," noted Jane Mackinnon, a shipowner's wife, who had come up from Campbelltown in Kintyre for the duration. "It was the subject of conversation everywhere, and everyone had a position to take up, for or against. It was an easy thing to show one's colors."

Moody forged into Glasgow with every tough ounce of a frame still burly rather than portly, with Sankey manfully pacing him. "The mind experiences a sense of fatigue in detailing their efforts," remarked a newspaper when the campaign was at its height. A weekday's first engagement would be the monster prayer meeting at noon for an hour. "One to two o'clock, conversation with individuals; four to five o'clock, Bible lecture, attended by some twelve or fifteen hundred; seven to half past eight, evangelistic meeting, with inquiry meeting at close; nine to ten o'clock, young men's meeting." Sabbath morning held an extra session in the City Hall and a sermon at some other church, but the afternoon was free from twelve-thirty to five. "He had strength and used it unsparingly," commented one of his Scottish friends, "but people seemed to think it had no limit." He kept one day a week for relaxing, normally Saturday.

Bible lectures and young men's meetings were alike remarkable. The former, being at four o'clock, drew the more fashionable since servants and shopkeepers, factory hands and their wives were immersed in the daily grind. "All around one, people were intensely interested," wrote Jane Mackinnon. "Three or four ministers in the pulpit itself and others on the stair, Mr. Sankey and the choir on the precentor's platform, and every inch of sitting and standing room occupied." Bible readings of the Moody-Moorhouse style awakened the People of the Guid Book to their ignorance of it. This simple Sunday school teaching for adults filled a void left by the involved exegesis that flowed ponderously from pulpits. Ministers swallowed pride and introduced Moody's method; in 1900 Sir George Adam Smith, the great biblical scholar, could write, "In

Scotland we owe to Mr. Moody a powerful revival of our Bible classes."

The young men's meetings at the end of an exhausting day brought out the very best in Moody, and that of Tuesday, February 24, became known across Scotland as the "Hundred-and-One Night." While Moody still preached at the City Hall, five Edinburgh students led by Henry Drummond gave "brief, solemn stirring appeals" in Ewing Place Church, "packed from floor to ceiling." As Hood Wilson followed, speaking on "Why Not Tonight?" Moody slipped in. The moment that Hood Wilson stopped, Moody said, quite quietly, "All those who are *sure* they are Christians, stand up!

"Sit down again, please! The three pews in front here. I want them cleared. Anyone who wants to take Christ as their Saviour, you all come forward now, so we can pray for you. Let us bow our heads as they come."

There was extraordinary movement in a tight silence that could be felt. "From every part of the building a stream began to flow." Moody lifted his eyes and prayed aloud. As James Stalker, one of the Edinburgh students, recalled, "the sense of Divine power became overwhelming, and I remember quite well turning round on the platform and hiding my face in my hands, unable to look on the scene any more." The front seats filled. Moody cleared the next rows, and the next.

An usher counted 101 people come forward. "Christian friends remained conversing with the anxious till about twelve o'clock." Toward the end a youth who said he "had been seeking Christ a long time," was going away "without relief. Mr. Moody came up and took me kindly by the hand," he recounted. "He looked at me—I might say he put his two eyes right through mine—and asked me if I would take Christ now. I could not speak, but my heart said, Yes."

Back in their hotel, the Edinburgh Five sat long into the small hours, "discussing the remarkable scene [they] had just witnessed," and Henry Drummond presented each afterwards with a finely bound New Testament which they all signed; his own copy he used in the next years until it was "worn to rags." One of the Glasgow ushers, William Oatts, who had the list of names and addresses of all the 101, kept touch with most of them for years. "Did these young fellows stand? Did the decision mean reality?" Over half a century later he claimed that for many it did; he met them, active Christians in Glasgow, London, Australia. And most of the 101 in the months immediately following that night worked hard among their generation of all ranks. A Moody campaign, as men had remarked already, was a spiritual incendiary—always igniting spiritual fires that burned long after the evangelists moved on.

"For the last 3 months I have had to refuse money all the time. At Edinburgh they wanted to raise me two or three thousand pounds but I would not let them I told them I would not take it." Thus Moody wrote to his Chicago friend Whittle on March 7, 1874.

Any unprejudiced observer could see that Moody had not "yielded to the temptations that powerfully assail his class. He [did] not give himself out to be coddled and petted by well meaning but injudicious admirers." Letters appeared in the papers, asserting the whole campaign to be a glorious hoax organized for gain by Barnum, the American showman. "Of course I have a good many enemies over here," Moody told Farwell, "who say I am a speculating Yankee." He refused to allow collections for campaign expenses, telling the committee to raise sufficient funds privately; in Scotland he appears occasionally to have accepted personal gifts "to myself for my own use," beyond hospitality and expenses, but sent much of what he received across the Atlantic to enable Whittle and Bliss to abandon business and tour America as another Moody and Sankey. "If you have not got Faith enough launch out on the strength of my faith," he exhorted Whittle. "Has not our God got as much money as the Watch Company & all he wants of us is to trust Him?"

Glasgow pocketbooks had opened wide; Scots who proverbially kept tight fists on sixpences itched to give pounds. A thirty-year-old chemical manufacturer named Campbell White, whose father owned the beautiful estate of Overtoun, asked Moody how he should use his growing fortune; John Colville, a young ironmaster, asked same. Moody needed only to lift his finger for money to flow. Where should he point? He had spoken at some of the big shipyards, warehouses, and factories, but he knew the force of his detractors' jeer that the poorest of Glasgow seldom came near his central services: the committee's ticket system tended to debar them. He had glimpsed extremes of destitution and unemployment. He knew that whiskey ruled the slums.

Moody turned the eyes of White, Colville, and their like, to consider the cry of Glasgow's poor.

Nor was it a matter merely of money. A text he used repeatedly was "To every man his work." The result was a surge of activity, spiritual and social, through channels old and new. The United Evangelistic Committee perpetuated itself as the Glasgow Evangelistic Association to begin a long, honorable career in evangelism and philanthropy—Poor Children's Day Refuges, Temperance Work, Fresh Air Fortnights, the Cripple Girls' League, the Glasgow Christian Institute, and a tent on Glasgow Green where on Sunday mornings young men brought in "the sleepers-out and other human derelicts . . . dejected, hungry and wretched-looking" for a free breakfast (if it was only tea and bread) and a service. A "Poor Children's Sabbath Dinner" started soon afterwards, in cooperation with an existing agency; a permanent hall rose; and, by 1918, five and a half million free meals for adults and children had been provided.

Economically, this was amelioration, not cure, as socialists were quick to point out with scorn at the end of the century, when Lord Overtoun (as Campbell White became) collided with Keir Hardie. Moody and his friends in 1874 could not grasp the roots of poverty when modern economic theories were almost unheard. Moreover, they believed that once a man's heart was purified and empowered by the Spirit of God he could rise above the worst circumstance.

For Glasgow's destitute children, the pathetic orphans of the inebriate, "hundreds of budding lives anchored down to vice," Moody brought in a munificent gift to William Quarrie's recently formed Orphan Homes of Scotland. Wherever he went, "Mr. Moody gave great attention to Young Men's Christian Associations, and at the height of the movement secured very large subscriptions for their foundation or expansion." Sir George Adam Smith's testimony is valuable because he held no brief for Moody, differed from him theologically, and worked in Glasgow for fifteen years. In 1898, he summed up one of the most important facets of the impact on Scotland: "We have forgotten how often Mr. Moody enforced the civic duties of our faith. Yet read again his addresses and articles of the time, and you will believe that in the seventies there was no preacher more practical or civic amongst us."

Moody stayed unmoved by "some very nasty letters" in the Glasgow press. "The enemy is thoroughly roused," Emma remarked. Apart from jokers and the scurrilous, the letter writers either objected that "the American brethren virtually and for the time being have superseded the pastors in the city"; or complained that "Calvinism is in abeyance."

During early spring, Moody detected a change of attitude among strangers, especially from the Highlands. This was reflected in some of the letters in his heavy daily postbag and in that of Hood Wilson, whose library had become "a perfect sea of letters, which were not only an inch deep on the large round table in the middle of the room, but covered chairs and shelves in every corner." Both men knew that a pamphlet, by the influential Highland preacher John Kennedy of Dingwall, written to damn them, had circulated among extreme Calvinists and dour conservatives of the remote depopulated northern and western Highlands. *Hyper-Evangelism: "Another Gospel" Though a Mighty Power* argued that "the present movement ignores the sovereignty and power of God," and that the emphasis on faith hindered the work of the Holy Spirit and denied "the utter spiritual impotence of souls 'dead in trespasses and sins.'" Dr. Kennedy blasted the inquiry room, the singing of "human" hymns, the use of organ music ("unscriptural, and therefore all who have subscribed the Confession of Faith are under solemn vow against it"), and asserted that prayer meetings had been turned into "factories of sensation."

Such diatribe was expected of rigid High Calvinism. Moody said he could have pointed out more faults in his work himself. This pamphlet would not account for the subtly poisoned atmosphere.

John Kennedy was a dignified prophet, preaching with Celtic fervor massively erudite sermons, which simple Highlanders treated with the utmost veneration. He knew Shakespeare, the poets, and the puritan divines—and he was an authority on cricket. He had charm and was widely traveled, having lately returned from America. Kennedy, of the Free Church, hated talk of reunion. Presbyterians of differing churches who united to work with Moody appeared betrayers of Calvinism. Not daring to confess this publicly, Kennedy cast around for means to cramp the movement, until a letter from a Chicago acquaintance dropped into his lap. Genuine Christian though he was, Kennedy distributed utterly unverified manuscript copies.

Weeks passed before Moody saw a copy and understood the puzzled glances, the shrugs, and the half hints.

The long letter from a strict Presbyterian lawyer in Chicago, an emigrant from the Highlands, John Mackay, contained legitimate if farfetched polemic against the YMCA and Moody's teaching. "He evidently wishes to get the people of Scotland drifted quietly from their moorings . . . . " But its core took quite another line, and Moody skimmed the pages amazed:

> . . . Mr. Moody came to Chicago a poor lad . . . he called at the office of a pious and wealthy merchant of this city (now a client of mine) and begged him as a friend and Christian to give him a place in his office as he wanted to get away from profanity and ungodliness . . . . Mr. Moody with his proverbial audacity and loud Christian professions worked himself into the confidence of the house. His employer had a lawsuit pending in the Court . . . it transpired that the opposing parties were possessed of secrets of the house. Suspicion at once rested on the saintly Mr. Moody . . . proved him the guilty man . . . . Moody stoutly denied the charge . . . . Undeniable proof . . . he confessed and was summarily discharged . . . Soon afterwards publicly declared his determination to discard all worldly pursuits, and to devote himself wholly to the Lord's work. Possessed of great vigor and unlimited cheek.

Moody wrote promptly to Farwell from Glasgow on May 7. "I heard a few hours ago of a letter that has been written from Chicago to a Dr. of Divinity in Scotland making me out a bad man." He begged Farwell to ask young Henderson (then the head of the house, a nephew of Moody's benefactor) for a letter expressing confidence in him:

> If I did anything unchristian while I was with Henderson I am not aware of it . . . . I was young and might have said and done things that I would not now, but I am grieved to think anyone in that house could say I am guilty of what his letter accuses me of . . . . No one knows me here and if my friends in Chicago do not stand by me, who will? for everyone in this country who is opposed to my preaching and revivals are doing all they can to break me down. I wish you would write me at once.

A formal request "for a thorough investigation into the truth or falsehood of these charges" reached Farwell from Kelman, chairman of the Scottish committee: "If the allegations contained in this letter are quite unfounded, please telegraph per cable to this effect and write to me more fully by post." Kelman foresaw an uninhibited effort by Kennedy to pillory Moody as a rogue at the imminent General Assembly of the Free Kirk.

Farwell had no difficulty in securing the signatures of thirty-five Chicago ministers to an endorsement of Moody's "Christian character," which he cabled to Edinburgh. Henderson wrote, "For fifteen years since Mr. Moody left us I have watched him, assisted him and believed in him," and told Farwell that the conversation upon which Mackay based the slanders was "intended to raise Moody in his estimation and could only be used as he used it by a willful perversion of its true intent."

Farwell demanded a retraction and since the "muleish Scotsman" would not retract, threatened Mackay with the law. Moody refused to prosecute. Farwell was disappointed. "I really think it would be a charitable act to make him pay $5,000 or $10,000 for his slanders, to be expended in evangelizing Dr. Kennedy's district in Scotland!"

Kennedy could not kill the Glasgow campaign. A meeting on one of the final days packed the Crystal Palace with registered converts, mostly under twenty-five and of the more educated classes. And on the last Sunday the Great Western Road had been black for three hours with a living stream of all sorts and conditions of men and women, mostly on foot because "vehicles were not easily to be had on a Sunday." Under the strong evening sun of a Scottish May, Moody preached in the Botanical Gardens from the box of a carriage to a crowd estimated at twenty or thirty thousand. No one could know the exact figure, which probably lay around fifteen thousand, and if through lack of a wind Moody was not audible to the edges, the singing was unforgettable. But to an age when vast meetings were less common it all appeared amazing.

16

Racked Hearts

On the morning of Wednesday, May 20, 1874, the Americans, "much fatigued by our incessant labors," went down to St. Enoch's station, without fuss or farewell deputation. Because they were about to plunge into two days of Edinburgh meetings before leaving for a heavy itinerary in the North, the two men "sought the seclusion and rest which a first-class railway carriage in Great Britain affords"; their women and the Moody children seem to have been parked thriftily in second or third class during the short journey, for the evangelists had a carriage to themselves.

Sankey had selected at Menzies' newspaper stall a penny weekly, the *Christian Age*, which specialized in American preaching, and while the train swayed and rattled through Glasgow suburbs, he scanned it eagerly, to find nothing to interest him except a sermon by Henry Ward Beecher. He gazed out at dull slag heaps and chimneys. Moody was immersed in Chicago mail. Shortly before Edinburgh, Sankey idly took up his paper again to look at the advertisements.

> For sale: A pretty Iron Church (including fittings, etc) . . . Ambrosial Tea—the most valuable tea ever grown . . . Shelford's Pianos, from 20 guineas upwards on EASY TERMS . . . Electricity is Life: Pulver-

macher's Patent Galvanic chain Bands, Belts . . . Hodder and Stoughton's Publications.

He ran his eyes down this vitally important book list: "Dr. Wheldon's new commentary . . . Rev. Paxton Hood's new work . . . One Thousand Gems from Henry Ward Beecher . . . The New Sunday School Hymnbook." He looked across at the next column, on the opposite page, and noticed an unsigned poem, titled "The Lost Sheep." It was set in bold type, on top of Beecher's sermon, but Sankey had missed it the first time. He read the lines carefully.

"Say, Moody. Here's a poem would make a fine evangelistic hymn—if it had a tune."

Moody glanced up. "Read it, Sankey."

Sankey did so "with all the vim and energy at my command. After I finished I looked at my friend Moody to see what the effect had been, only to discover that he had not heard a word, so absorbed was he in a letter. My chagrin can be better imagined than described."

Sankey popped the poem into his scrapbook. During the press of meetings in Edinburgh that afternoon and evening a phrase or two of a possible tune formed half-consciously in his mind. Next noon in the Free Church Assembly Hall the theme was "The Good Shepherd." Several ministers spoke, then Moody as chairman, then white-haired Horatius Bonar, who dwelt briefly but eloquently on the "Shepherd Work of Christ," carving a deep impression on his sympathetic audience. In the pulpit, Moody turned to Sankey at the harmonium: "Have you a solo appropriate for this subject, to close the service with?"

Sankey had not. "Greatly troubled," he dismissed thought of singing a metrical version of the Twenty-third Psalm because it had already been used twice at that meeting, and would be no solo:

> I knew that every Scotchman in the audience would join me . . . At this moment I seemed to hear a voice saying: "Sing the hymn you found on the train!" But I thought this impossible, as no music had ever been written for that hymn. The seconds ticked. Moody waited. The audience stirred. Again came the thought, "Sing that hymn!"
> Placing the little newspaper slip on the organ in front of me, I lifted my heart in prayer, asking God to help me so to sing that the people might hear and understand. Laying my hands upon the organ I struck the key of A-flat and began to sing:

> There were ninety and nine that safely lay
> In the shelter of the fold;
> But one was out on the hills away,
> Far off from the gates of gold—
> Away on the mountains wild and bare,
> Away from the tender Shepherd's care,
> Away from the tender Shepherd's care.

After the first verse I was very glad I had got through, but overwhelmed with fear that the tune for the next verse would be greatly different from the first. But again looking up to the Lord for help in this most trying moment, He gave me again the same tune for all the remaining verses, note for note.

As the impromptu melody, pibroch-like, redolent of moor, mist, and forest, rose little by little in pitch and tension to its peak in the fifth line, falling right back in half in the last line to point rest, every man and woman saw the Good Shepherd leave the ninety and nine, climb the rough road, and cross deep waters and thorn thickets of storm-racked mountain, to find His one lost sheep, "sick and helpless and ready to die." Then Sankey's voice rang vibrant with triumph:

> But all through the mountains, thunder riven,
> And up from the rocky steep,
> There arose a cry to the gate of heaven,
> "Rejoice! I have found My sheep!"
> And the angels echoed around the throne:
> "Rejoice, for the Lord brings back His own!
> Rejoice, for the Lord brings back His own."

Sankey records: "As the music ceased, a great sigh seemed to go up from the meeting." Moody, greatly moved, brushing tears from his eyes, hurried from the pulpit and picked up the slip of newsprint.

"Sankey, where did you get that hymn? I never heard the like of it in my life!"

Sankey—with half the audience—in tears, the Victorian's inevitable release from emotional tension, replied solemnly: "Mr. Moody, that's the hymn I read to you yesterday on the train, which you did not hear."

"The Ninety and Nine" swept Scotland. A short time afterwards,

Sankey received a note of thanks from a woman for singing the poem of her deceased sister. It had been written in 1868 by Elizabeth Clephane, daughter of Andrew Clephane, the late sheriff of Fife, at the age of thirty-eight; she had died the following year. She had been left an orphan in childhood with two sisters and a brother, George, a wastrel packed off to Canada as a "remittance man" (the contemporary method by which black sheep of "good" families were given an allowance dependent on their remaining in the colonies). George fell in a drunken stupor on a country road late at night in May 1851, near Fergus in Ontario, where he was found dying the following morning. Elizabeth had liked to fancy that in his last hours this lost sheep of a brother "had found pardon and peace through the Cross."

When, sixteen years later, a cousin had begged her for a poem to print in *The Children's Hour*, Elizabeth had recalled her grief and hopes and written the five stanzas. Though it was copied by one or two other papers, it remained little known until Sankey found it. Her single other hymn, "Beneath the Cross of Jesus," also carries one of the few Sankey tunes to survive, written at Dr. Barnardo's house in the East End during the London campaign of 1875.

"The Ninety and Nine" was not Sankey's best, but it was his most popular hymn and is still to be found in hymnbooks, including the *English Hymnal*. With that song, Sankey and the hymns he introduced were woven warp and woof into the Britain—and later, into the America—of the seventies and after. His music spread around the world. *Sacred Songs and Solos* and its American counterpart, *Gospel Songs*, were said to have sold between 50 and 80 million copies in the first fifty years. If greatness were to be estimated by sales, or by the tally of persons decisively influenced, directly or indirectly, Sankey was great. It has been suggested that fewer people listened to actual performances of Bach's works during the entire nineteenth century than heard Sankey sing in the year 1875.[1]

The music and the musicians of which Sankey was archetype are derided. The name, if remembered, is mud.

Sankey is judged in the twentieth century for his hymnbook and compositions and not, as in fairness he ought to be, for his singing. He was essentially a singer; composing and arranging were his

---

[1] Robert M. Stevenson, *Patterns of Protestant Church Music* (Durham, N.C.: Duke University Press, 1953).

secondary activities. To him the melody was all-important. Without formal training in choral writing, accustomed to accompanying himself on the simplest instrument, Sankey showed little interest in arrangement, and his harmonies were drab, stilted, and limited generally to three basic chords: the tonic, dominant, and subdominant. The songs reflected the tinkling taste of the age, the nadir of English music. Yet many intensely lyrical songs of Ira David Sankey and Philip Bliss imply more than they disclose and, if harmonized, create for a generation of a more educated ear the profound impression that they wrought on the late Victorians. "Grace 'Tis a Charming Sound," "Thou Didst Leave Thy Throne," and "Whosoever Heareth" can make suitable congregational music, while a voice approximating Sankey's timbre may give Bliss's finest composition, "Man of Sorrows," a pathos as genuine as that of Handel's "Behold and See."

It is said that gospel songs formed the folk music of hymnody, that Sankey was the Stephen Foster of sacred music. His was not a conscious use of folk tunes. But Sankey, Bliss, Bradbury, and the others lived close enough to ordinary folk to reflect their feelings. A Glasgow journalist wrote:

> Much of it is so Scottish and Irish in its construction, that to our people, familiar with such music, it is sometimes difficult to realize that what we hear is sacred song . . . Is it not possible that this may be why these simple songs have found such a direct and wonderful entrance to the Scottish heart?

Most of Sankey's songs began as solos, each with a chorus that could be memorized by the masses who could not read. For congregational singing he would choose established hymnody—metrical psalms (in Scotland) and (in England) Watts or Wesley and hymns of the Evangelical Revival, or the recent hymns of Lyte and Havergal. Popularity forced solos into a choral frame for which they were not designed. The effect was worse when attempted by a small congregation. Sankey music needs one singer—or massed voices. "Even the critical musician," wrote a London musical paper in 1875,

> will allow its prodigious grandeur—a grandeur far different from that of a Handel Festival, but more impressive, as it is natural, spontaneous and enthusiastic. No puerility in the words no consecu-

tive fifths or solecisms in the music affects those who sing; and the infantile tune becomes magnificent in the surge of ten thousand voices.

Yet the next generations remembered and judged Sankey as strummed endlessly by amateurs at cottage pianos.

Like all composers, Sankey and Bliss wrote more bad music than good. Most composers bury the bad, but the gospel hymn writers could not do that—the bad had been collected and perpetuated by popular demand before time weeded out the chaff. And popularity often sprang from nonmusical factors; hymns were judged by their effect, which might be caused by merely temporary social situations.

The gospel songs were written with a limited purpose: what Sankey called "preaching and teaching in song." He once remarked,

> I wish people would get the distinction, that one class of hymns are to teach, and the other, such as "Praise God from Whom All Blessings Flow" and "Jesus Lover of My Soul" are hymns in which the whole congregation can praise God.

In the teaching hymn, a development of the Sunday school music that emerged during the 1860s in America, words are vital. Sankey "sings the words and brings out their full meaning and expression. The music is made subservient, and in time and accent is constantly varied so as to *fit the words*." He was as genuine a preacher as Moody, and singing was his natural medium: "I sang from childhood, and was literally full and running over with music." Sankey sang as Moody preached—to implant simple truths, and to evoke response. Professional musicians, who claimed that Sankey demeaned music from a fine art by using it as a means to an end, were virtually decrying use of any art for religious purposes; the fact that his taste was no better than his contemporaries' is immaterial.

Sankey created a vogue. A host of imitators arose, not all sincere, to stir emotions, soften audiences, and make bad music a substitute for prayer or good preaching. Posterity has judged Sankey by the imitators or by his third-rate interpreters. But the impression he made upon Britain and America can be understood only by seeing him as man, singer, and evangelist.

As man, he was "polished, pleasant, sunshiny," and "very

friendly in his manner." He was easier to know than Moody—less impatient and less brusque, jovial and deeply spiritual—but engagingly human—with a touch of the absurd never far away. "Sankey," said Moody at dinner in an English hotel one night, as Sankey was about to start on his favorite dish of steak and fried onions. "Sankey, do you expect to speak to anxious souls tonight?"

"Why, yes."

"Then put down those onions!"

Sankey paused. "Well! I like my onions, but I like to lead souls to Jesus, so I guess the onions will have to go."

His untrained baritone voice of moderate compass, slightly rough but round and full, and with that quality of "sweetness" much prized in his age, had what Hitchcock of Chicago called an "indescribable quality which, with his sympathetic nature, seldom failed to reach the most hidden recesses of the heart." It was this capacity to penetrate, to create spiritual longing, soften prejudice, and bend wills that was Sankey's distinctive gift. "He racked the hearts of all classes, rich and poor," wrote an Englishwoman. The quality of his voice cannot explain this; had he come before the public as a concert performer he would have made small stir. Nor may it be dismissed as a trick. Sankey, like Moody, had a horror of consciously whipped-up emotion. Probably he did sometimes force the emotional temperature, for the line between devotional awareness and mental excitement is thin, but his aim was to teach, to confront, to draw his hearers to God.

He was preeminently an evangelist, with the true minister's power of submitting himself to be a vehicle of the Divine. "Mr. Moody had just given an impressive address," wrote a Scots lad, a trained singer,

> and as he closed, a sigh of relief from nervous tension seemed to pass over the gathering. Mr. Sankey took his seat at the little harmonium, sounded a few chords, and said "There were ninety and nine." Not a sound was heard as he unfolded the story. The people forgot that he was singing—he was telling an old story with a new charm. It was enthralling. As he uttered the last words Moody's hand was up, and heads and hearts were bowed before God, while sheep who had wandered were gathered into the fold.

"Mr. Sankey sings with the conviction that souls are receiving Jesus between one note and the next," wrote an Edinburgh woman.

When you hear "The Ninety and Nine" being sung you know of a truth that down in this corner, up in that gallery, behind that pillar which hides the singer's face from the listener, the hand of Jesus has been finding this and that and yonder lost one, to place them in His fold.

17

The Road to London

Through that whole summer of 1874 revival burned over Scotland. John McNeill wrote poetically half a century on:

> Across all the years, my heart still kindles at the glory of that time. I got my soul and my Saviour out of it. I feel like crying out to the dwindling survivors of that generation; crying out to remind themselves of that mighty rush and sweep, when all over the land the souls of men were bound before the Lord, like the standing corn in a harvest wind!

Moody, using a different metaphor, said he was merely shaking the trees: the fruit had long ripened under faithful teaching by the churches. Once the shaking began and the harvest wind blew, the effect reached far beyond where Moody and Sankey happened to be; indeed, the "greatest results comparatively have been reported from districts which they have not visited." Henry Drummond and other students were sent—casually but effectively—to places where the Americans had no time for in Scotland, and to northern England where they had been already, and local clergy passed on the fiery cross. Andrew Murray of South Africa, returning to Scotland a few years after Moody's visit, noticed "very distinctly the influence of Mr. Moody's work. There is much more readiness to talk out, and much more warmth . . . The whole religious tone of

Scotland has been lifted up and brightened most remarkably."

Sankey went south early in August 1874, to rejoin Fanny, the new baby, Ira, and the older children fresh from America. But from late May until early September Moody worked in the north of Scotland until upon their twelfth wedding day, feasting on the views, the Moodys with their children steamed down Loch Ness and the Caledonian Canal (even Moody could not be seasick) to preach at Oban. Next day they sailed through the glorious scenery of the islands. Late in the evening after a carriage drive of forty miles, "very, very tired, Willie fast asleep, [little] Emma nearly so," they reached the home of Peter and Jane Mackinnon at Campbelltown.

Now that they had Moody "in [their] very home, to know him and talk to him in ordinary life," Jane scribbled notes of all he said and did and was. She fell in love with ten-year-old Emma because she reminded her of their own dead child; this may have been the first step toward becoming Mrs. Moody's greatest friend on either side of the Atlantic. Peter Mackinnon, who was a partner of the British India Line, in the course of several years became to Moody "more of a father than any man that has crossed my path."

Of the Campbelltown mission Jane treasured most the little incidents and facets: How Moody came back after a meeting on a windy night, remarking "the gas made such a noise, it roared and I had to roar, and it was a battle between us, but I think I won"; how when the beadle kept opening a door that Moody shut because a draft interfered with the inquiry work, he locked it and put the key in his pocket; how he would inspect a church for ventilation before speaking; "he had all his wits about him, even for the smallest details." She noticed his decisiveness: "You just listen to me, and do what I tell you." And his adaptability in the services: "He said he never knew, even a few minutes before, what he was going to do . . . I suppose he asks guidance at every step, and is sure he gets it."

Jane Mackinnon found both Moodys to be good companions. "I liked the combination of playfulness and seriousness in Mr. Moody . . . It was delightful having him at leisure; he is so simple, unaffected and lovable, plays so heartily with the children, and makes fun with those who can receive it. He is brimful of humor." He played croquet, helped the children catch crabs on the beach, and when they all went for a drive in the hills, "we had a delightful little time, race, scramble, lunch, fun."

As to Emma, Mrs. Mackinnon said,

One day was enough to show what a source of strength and comfort she was to her husband. The more I saw of her afterwards, the more convinced I was that a great deal of his usefulness was owing to her, not only in the work she did for him, relieving him of all correspondence, but also from her character. Her independence of thought . . . her calmness, meeting so quietly his impulsiveness, her humility.

When telegrams poured in, urging Moody to squeeze in a visit to yet another place and he would ask her, "Which way should I go? I really don't know what to do." Emma would not sway him. "You decide, and tell me, and I'll write." "Dear, uncomplaining Mrs. Moody"—Jane had not adjectives enough—"so patient, quiet, bright, humble; one rarely meets just so many qualities in one woman."

But Emma had the last word. That very week from the Mackinnons' house, two days before leaving Scotland at the close of those formidable nine months, she wrote to her mother in Chicago: "Mr. Moody is nicer and kinder every day. He is a gem of a husband. I ought to be *very happy*."

The Moodys crossed to Ireland to spend five weeks with Sankey in Belfast, where the Glasgow scenes were repeated. The Belfast memories of the Moodys ranged from the sublime to the ridiculous—from the "immense audience" on a Sunday afternoon in Templemore Park, where Moody preached downwind from a platform rigged on a couple of wagons, to their host's abominable pet monkey, which knew perfectly well that Mrs. Moody was scared of it. One evening the monkey hid itself in the chandelier above the dining room table and leaped onto her head: "One of the few times I ever heard her scream," her daughter tells.

Moody snorted at a warning to avoid Dublin, the capital of the whole strife-infested island, with its Roman Catholic majority, and the first Dublin meeting drew great crowds. There followed the slowest grind since Edinburgh, to reach a climax that was reckoned to surpass any in Scotland. For the first time Moody and Sankey had broad support from Episcopalians, including several bishops of the recently disestablished Church of Ireland. Moody astounded the Irish by refusing to attack Roman Catholics, who therefore did not scruple to attend. The campaign became the talk of the town, Irish volubility giving Emma choice snippets: "Shure and it's Mr. Sankey I like best. And which would it be you prefer, ma'am?" At a music hall, one comedian said to the other:

"I am rather Moody tonight. How do you feel?"

"Sankeymonious!"

The gallery hissed. Someone started singing "Hold the Fort," which the whole audience took up till the comedians fled to the wings.

The Dublin correspondent of *The Times*, bringing Moody and Sankey for the first time to London breakfast tables in November 1874, commended the mission as "the most remarkable ever witnessed in Ireland," which had "a character essentially different and seemed to possess elements of vitality which were wanting in others." He noticed especially the "absence of any effort at self-display but rather a sensitive avoidance of it" and the "reverence and devotion" of the services. Among the thousands who heard the evangelist was a youth called George Bernard Shaw. Five months later, reading of the London campaign, he wrote a letter to *Public Opinion*, ascribing it all to publicity, curiosity, novelty, and excitement; as to converts, the effect was "a tendency to make them highly objectionable members of society." The editor printed the letter of April 3, 1875; thus, by a quirk of history, Moody was responsible for Bernard Shaw's first appearance in print.

The campaign closed with a great "Christian Convention for Ireland." Railway companies brought ministers and laity at reduced fares from every corner of the unpartitioned land to the Exhibition Palace, its "long vista lined on both sides with festoons of climbing plants, with two beautiful fountains in the center." Once again the world wondered at the submerging of bitter sectarian feelings: "It was the first time that all these ministers had met on a platform broader than their churches'. Moody's touch could be felt in the committee's arrangement that clergymen from a distance were lodged with clerical families of denominations other than their own.

Of the several thousand converts reported from Dublin, the most charming of stories came through a young American visitor twenty-five years later, who, on asking the Dublin YMCA to find him lodgings, was escorted to a nearby house. The man who opened the door shook his head; they were no longer taking lodgers. The YMCA member said: "The gentleman comes from America."

"Oh, it's from America you are? Then come along in. You shall certainly stay."

When at the end of a week the American asked for the bill, the landlady said there was none; pressed she replied that the only payment could be another week free. He argued. She exclaimed,

> Our home was the home of a drunkard. Through the influence of one of your Americans, Mr. D. L. Moody, my husband was converted and my home is now a Christian home. It is very little we can do to show our appreciation, but hospitality is one of the few things we can do and we hope you will not take that pleasure away from us.

At the end of November the Americans crossed the Irish Sea, a "very fine smooth passage, but there was a slight roll." Jane Mackinnon saw Moody turn distinctly green. "I was naughty enough to enjoy his downcast look and to see him not master of the situation."

They traveled to Manchester, Sheffield, Birmingham—and over all hung the unspoken question, Would Moody fail in London?

They arrived at Manchester in the rain—the Albert Hall in the city where Moody might have begun in '73 at some back-street chapel. Little 'Arry Moorhouse, aiding his old friend, rejoiced that "success has not made him proud. He uses his ten talents, I use my one and we both together praise the Lord for using us at all." Moody spent Christmas in the North London suburb, where Emma stayed because Willie was unwell. She had written on December 22, "I think I am more of a baby than either of the children, for I had really felt that I should have had hard work on Christmas not to be homesick without him." When he left again, the family had "an attack of influenza all around" and retreated to Bournemouth.

They stopped at Sheffield over the New Year. "There is a degree of religious feeling in the town," a Church of England newspaper, the *Record*, reported, "which has not been equalled for years." In Birmingham, during the icy January of 1875, the effect could be gauged by doggerel sold on the curbs and in the Bull Ring:

> Oh, the town's upside down, everybody seems mad,
> When they come to their senses we all shall feel glad,
> For the rich and the poor, and the good and the bad,
> Are gone mad over Moody and Sankey.

After the services at Bingley Hall, night after night, in the words of a convert looking back after fifty-three years, "groups of people would be collected here and there, on gallery and floor, round some worker in the mission, anxiously inquiring for the way of salvation, confessing sin or doubt or difficulty." An Anglican clergyman wrote, "Such a chance of guiding souls comes only once in a lifetime."

A few days' rest in Bournemouth, then on to snowy Liverpool in February, where the local committee had erected a monster auditorium of timber. At Liverpool, Moody had an awful premonition of danger that drove him to take such precautions that he began to wonder whether overwork had unhinged his mind—until one evening the police told him they had just caught an escaped lunatic whom Confederate ghosts goaded to murder the Yankee preacher.

As he was about to leave a city, Moody would summon young Henry Drummond from the previous place, generally by telegram, "in a great hurry scurry," to work together the final days and continue on his own as Moody moved onward, each week bringing London nearer, vast critical London, which he must face with his stock of sermons—not only used again and again but now printed in newspapers and pirated by pamphleteers.

All Britain was singing. From Liverpool Moody scrawled a page to Whittle about Bliss:

> I am delighted with his music. I do not think he has got his equal on earth at this time & raised up of God to do the work that he is doing, his hymns are all ready sung around the world, we are using them to do a great work in this country. To let you know something of how they are liked we are selling of the penny book 250,000 per month they are going all over the United Kingdom & God is using them as much as he did Wesley's hymns in the days of the Wesleys. Tell Bliss to keep at it, God bless him is my earnest prayer.

The august Dr. Dale, of Carr's Lane Congregational Church, in Birmingham, theologian, preacher, and politician—felt puzzled. He had been expecting a revival, for religious life had been touched with expectancy two or three years, but he "certainly did not suppose" it would come through "two American strangers."

Watching the attentive faces of the great crowd at Bingley Hall

> [people] of all sorts, young and old, rich and poor, keen tradesmen, manufacturers and merchants and young ladies who had just left school, rough boys who knew more about dogs and pigeons than about books, and cultivated women—I could not understand it.

He told Moody: "The work is most plainly of God, for I can see no relation between yourself and what you have done." Moody laughed and replied, "I should be very sorry if it were otherwise."

Many were puzzled. Even those who ascribed the movement's force to the tremendous wave of prayer it generated wondered why this particular man, an American at that, should be the focal point.

The secret was partly the way Moody preached. "Perfect naturalness," Dale described it. "He talks in a perfectly unconstrained and straightforward way, just as he would talk to half a dozen old friends at his fireside."

In an age of ponderous English sermons when Spurgeon, most popular of all preachers, mouthed rolling periods, piled metaphor upon metaphor, Moody merely chatted, "to thirteen thousand as to thirteen," on what the Bible showed him. He made it alive in the context of every day: Daniel in the lions' den takes out his watch to check if it is the hour of prayer. Scoffers before the Flood "talk it over in the corner groceries, evenings: 'Not much sign of old Noah's rain-storm yet!'" Bartimaeus, suddenly seeing ("the first object that met his gaze was the Son of God Himself"), rushes into Jericho,

> and he says, "I will go and see my wife and tell her about it"—a young convert always wants to talk to his friends about salvation. Away he goes down the street 'n' he meets a man who passes him 'n' goes on a few yards 'n' then turns round 'n' says, "Bartimeus, is that you?"
>
> "Yes."
>
> "Well, I thought it was, but I couldn't believe my eyes! How've you gotten your sight?"
>
> "Oh, I just met Jesus of Nazareth outside the city and asked Him to have mercy on me."
>
> "Jesus of Nazareth! What? Is he in this part of the country?"
>
> "Sure. Right here in Jericho."
>
> "I *should* like to see him!" and away he runs down the street . . .

It's Zaccheus (or "Zakkus," as Moody would say) soon in the

sycamore tree. And thus the sermon leads to another scene of Christ meeting a man in his need. "Sin, gloom and darkness flee away. Light, peace, joy burst into the soul."

Moody had the gift of fading from his hearers' consciousness. As one recalled,

> Throughout his address you entirely forgot the man, so full was he of his message and so held were you by his earnestness, intensity and forceful appeal. He had many illustrations drawn from his personal experiences, but never did self appear prominent . . . He was completely absorbed in the message and in getting it over to the mind, heart and conscience of those listening.

At one Liverpool meeting for men, a force of rationalists was reported present. In the speakers' room before the service, F. B. Meyer was awed by Moody's prayer, his overpowering "burden of heart."

Moody preached. Large numbers stayed for the after-meeting. Moody came down from the platform, stood on a chair,

> and launched out in a wonderful discourse. His incentives against sin, and his lashings of the conscience, were awful. He seemed to be wrestling with an unseen power. Beneath those burning words men's faces grew pale under a conviction of the broken law of God. Then he began with the wooings of the Gospel, in a strain of tender and heartbreaking entreaty; and before he was through the whole audience seemed completely broken. One man arose and said, "Mr. Moody, I want to be a Christian." It seemed but a moment when forty or fifty men were on their feet.

Moody's message sprang upon an England in which basic thought-forms were strongly Christian, and in which only the lowest people knew nothing of the Bible. He touched English religion at its points of sharpest need. As he said, "The Church is dying of respectability," smothered by its own success.

By the 1870s, the Evangelical Revival had filtered into every nook and cranny to dominate much of the outlook even of those, whether Tractarians or new-fashioned agnostics, repudiating its tenets, with thousands upon thousands of the unthinking mass who obeyed evangelicalism's dictates yet lived untouched by its heart. Beliefs and ethics that had been revolutionary in the eighteenth century were now necessary for promotion or a good name. Sins of the flesh had to be concealed behind a veneer of the spirit. The Golden Rule had changed: "Thou shalt not be found out." Moreover, reaction from past bawdiness had created prudery in the present, while inequality of the sexes never was more marked than in Victorian damnation of "fallen women," whose seducers or patrons, if reasonably discreet, flourished unabashed, undamned.

Moody pierced this screen of hypocrisy.

More widespread lay the diluted Christianity that supposed that heaven was earned by goodness and hell by being wicked, used fear of hell as a sanction to protect the accepted code, and knew nothing of grace. Against this Moody proclaimed eternal life as the gift of God to the undeserving. He did not deny eternal punishment for those who refused this gift, "but I believe that the magnet that goes down to the bottom of the pit is the love of Jesus." He repudiated the nicely calculated less or more of moralizers.

> When the prodigal came home, grace met him and embraced him. Law said, Stone him!—grace said, Embrace him! Law said, Smite him!—grace said, Kiss him! Law went after him and bound him. Grace said, Loose him and let him go! Law tells me how crooked I am; grace comes and makes me straight.

Moody proclaimed that God wanted men more than they wanted Him, that salvation was not a grudged reward for a consistent climb into goodness, but the new birth of a repentant sinner into the life of Christ. "Instant salvation," he called it again and again. "He preached," wrote Dale, "in a manner that produced the sort of effect produced by Luther, and provoked similar criticism. He exulted in the free grace of God . . . His joy was contagious. Men leaped out of darkness into light, and lived a Christian life afterwards."

It had been so in the days of Wesley and Whitefield, and in Ulster and parts of Scotland in '59, but during recent years only here and there among individuals, or in limited sectors, such as that of the very poor who came to the appeal of General Booth and his new Salvation Army. Moody was bringing this joy to all classes. In each city the leaps out of darkness came first among the middle class, then among the poor, then the rich and leisured. That was in the provinces; for the movement to become national, he must win London.

Dale saw this "instant transition take place with nearly every person with whom I talked" at the close of after-meetings in Birmingham. "They had come up into the gallery anxious, restless, feeling after God in the darkness," but after a conversation of fifteen or twenty minutes "their faces were filled with joy, and they left me not only at peace with God but filled with joy . . . . These people carried their new joy with them to their homes and their workshops. It could not be hid."

Nine years later Dale told a friend that of the 200 who joined his own church through Moody's influence, three quarters "have stood well."

And thirty-five years later, Charles E. Brown, another Birmingham convert, described his own very typical experiences. "A lonely and miserable lad—embittered," he had followed the crowd to Bingley Hall, heard Moody and

> thought nothing of it. I was scornful in my spirit. But there was some fascination about the man that brought me there the next night. An address given that night on "Excuses" tore away from my heart every shred of excuse that stood between my soul and Jesus Christ. At the end of that address, in that great assembly of eighteen thousand people, I yielded up my life to Jesus Christ. I was one of the multitude who never gave in their names. I have lived an unworthy Christian life since that day, and of all men in the Christian ministry I am probably the most unworthy, but the last influence coming on top of a mother's prayers and a Sunday school teacher's letters, the last influence that led me to surrender my unworthy life to Jesus Christ came from the Spirit of God through the lips of D. L. Moody.

18

Dockers and Duchesses

Police Constable George Ling of the A, or Westminster, Division Metropolitan Police, aged twenty-three, thought it "very remarkable" he should be on duty at the preparatory reception to Moody and Sankey on March 8, 1875, because his father in Norfolk had asked him to send newspaper reports of the coming campaign—not that the constable cared about that sort of thing.

Ling's post in Exeter Hall was at the bottom of the wide stairs, and he heard Sankey's voice clearly through the doors. This "gave me the desire to attend their meetings to hear the evangelists. The result was my conversion." Becoming Queen Victoria's personal police constable, in attendance for many years, he held evangelistic services at the Windsor YMCA, and, when the Queen was at Osborne, taught a men's Bible class at Cowes.

George Ling was one of thousands transformed during Moody and Sankey's London mission between March and July 1875.

A vigorous committee—clergy, members of Parliament, high-ranking officers—had flooded London with notices, had organized visitation of the entire capital, and, for a start, had booked the Agricultural Hall in Islington, then north London's principal middle-class area, for ten weeks at a weekly rent of fifty pounds. This home of the annual prize cattle show had been adapted by the contractor, Mr. Sharman, to hold over fifteen thousand chairs.

When the crowds poured in, two hours before the opening service on Tuesday, March 9, they saw the west end arranged in rising steps, which to the *Illustrated London News* gave the "appearance of a gigantic infant school." The red baize dais had seats on the left for participants and distinguished guests; in the center, "a kind of railed pulpit or reading desk"; to the right, the voluntary choir of nearly two hundred voices. All round the hall red banners proclaimed texts such as: "Repent ye and believe the gospel"; "The gift of God is eternal life"; "Ye must be born again"; and, "They shall sing in the ways of the Lord." Gas jets hung in chandeliers and in three lines down the side and two or three semicircular arches over the center, making the crowded building hot as well as light, and leaving a mist that spoiled the view from the gallery. The enormous sounding-board over the dais proved ineffective, and after ten days a large quantity of thick galvanized wire was suspended from the roof, but replaced later by a canvas awning.

At seven-thirty Moody and Sankey stepped onto the dais. Moody's opening words created a sensation: "Let us rise and sing to the praise of God, Let us praise Him for what He is *going to do* in London." The whole audience sang the doxology.

The service proceded on the familiar plan, described by the *Daily Telegraph* as "the interchange of precept and song, the omission of anything that could tend to monotony, and a constant opportunity for all to take part in the service." The *Daily Telegraph* correspondent, who must have had a bad place, for he described Moody as tall, if stout, with a "not unintellectual cast of countenance," was relieved to discover him "altogether as unlike the conventional 'ranter' as it is possible to conceive," and, with unconscious snobbery, assured readers that Moody had little American about him except for "a strange Western twang," and that Sankey "might be mistaken for an Englishman anywhere."

Apart from two isolated incidents, sixteen or seventeen thousand listened to him in perfect quiet, "except for the occasional coughing which always attends the gathering of a vast congregation in England." Moody spoke in his usual style, polished a little since Edinburgh, but still very much his own—"straightforward, racy," recorded *The Times* in a remarkably friendly article. He was "full of American humor, often it must be owned, a little vulgar" because he described venerable Bible narratives "as if they were good

American stories picked up in Chicago." But, for all that, with his "strong clear voice," Moody showed his listeners the "means of becoming better men and women, and of having a better hope in this world and the next."

Thus, quietly, the evening moved towards its climax. Moody said:

> God has laid it upon the heart of the world to pray for London. It must be that God has something good in store for London; the Son of man is coming to London to seek and to save that which was lost. And I pray that the Good Shepherd may enter this hall tonight and may come to many a heart and that you may hear the still, small voice: "Behold, I stand at the door, and knock: if any man hear My voice, and open the door, I will come in to him, and will sup with him, and he with Me." [Rev. 3:20] O friends! open the door tonight and let the heavenly visitor in. Do not turn Him away any longer. Do not say with Felix, "Go thy way this time, and when I have a convenient season I will call for thee." Make this a convenient season. Make this the night of your Salvation. Receive the gift of God tonight and open the door of your heart and say: "Welcome, thrice welcome into this heart of mine!"

Moody had warned his sympathizers:

> We must expect opposition. If you think a great work is to be done here without opposition you will be greatly mistaken. The opposition will be bitter . . . . There will be many bitter things said, and many lies started, and as someone has said, a lie will get half round the world before the truth gets its boots on!

Despite the friendly tone of *The Times* and several other papers, a shower of vituperative printers' ink splattered the evangelists.

High church Tories in London clubs and prim maiden aunts read in the *Morning Post*: "Their teaching is wild, baseless, and uncertain . . . . Moody and Sankey will be a puff in the wind." Coachmen and bartenders thumbing through the *Morning Advertiser* were told, "There must have been thousands in that crowd of uplifted faces who looked with horror and shame on the illiterate preacher making little better than a travesty of all they held sacred." Moody's accent was called "broadly and vulgarly American." The word *vulgar* was worked hard in the London press, to deride Moody's accent and his preaching. The *Saturday Review* decided, from afar, that he was "a ranter of the most vulgar type," whose mission appeared to be "to degrade religion to the level of the 'penny gaff,' an itinerant gutter show like "Punch and Judy." "Mr. Sankey's singing is as vulgar as Mr. Moody's preaching," said *Vanity Fair*, publishing one of its famous cartoons.

Punch called them "comic evangelists" and brought out a long poem, beginning:

> At Islington Hall those Revivalists Yankee,
> Pious pair D. L. Moody and Ira D. Sankey,
> Are drawing, they tell us, immense congregations
> By eccentric devotions and droll ministrations.
> Their manner seems strangely at odds with their matter,
> The former grotesque and most serious the latter.
> They proclaim Gospel truths, in spite of grave prepossessions,
> In colloquial slang, and commercial expressions.
> State Scriptural facts in American phrases,
> And interpolate jokes 'twixt their prayers and their praises!

Mr. Punch meant no harm and the next week apologized, rather lamely.

Scurrilous libels circulated: "Where the corpulent old ex-pounder is known he is regarded as a selfish, sensual, hypocritical variegator of facts." According to rumor, Sankey started as a "nigger minstrel" but found evangelism paid better, and both were amassing fortunes from hymnbooks, commission on sales of organs, gifts of admirers, penny lives, and pictures hawked in the streets. On their return to the "land of the everlasting dollar," they would "gaze upon their cosy homesteads purchased with good English gold, and with a merry twinkle of the eye exclaim, 'We have spoiled the Egyptians, I *guess*.'"

Moody had done his utmost to suppress the "lives." He refused to be photographed, rejecting lucrative offers and turning his back, should an amateur set up cumbrous camera on tripod and dive under the black cloth. Unauthorized publications were so imaginative that an earnest sympathizer hastily issued a pamphlet entitled "Mr. Moody Not a Jew."

As to *Sacred Songs and Solos*, Moody and Sankey had been using the mounting royalties to defray personal and family expenses until, on January 1, 1875, an enlarged edition was published, of which sales would be enormous. The evangelists already had sufficient funds to cover expenses until the end of their stay. The London committee refused to touch the money. Moody announced that Sankey and he had asked the publishers, as of January 1, to "hand over the royalty upon all our hymnbooks to one of your leading citizens, Mr. Hugh Matheson, who will devote the same to such charitable objects as may be decided upon."

Strict Baptists and high Calvinists wrote tracts ("this Goliath of Free Will . . . Mr. Moody has *no* good seed to sow"). Even Spurgeon, commending and supporting him publicly, was annoyed privately because Moody refused his "very dictatorial" advice to attack the Church of England. In the East End, Spurgeon "scattered Baptist papers" before Moody's arrival, urging converts to be rebaptized. This, as Moody told Whittle in 1876, created resentment, and "few converts went into Baptist churches."[1]

Despite libel and criticism, Agricultural Hall attendance, which had dropped slightly the second night, rose after more space had been arranged, to an estimated 20,000 nightly except Saturdays, the evangelists' day off; Sunday meetings were early morning and late evening, to avoid interfering with churches. The figures were probably exaggerated by several thousands, but for a nightly draw were unprecedented; to the England of 1875, they were fantastic.

The Lord Chancellor of Disraeli's new Conservative Government, Cairns, an Ulsterman, attended frequently; he was the second of those two who, in Moody's view, helped most in Britain, "for people said if the Lord Chancellor came to my services they had better come too."

Gladstone, lately fallen from power and now leader of the opposition, talked privately with Moody and once or twice sat on the platform among the lay and clerical supporters from every denomination. A high churchman from an evangelical background, "Gladstone, Moody says is a converted man and a true and humble Christian." A young Scotsman heard Gladstone exclaim: "I thank God I have lived to see the day when He should bless His church on earth by the gift of a man able to preach the gospel of Christ as we have just heard it preached!" At that, Matthew Arnold, standing beside him, said: "Mr. Gladstone, I would give all I have if only I could believe it."

Gladstone envied the man whose voice night after night reached so far in an age without mechanical aids: "I wish I had your chest, Mr. Moody!"

[1] This new sidelight on Spurgeon comes from the entry for May 3, 1876, in the unpublished diary of D. W. Whittle, recording a conversation with Moody that day at Augusta, Georgia.

"And I wish I had your head on top of it!"

The aged Lord Shaftesbury, to his surprise, had not been asked "to join them on their committees—or to give my [?] name[2] or to express any sympathy," merely for a contribution. He received no invitation to the preparatory reception at Exeter Hall. "I shall wait to be called. I shall avoid intrusion, or obtrusion, of any kind."

From the distance of his house in Grosvenor Square, he rejoiced at first reports, yet puzzled because

> from all I read and hear they "present the Gospel," but, I think, an imperfect Gospel—They preach Christ but not "Christ Crucified!" How then does the Divine Favor so rest upon them? It is almost impossible now to regard the power and influence, as not superhuman.

Shaftesbury was a little troubled, lest they made the "terms of life" too easy: "Salvation is thrown broadcast; and almost at the heads of the Hearers."

By March 25 he was writing:

> The success of Moody and Sankey not only [?] unabated but increased. It seems more and more a supernatural character. It comes at a time when the masses are lying in indifference, and are nevertheless impressible. They are sleepy, but have no objection to listen. They will not seek, but they may be found. It looks amazingly like the "right man, at the right hour."

The next day, Good Friday, Shaftesbury went for the first time and gladly admitted that they "preach Christ Crucified." He was "deeply impressed; the more impressed, because of the imperfection of the whole thing." Down at his Dorset mansion the following week, he stood at his tall desk and scrawled page after page of diary. How Sankey's song, so simple, went "to the inmost soul, and seemed to empty it of everything, but thought of the good, tender, and lowly Shepherd." Moody's voice was "bad and ill managed," the language colloquial, and Shaftesbury a little scandalized that the anecdotes were "oftentimes bordering on the 'humorous,' almost to the extent of provoking a laugh!" (This must have been a masterly understatement dictated by the earl's old-fashioned sense of propriety; unless Good Friday had muted Moody.) There was

[2] Shaftebury's handwriting in his diary is very hard to decipher.

nothing externally to win, perhaps something to repel, "and yet the result is striking, effective, touching and leading to much thought . . . the Holy Spirit can work out of feeble materials. Is it not so today?"

He launched into a meditation, about how, when bishops were lecturing right and left "upon Homiletics and the persuasion of the Masses—Here come two simple, unlettered men from the other side of the Atlantic . . . " Untrained, unskilled, having no denomination; on the other hand, not sinister: "They are calm, without an approach to the Fanatical, or even the Eccentric. They seek neither to terrify, nor to puff up; eschew controversy and flatter no passions!" Yet thousands of all degrees, "workpeople, shopkeepers, merchants and lawyers, clergy and laity alike confess the power and cannot explain it." Shaftesbury repeated that there must be "something in it superhuman." God had chosen the foolish things of the world to confound the wise. Dipping his quill (they were going out, but he still used one) and hovering over the top of the right-hand page, he thought of the greatest Tractarian preacher of the day and scrawled, "Moody will do more in an hour than Canon Liddon in a century!"[3]

Thenceforth Shaftesbury gave Moody the full weight of his prestige and wisdom. At a discussion of committee and sympathizers on the morning of April 7, Shaftesbury more than anyone else directed Moody to the scene of his most remarkable influence.

Shaftesbury pointed out that the Agricultural Hall had not attracted widely either "the lowest grades of the people" or the upper classes. (The *Saturday Review* had jeered that it was filled "by smug, self-satisfied, middle-class respectability, smirkingly confident of its own spiritual security.") For the former, a vast temporary structure was being hammered together in the East End on Bow Common. For the wealthy, afternoon Bible Readings would start the next week in The Queen's Opera House in the Haymarket, but Shaftesbury, the "Poor Man's Earl," "in a most earnest and powerful appeal to Mr. M., which carried with it, as appeared from the cheering, the general sympathy of all present,"

---

[3] Liddon of St. Paul's might have been chagrined had he read this. A year later, on Whitsunday 1876, in an Oxford University Sermon, he paid a glowing tribute to Moody and Sankey, although to his mind "they knew little or nothing of . . . sacramental channels whereby the life of grace is planted and maintained in the soul."

urged evening meetings there too.

> In the Opera House your preaching will be heard by multitudes who will throng in of an evening from the university clubs, the naval and military and other clubs in the neighborhood. There will be many of high intellectual and social position who will thus have the Gospel brought nearer to them, and not only these but many tradesmen and shopkeepers and their dependents who cannot or will not go to Islington.

Moody disagreed. He wanted to extend the Islington mission beyond schedule to the end of May, when he was due to begin in South London. Why should he abandon a hall of twenty thousand for the five thousand of the Opera House? Privately, he did not relish being thrown to the lions of the aristocracy. He could just imagine them: "Aw, my deah fellah, have you heard these—aw—vulgah Yankees, awfully funny, what!"

In any event, the impact of the East End Bible Readings caused him to hand the Agricultural Hall to an associate nine days early on May 9.

When he had to begin in East London, Moody announced that for a while there would be *two* evangelistic services each evening: Bow at 7:30 P.M. and Haymarket at 9:00 P.M. On Bow Common, in the newly-rigged gaslit monstrosity with galvanized iron roof and sawdust floor, he preached each evening to eight or nine thousand of the sort he loved most to be among—he might have been back in Illinois Street. At half past eight, he and Sankey jumped into a brougham, trotting as swiftly as traffic allowed up Mile End Road and through the city, under shored-up Temple Bar and round Trafalgar Square to the Haymarket—from the East End to the West, from a world of slums and squalor to that of great mansions and the royal parks, from dockers to duchesses. Arthur Kinnaird (afterwards 11th Lord Kinnaird) then aged twenty-eight, told Will Moody in 1900:

> Nothing showed the wonderful adaptability of your father more . . . coming from Bow Road, the poorest part of the East End, to the very antipodes of it all in character and surroundings, and yet at once hitting on the right note of dealing with the new conditions.

St. James's, Mayfair, and Westminster lay close; Belgravia was a short carriage drive—the heart of fashionable London, proud,

close-knit, and still fairly exclusive—a society of privilege, pleasure, and wealth. The stage of the Opera House (it replaced the
one that burned in 1867 and was demolished in 1892 to be rebuilt as
Her Majesty's Theatre) served as the platform for committee and
clergy, with Moody's reading desk in the center, and the auditorium, except for the pit and the galleries high above, consisted
of stalls and circles of boxes. An indignant box-renter, Mr. Leader,
sought an injunction from the Court of Clancery to prevent the
theater's use for untheatrical purposes. Refused the injunction, but
awarded costs and nominal damages, Mr. Leader and several
others kept their private boxes locked and empty.[4]

"The scene in the Haymarket baffles description," wrote an
eyewitness. "It was literally blocked with the carriages of the
aristocratic and plutocratic of the land; and the struggle for
admission was perhaps even more severe in the West than in the
East." "When we got to the Opera House," wrote another,

> we found an immense crowd outside. We got a place at the very top of
> the highest gallery, and although at that distance Mr. Moody seemed a
> tiny figure of a man, every word, even his whispered words, were
> heard . . . . I was struck with the impression which Mr. Sankey's singing
> made on the audience.

The Duchess of Sutherland "insists upon going every day." The
Sutherlands had entertained Moody at Dunrobin Castle in the
Highlands, the Duchess a chieftain and a countess in her own right
and lately Mistress of the Robes, the Duke the owner of more acres
than any man in Europe. "God bless you," wrote the Duke to
Moody, "I shall never forget what I have heard from you. If you
knew what a life mine is, in ways I was not able to tell you the other
day, and what a terrible story mine has been, you would pray for me
much." In another note the Duke thanked the former farmhand
from Northfield "for all the joy and strength our dear Lord has
given me through you, and I pray that your wonderful work may be
more and more blessed."

The Duchess would collect bevies of friends and relations at
palatial Stafford House (now Lancaster House) and whisk them in
the ducal carriage along Pall Mall to the Haymarket. Some of them

---

[4] I regret to state that the motion to stop Moody from using the Opera House was
put to the court by my great-uncle by marriage, J. W. Chitty, Q.C., afterwards a
Lord Justice.

hated it: "The mixture of religious fervor and the most intense toadyism of the Duchess," a Lady Barker sourly told a dinner party, "was horribly disgusting."

"Moody's and Sankey's meetings were quite noticeably one of the events of the Season," a visitor to London noted. Nearly everybody who was anybody went at least once, from high motives or low; it was the talk of ballrooms and garden parties and rides in Rotten Row. Moody had an impact on the aristocratic because he was quite unaware when he rode roughshod over prejudices, privileges, and attitudes. They tolerated from him what they would have resented from an Englishman.

To one of the first Bible Readings came the Princess of Wales, the ravishingly beautiful thirty-year-old Alexandra, entering the royal box a few minutes before the service. Sankey burst into the backstage room, his eyes popping, and his hands nervously straightening his bow tie and whiskers.

"Moody, the *Princess of Wales* has just arrived!"

Moody, talking to a young English helper, glanced up. "May she be blessed. I'll be out in a minute. Now, Inglis, as I was saying . . . "

Inglis reported his impression:

> What a difference between the two men. There is Sankey, all in a flutter. Moody takes it as a matter of course. When we came out on the platform, I watched them. Mr. Moody rolled into his chair like a New England farmer. There he stood with a tweed suit on, pockets full of papers and said, in his usual way, "Hymn number so-and-so, let's all rise and sing it."

The princess, who seemed to know the hymns already, attended on two or three occasions and told an evangelical peer, Lord Radstock, that Moody had been a definite help to her.[5]

One of the Ladies of the Bedchamber, the Dowager Countess of Gainsborough, decided to write to the Queen.

[5] His son, the late Lord Radstock, told me this in 1952.

19

Climax in Britain

17 Hyde Park Sq. April 26th, 1875. Private.

Madam—I have been thinking Your Majesty would like once to hear these American Evangelists, who are so occupying men's minds at this time—& drawing such crowds to hear them. It would interest Your Majesty I am sure, very much and if Your Majesty wished it, might it not be?—There is the Royal box, which Your Majesty could go to quite privately . . . . I have the honour to be Your Majesty's devotedly attached and faithful old servant and Subject—F. Gainsborough.

Windsor Castle, 27th April 1875.

Dear Fanny—I received your letter yesterday on the subject of Moody and Sankey, "the American Evangelists." It would never do for *me* to go to a public place to hear them, or anything of that sort, nor, as you know, do I go to *any large public places now.*

But independently of that, though I am sure they are very good and sincere people, it is not the *sort* of religious performance which I like. This sensational style of excitement like the Revivals is not the religion which *can last*, and is not, I think, wholesome for the mind or heart, though there may be instances where it does good.

The Queen concluded her unconsciously ironic letter:

> Eloquent, simple preaching, with plain practical teaching, seem to me far more likely to do *real* and *permanent* good, and this can surely be heard in all Protestant Churches, whether in the Established Church or amongst Dissenters, *if* the Ministers are thoroughly earnest.[1]

The only Moody to get near the Queen remained little Willie, who at York station back in '73 had darted under a barrier when the Queen's train was in, and for his rapt stare received a royal smile.

Round the corner from Lady Gainsborough's was the London house of a rich retired tea planter in his fifties, with Franz Josef whiskers, who regarded Moody not with the Queen's distaste so much as a blend of amusement and sporting admiration: "There must be some good about the man, or he would never be abused so much by the papers."

Edward Studd had made a fortune in North India. He owned a fine country house, Tedworth Hall in Wiltshire, and was Master of Fox Hounds, with a passion for the turf. He had lately bought the best horse ever to come his way, entered it in an important race, and sent a hot tip to another retired planter named Vincent, a keen racing man, "Put every penny you can on my horse." In a few days he accosted Vincent in London: "How much money have you put on my horse?"

"Nothing!"

"You're the biggest fool I ever saw. Didn't I tell you what a good horse it was? But though you are a fool, come along and dine with me. My family are all in the country and you shall say where we shall go after dinner."

Unknown to Studd, Vincent had been in Dublin for the Punchestown Races the previous autumn and had annoyingly missed the steamer home. Wandering around to find a show, he saw a theater advertisement for, he supposed, a two-man American vaudeville, and he went in.

Dinner at Studd's over and the port sipped, the host lit a cigar. "Now where shall we go to amuse ourselves?"

"The Queen's Opera House."

"What? Isn't that where these fellows Moody and Sankey are? Oh, no, this isn't Sunday. We will go to the theater or a concert."

"No, you are a man of your word. You said you would go where I chose."

[1] Quoted by permission from the *Letters of Queen Victoria*, published by John Murray.

Thoroughly grumpy when they reached the Haymarket, Studd
was relieved to see that they were too late, and the place was
obviously full. Vincent pulled out his card case and scribbled on a
card: "Come and get us in. I have a wealthy sporting gentleman
with me but will never get him here again if we do not get a seat,"
and sent it in to a committeeman he knew. Studd found himself
following Vincent through the green-room door onto the stage and
placed right under Moody's nose.

He never took his eyes off Moody until the end of the address.
"The fellow has just told me everything I've ever done!" he
exclaimed. "I'll come and hear him again," and did so night after
night until his conversion.

Afterwards he asked Moody: "I want to be straight with you.
Now I am a Christian, shall I have to give up racing and shooting
and hunting and theaters and balls?"

"Mr. Studd, you've been straight with me, I will be straight with
you. Racing means betting and betting means gambling. I don't see
how a gambler is going to be a Christian. Do the other things as
long as you like."

Studd pressed the point. What did Moody really advise about the
theater and cards?

"Mr. Studd, you have children and people you love. You're now a
saved man; you want to get them saved. God will give you some
souls, and as soon as ever you have won a soul, you won't care about
any of the other things."

Studd lived a bare two years, but it was said at his funeral that he
did more in two years than most Christians do in twenty. He
withdrew from the Turf, turned the great hall at Tedworth into a
meeting room, wrote to his friends about their souls and laughed
when they replied rudely, called on his tailor and his shirtmaker
and the man from whom he had bought his cigars, and spoke of
Christ. "All I can say," said his coachman, "is that though there's the
same skin, there's a new man inside."

Edward Studd's three eldest boys were at Eton. To that bastion of
privilege, nursery of statemen, Moody and Sankey were invited.
The resultant uproar disclosed the depth of their penetration into
British life.

It was not Edward Studd's doing. The astonishing storm in a

teacup began on Saturday, June 12, when Quintin Hogg and John Graham, M.P., both Old Etonians and the latter a parent, called on old Provost Goodford with a formal introduction from Gladstone.

Because several of the senior boys wanted to hear Moody and Sankey, Graham wished to hire a tent to be erected in South Meadow, private land near the College, and to admit boys by free ticket for an hour's service on Tuesday, June 22. The Provost was understood to say he would not oppose the effort (afterwards he denied it). The Headmaster, Dr. Hornby, said he could not give sanction or connect himself or the school, but "in the event of their coming to preach once in our neighborhood I should not feel bound to put any special restriction upon our boys on the day selected." In other words, "Go ahead as a private arrangement."

Three days before the chosen Tuesday, another parent, Edward Knatchbull-Hugessen, M.P., lately Under-Secretary for the Colonies and a staunch high churchman, came down to Eton. He saw the tent, heard a revival meeting would be "held under the protection of forty policemen," and stood aghast at the idea of Eton boys being subjected to the "semidramatic performances which have lately caused so much excitement in London."

Knatchbull-Hugessen was a great-nephew of Jane Austen, and a writer himself. *Whispers from Fairy Land* had come out the year previous: *Higgledy-Piggledy* was published in 1875. He at once resolved to slay the dreadful American dragon that threatened to blow down the walls of Eton.

K-H attacked the Provost, Lord Lyttleton, the Chairman of the Governing Body, and the Headmaster. K-H wrote to *The Times* and the *Morning Post*: "I had always imagined that the religious instruction afforded at Eton was full and satisfactory"; the letters appeared on Monday, the twenty-first, and Eton authorities were deluged with telegrams for and against. The dragon-slayer secured seventy-four signatures from fellow M.P.'s, all Old Etonians or parents, to an urgent protest, to which the Headmaster replied calmly: "I have never heard this language used with reference to the Windsor Fair of old days, or the present Windsor Races and Steeplechases."

Just after 5.00 P.M. that Monday evening, the Marquess of Bath ("frozen down into the very exemplar of an immaculate, unemotional self-possessed British aristocrat") rose in the House of Lords to ask Lord Lyttleton whether the Provost and Headmaster had given sanction to the visit of Moody and Sankey. "Nothing," he declared, "can be more fatal to the discipline of the school, nothing more calculated to interfere with good regulation in the management of the boys!" Lord Lyttleton made a rambling reply, two other Governors spoke, Lord Shaftesbury rebuked Bath, saying, "In a matter of such importance, and one in which the feelings of the country are excited, the House ought to have had full notice." The Duke of Richmond, Leader of the House, moved that they proceed to business, the Poor Law (Paupers' Order of Removal) Bill.

The next morning the newspapers laughed:

> . . . discussed with as much heat as if it had threatened the peace of Europe . . . Such a prodigious agitation . . . Now we really hope the Governing Body of our greatest Public School will not be induced to make itself ridiculous . . . Leave the preachers alone and the boys alone.

Sankey put on his very best tie; Moody, saying the Eton affair was doing great good by making aristocrats show their colors, stuffed his pockets with papers. The two men caught the Windsor train.

Dispute had blown so hot in the school that the Buckinghamshire police said they would not be responsible for order in the tent, and Graham and Hogg had no option but to abandon plans for its use. The Mayor of Windsor agreed to lease Windsor town hall and disappeared by the 11:00 train. He could not have gone far—probably to London—for at 1:00 P.M. the Superintendent of Police of the Royal Borough reached him to say: "The Eton boys have purchased a large quantity of eggs! There will be a breach of the peace!" The Mayor wrote out a telegram. Shortly before 3:00, when boys already were gathering, a policeman pinned a notice on the door: No Meeting Today.

A linen draper offered his large garden opposite. And there on that sunny June afternoon, standing on a chair in the shade of a chestnut tree before some hundred and fifty to two hundred boys, four masters, and two or three hundred parents, Old Etonians, and townsfolk, all listening quietly, Sankey sang and Moody preached. Attentive audience, decorous meeting. *The Times* said it was "impossible to see" how Moody could have done the boys "the slightest harm."

Edward Studd was not singled out among those present. Nor were his sons Kynaston, George, and Charlie. No one realized that those four were to be the link between Moody's work for a nation and his work for a world.

The Lord Chancellor, who was a Presbyterian, urged the Archbishop of Canterbury, A. C. Tait, to give Moody and Sankey "some official countenance." Churchmen and dissenters were learning to love, working together in the campaign, but numerous Anglican clergy stood aloof while others pressed the Archbishop to come out for Moody. After "communicating with parochial clergymen of various opinions," Tait wrote a long letter to Cairns for publication in the press.

The Archbishop, a broad churchman, expressed "the deepest interest in a movement which . . . has been so wonderfully blessed in drawing together great masses to hear simple addresses on the great Gospel doctrines." He prayed it might "bring a blessing to many souls" and rejoiced that it was "conducted on so great a scale and with such apparent success." But he would not give "any direct sanction." His chief objection lay in the "after meetings for confession of sin and guidance of the conscience," of which his minute and careful inquiries in all directions (as his biographers described them) had apparently provided a false picture. But he quoted Moses, "Would God that all the Lord's people were prophets!" and ended with a broad hint to the clergy to "assist all of their people who seem to be awakened by this preaching."

Cairns was deeply disappointed; Dr. Dale of Birmingham was indignant. Yet it was truly said to be "the first occasion on which an Archbishop [had] so courageously allowed his sympathy with the efforts of lay missionaries," and the most friendly official word to non-churchmen since the Exclusion of 1662. Tait's attitude to Moody differed profoundly from that of his predecessors to Wesley and Whitefield, Anglicans though they were. The Archbishop's letter was a milestone on the long road toward reunion.

Londoners had taken Moody and Sankey into their hearts. Errand boys whistled, and barrel organs, instead of "Pop Goes the Weasel," ground out "Hold the Fort"; indeed, the common expression "hold the fort" dates from that time. In the last weeks, great services were held simultaneously at different centers, each in charge of associates, with Moody and Sankey now here, now there. A plan for them to give a month to each quarter of the capital was abandoned because "the people flock to whatever part the Americans are laboring in," one reason Moody at the time doubted the value of the London campaign, a doubt he lived to discard.

Any attempt to interpret those four and a half months in terms of statistics is utterly misleading. The attendance figure calculated by enthusiasts, 2,530,000, is as meaningless as the announcement of the total cost: £28,396 19s. 6d. The latter ignores the evangelists' services, given free of charge, and the considerable outlay by helpers who met their own out-of-pocket expenses; the former ignores the enormous number of frequent attenders. Nevertheless, it cannot be doubted that Moody was heard and seen by at least a million and a half in London in 1875, long before radio and television made mass audiences usual.

Equally deceptive is any statistical assessment of conversions, a practice Moody deplored. Every letter from clergy who denigrated the mission's lasting effect on church membership could be balanced by contrary, favorable evidence.[2] Much depended on whether a church encouraged or rebuffed converts, whose spiritual health in after years was not Moody's responsibility, although his contention that a man should give to newfound faith lips and legs and hands could bring rapid—sometimes overrapid—progress.

The mission had plumbed the depths. "Such tales of woe I've heard in Moody's inquiry room," said Drummond, "that I've felt I must go and change my very clothes after the contact." The wider value lay in the atmosphere or spirit generated. Not only were dockers said to swear less after the East End campaign, but duchesses were no longer ashamed to talk openly about God. After Moody, English religion became warmer and more personal. When the full force of rationalism and extreme lighter criticism and the battle between science and religion—all hitherto limited in impact—burst upon the English educated classes in the late seventies, thousands throughout England who might have been swept from a cheerless, formal faith into agnosticism were secure in the friendship of Christ.

Moody caught up and pushed forward movements that were already active or stirring—Dr. Barnardo's, the Shoe Black brigade,

---

[2] Dr. William G. McLoughlin, in his *Modern Revivalism* (1959), quotes an adverse comment made by an East End minister in November 1875, of which he found a copy "among the Moody papers in the possession of Mrs. Emma Moody Powell of East Northfield," but he quite omits the favorable comments, made by three other ministers, of the same date, which are also in Mrs. Powell's papers.

ragged schools, "rescue" missions, temperance crusades, the YMCA, and children's missions. He gave discriminating encouragement to the feeling after "practical holiness" which led, in late July 1875, to the first Keswick Convention. Church of England parish missions had been held for six years past; by persuading Hay Aitken to abandon his Liverpool living to be a full-time missionary, and by going down to the House of Commons and sending in his card to several wealthy allies and getting them to write cheques, Moody was virtual founder of the Church Parochial Mission Society, which operated for decades.

At the farewell reception to Moody and Sankey, Lord Shaftesbury, who had been conspicuously absent at the welcome five months earlier, said: "I have been conversant for many years with the people of this metropolis, and I may tell you that wherever I go I find traces of these men, of the feeling they have produced, of the stamp that, I hope, will be indelible to many." And thirty-four years later, Eugene Stock, Lay Secretary of the Church Missionary Society, with a finger in most London pies for fifty years, wrote of "that wonderful mission" of 1875:

> The Church of England has little idea what she owes to it, both in the general standard it set of *reality* in religion, and in the men and women whom it influenced—scores and scores of now honored clergymen and laymen and women, yes, even bishops.

The closing service filled the great temporary building in South London on July 13. After a short holiday—the Moodys in Wales and the Sankeys in Switzerland (where "about fifty beautiful Swiss singers came and sang hymns under my window")—they sailed from Liverpool on August 4. Moody wrote to Hitchcock in Chicago:

> Tears often come to my eyes as I think of you all. I shall be delighted to take you by the hand again. I do not think you know how much I have thought of you all in the last two years and now the time is so near for me to go to you I am just homesick to see you all again.

The influence upon Moody of those two years was unfathomable. His physique had not bent under "the terrible strain which he never seems to feel at all"; so Drummond wrote from London. Charm and irrepressible gaiety had kept their bloom. He remained unspoiled. His intimate friend, D. W. Whittle, soon after the return to America, marveled that the only change I see in him now is a growth in conscious power, and a speaking with added weight and conviction. He is thoroughly and wholly conscious that it is all of God. Praying alone with him I found him humble as a child before God. Out in the work with him I found him bold as a lion before men. No hesitation. No shrinking. No timidity.

And instead of being emptied to the last dregs, Moody had even more knowledge and sharper insight, for he was always like a sponge, soaking up consciously and unconsciously. A Scotswoman, Mrs. Barbour, who had known Moody in Edinburgh right at the start in December 1873, watched him in London in the summer of 1875. "He has given up a great deal of those peculiar out-of-the-way things he was wont to say. He is much calmer and exceedingly self-possessed; he is what I would call 'combed down,' though not a whit less fervent and earnest."

Britain had brought Moody to maturity. It had given him international fame.

At the early age of thirty-eight, he had reached a dangerous eminence. The world had yet to see whether he would slip or climb.

PART THREE

Remaking America, 1875-1881

20

Chickens at Northfield

Widow Moody's chickens at Northfield were for D. L. Moody as decisive as Mrs. O'Leary's cow, popularly supposed to have caused the Chicago fire.

Moody and Sankey and their families entered New York harbor on August 14, not knowing what the attitude of their countrymen would be toward them. The *New York Times* still asserted that they had been sent to England by Barnum the showman; thousands would have agreed with a Mr. Portal, an elderly Episcopal clergyman from Philadelphia, who remarked at a London luncheon party: "America had heard with amazement and shock how they were run after. They owed their success partly to their cheek, partly to their music." Other ministers sent urgent invitations or pleaded for their cities through laymen such as Farwell, Wanamaker, and Stuart, who had crossed the Atlantic to join the London campaign.

Moody and Sankey returned as international figures, distinguished Americans. A horde of reporters met the steamer *Spain*, and Moody would say nothing of the future except, "I am going right up to Northfield, Massachusetts, to see my mother."

The Moodys reached Northfield on August 16, driven from South Vernon depot by George in an aged buggy drawn by a plodding farm horse (Samuel followed in a wagon with their baggage), over the Connecticut by the railroad toll bridge, and up the hill into the avenue of elms in summer splendor, to Betsey's little home.

Betsey, seventy, venerable in her white widow's cap, had deep pride in her Dwight, for the crowds he had drawn and the fame he had won, even if he had hobnobbed with English dukes. She did not approve of what he preached. She had decided she would be "a Unitarian till I die."

They squeezed themselves into the small frame house that already contained Betsey and the unmarried brothers Edwin and the beloved Samuel—red-bearded, short, epileptic, and frail—the town tax collector yet popular, and a little amused in his intellectual way at Dwight's revivalism. Moody could not see too much of him. Together they drove about the lanes. Alone or with his children Moody climbed the glorious hills and valleys where once he had pastured cows, picked berries, and gathered chestnuts, and from the bleakness of New York's next winter he would often "think of the pleasant hours we had at the old home last summmer and the children will have it there's no place on earth like the old house at Northfield."

He called on his relations. "One rainy day," A Holton cousin who was Willie's age wrote:

> a man with a full dark brown beard drove into our yard and talked with Father. He was in a covered carriage and had the storm apron buttoned up to his neck and drove with the lines through a slit in the apron made for that purpose. He seemed carefree and happy as a child.

Moody intended those short weeks to be recreation for body and soul: his own body ("He weighs 220 pounds, hard, compact flesh," D. W. Whittle noted nine months later) needing exercise and country air, and his soul crying for study and quiet before bustling away to Chicago or wherever the future lay. Jabez T. Sunderland, the young minister of First Parish Church, which Betsey's family attended, had been a Baptist in Chicago before turning Unitarian. He presumed upon previous acquaintanceship in the West to invite this distinguished native son to occupy the pulpit on a Sunday— Jabez T. was a liberal man; he allowed his wife to preach sometimes, wearing daring grass-green gloves.

Moody refused. "Those who believe in Unitarianism insult

Christ, and whoever insults Christ insults me." The invitation fired him. Family, cousins, neighbors, the whole countryside, "cold unitarians . . . My heart burned to draw them to Christ." The "Orthodox," or Trinitarian, minister, T. J. Clark, was in no hurry to see Moody disturb the placid moderation of Northfield religion, but grudgingly agreed to an extra service in Second Parish Church, the old four-pointer, on Sunday afternoon, September fifth.

Betsey came from pride, determined not to budge from her convictions. Samuel came, too. Everybody did. "Early as we were the church was already half full," found one family from across the river. "The ushers had begun the farthest back and filled the seats solid as they went. Mr. Moody was in the pulpit giving out hymns." Within a few minutes, the place was bulging—literally: the under-pinning was giving way. George Moody walked swiftly up the aisle as they sang and murmured urgently in Moody's ear. At the end of the verse, Moody lifted a hand. With that wonderful smile, he said in his usual tone: "The place is full. Many are still outside. I'll preach on the steps so all can hear. While we sing the next number all will go out, beginning at the rear." They sat around on the grass and the dusty street, a small boy up an apple tree, and when they saw the old white building spreading dangerously, perceptive townsfolk understood that Moody's skill in emptying the congrega-tion swiftly had averted panic and disaster. Before the next meetings the deacons shored it up.

Sankey perched his little organ on the narrow covered platform designed for churchgoers to step off wagons without wetting feet, and sang "The Ninety and Nine." On that still summer afternoon the words sung so distinctly were wafted by the water to be heard, amazedly, no less than a mile across the Connecticut by a Mr. Caldwell, who had refused in anger to attend the service. As he sat on his porch, stirrings of conscience at the words of the distant song led to his conversion.

Moody's subject was Zaccheus. Northfield folk never forgot that "quiet Sunday afternoon." After seventy years, W. T. Holton, son of Moody's first cousin Jonathan, who farmed across the Connecticut River at Gill, could remember the details.

> The sun shining over the distant hills from the far side of the river; the air, so calm that not a leaf stirred; not a sound to disturb the quiet except the low murmur of voices from little groups as they discussed

in subdued tones the meeting and sermon. The familiar surroundings of the town and the faces of the neighbors were only a little more real than the scenes that had been vividly portrayed by the speaker . . . . With these scenes diverting us we were loath to do anything to break the spell, but the crowd gradually dispersed and we realized that evening chores must be done after driving several miles behind an old farm horse.[1]

Sankey, Whittle, and Bliss having been sent for to confer about the future, Moody used them for two weeks of special services and in other ways. One afternoon the four friends went over in the flat-bottomed ferry to dine with Uncle Cyrus, and Moody told Bliss and Sankey to sing while he helped Stebbins, the ferryman, pull on the hawser. Whittle wrote in his diary: "We all thought we crossed slowly. Sankey after a third or fourth song looked round and discovered Moody holding onto the wire and pulling back while the ferryman pulled forward." Moody wanted Stebbins to hear soul-saving hymns, loved to hear Sankey and Bliss, and roared with laughter when found out. Bliss struck up his 'Pull for the Shore, Sailor,' and by watching Moody [we] reached the land."

Up and down Main Street wandered inquisitive strangers, hoping for a glimpse of the great evangelists. By special trains from Brattleboro, by buggy and wagon and surrey, the district converged upon the Orthodox Church. (But the town blacksmith "hated me, spoke most bitterly against me. The smithy was the rendezvous of all the strong opposition men.")

Betsey did not shirk, confident in convictions that had withstood her son since his crazy days. On the hills, alone, or with his friends, Moody wrestled in prayer. Some song, some graphic Bible story pierced her shield of moral confidence, but she gave no sign until on one of the last evenings, when Moody invited those to rise in their places who wished to acknowledge Christ as Son of God and trust in Him as Savior, "that we might pray for you," Betsey rose. Moody was so overcome that he could barely ask one of the others to lead the prayer.

---

[1] W. T. Holton ascribed the collapsing church incident to this service in the summer of 1875, but Eva Stebbins Callender, who also remembered it as a child, remembered it on a warm summer day of some unspecified later year of this period. George Moody's son Ambert (aged twelve in 1875) gave no date. There is doubt also if Sankey was correct in assigning the song-across-the-river incident to the first Sunday.

D. L. Moody
at age 23.

Emma Revell Moody at age 19.
Moody Bible Institute.

D. L. Moody at the time of his
marriage, age 25 (1862). *Moody
Bible Institute.*

D. L. Moody with J. V. Farwell and some of the young ragamuffins gathered off the Chicago streets to go to Sunday school (1858). *Moody Bible Institute.*

D. L. Moody and his wife, with grandchildren (1899). *Northfield Schools, Northfield, Mass.*

Emma R. Moody

Portrait of D. L. Moody
(1867) by G. P. A. Healy.
Moody Bible Institute.

Moody conducting a service at the Agricultural Hall, in London, with Sankey behind the organ. *Moody Bible Institute.*

On the last night Samuel stood. His was no passing emotion. Like a river suddenly undammed, love poured out of him. In the short remainder of his life, "my long-sought brother . . . took a leading part in religious meetings. He went and talked with weak brothers and set them on their feet. He searched for souls on both sides of the Connecticut River, in both sides of the valley." When Northfield formed a YMCA, Samuel was elected president.

Now that Betsey and Samuel loved Moody for his work, as well as for his own sake, his roots thrust into Northfield. From being a center of cold if unmilitant Unitarianism, it became a focus of "the greatest revival ever known in that part of the state. By the following winter," W. T. Holton remembered, "for miles around prayer meetings were held in most every schoolhouse and often in private homes; while active workers, speakers, and singers alike would go round in crowds." When Whittle stayed in Northfield the next summer, he wrote:

> A wonderful work has gone on here in this community for the past year . . . Moody is loved by everybody high and low, and has the confidence of all. He greatly enjoys the results of his labors here in his native town. The testimony of the converts delights him, and their shrewd, pithy illustrations are treasured up by him for use in his work. He is a man among men and thoroughly at home with them.

Moody needed roots in the soil. He had been able to serve Chicago because, beyond the acres of city slum, he had seen in his imagination the valley and the river and the hills—Northfield, not dryly Unitarian, but a redeemed Northfield, active in the cause of Christ. The dream would be fulfilled; Northfield would mean more to him, and he to it, than either could imagine in 1875.

Nevertheless, for all that wonderful homecoming, he would again have made his home in Chicago, except for Betsey's chickens.

They were trespassing beyond Betsey's fence into the cornfield of Elisha Alexander, whose larger house stood to the northwest, higher up the hill. Uncle 'Lisha, as everybody called him, a distant relative two years younger than Betsey, was deputy-sheriff, shrewd trader, chief creditor of the townfolk, an important man. He was annoyed. He would not have Widow Moody's hens stealing his corn, and he let her know it.

Moody, spanking down a lane in a buggy, pulled up sharp when he saw Uncle 'Lisha.

"I want to buy a strip of that field."

"No. I don't care to sell unless it's the whole place."

"How many acres?"

"Twelve."

"How much?"

"Well," said Alexander, relishing the prospect of a long hard dispute lasting months, and determined to start really high, "I'll take thirty-five hundred dollars for the whole place with house and barns."

"I'll take it!"

This leap into real estate was intended to be brief; the farm would be resold except for the chicken strip. On reflection, Moody decided to keep the whole, at least for the next few years when they would be working in cities of the East, because it could be their base, their summer home. The Homestead stood on the high road with a magnificent view down to the river and away to Brattleboro Mountain, in typical New England style, substantial, not grandiose.

He had been able to buy because Edward Studd had pressed upon him a personal gift of £500, approximating $2,500. Twice Studd's check was returned, until he begged Farwell, "How can I get it into Moody's hand without offending him?" They succeeded because the third time Moody did not wish to hurt Studd's feelings. Thus Edward Studd, the Englishman from India, stands at the crossroads of Moody's life, by a check in 1875 and by his sons in the next decade.

The source of the remaining $1,000 (and $2,500 spent on alterations) is not known, but since Moody had served two years without pay it hardly could be grudged.

Now came the Great Renunciation.

Royalties on sales in Britain of *Sacred Songs and Solos* for the first six months of 1875 totaled slightly over £5,600. The English trustee, Matheson, declined to give a British charity the earnings of Americans and after discussions with Moody, Farwell, and Sankey in London, decided that the fund should help to complete the Chicago Avenue Church, which had lost its leaders for two years. He sent the church $27,000. Larger royalties would accrue from the most popular hymnbook in Britain, and already Morgan and

Scott had issued a first slim volume of sermons (the vernacular Moody was polished anonymously by Drummond). *Sacred Songs and Solos* could not be published in the United States because of copyrights, but an American counterpart was in preparation, *Gospel Songs*.

Moody said: "I am not going to give any man ground for saying we're making a gain out of preaching the Gospel." While Sankey, Bliss, and Moody were at Northfield that September 1875, they sent for William E. Dodge, Jr., a New York businessman and philanthropist, and made him draw up a trust to which all royalties would be paid. Not discerning yet this money's possibilities, the trustees at first distributed it to worthy but casual claims: "If you can hold the Association for a few months we can lift the debt," Moody, in October 1875, told Farwell, who was helping the Chicago YMCA. "I do not want you to say anything, but I think we will make enough from the hymnbooks."

More than $357,000 poured into the trust over the next ten years, in an age when one dollar went far, and at Moody's death an estimated million and a quarter had been earned by the hymns.

When he abandoned a business career he had discarded the means of a fortune. Riches came unasked. He refused them, a brave act, because wealth was post-Civil War America's one gauge of success. He did not even retain an annual sum to keep his wife and family, but merely bought a life insurance of $1,500 a year for Emma on his death, relied on occasional spontaneous gifts from wealthy friends, together with modest privately raised honoraria for American campaigns, and (from the later eighties) some income from books. The latter went directly to Mrs. Moody, who kept the accounts and paid all family, household, and farm bills. Moody maintained a reasonable standard of living, sent his sons to college, and showed constant generosity to his relatives, but from time to time, while vast sums flowed into the hymnbook fund, Moody ran distinctly short.

Sankey's sacrifice, however, was sharper. Brought up in prosperity, he had thrown away a good salary and pension rights. He had refused large offers, and God had brought this unexpected wealth. Sankey loved money, loved to be smart and comfortable. Moody never noticed surroundings or clothes. Moody always would have work; Sankey's voice might fail. Yet he signed away his earnings.

The Trust lawyer told Paul Moody that his father "did not seem
to care what happened to the money, provided he wasn't bothered
with it." Paul considered Moody "scared of money." Moody never
forgot the struggle to give up business, and if he loved to play the
philanthropist he dared not face the temptations of a rich man. Of
Marshall Field, Lieter, "and other men of our age in Chicago who
had succeeded in business and become wealthy," Moody said to
Whittle (in 1884):

> Whenever I think of them and the worldly influences that surround
> them and their families, I feel so thankful to God for being right out of
> the whole of it. What should I want of their money? I have had more
> money to give away to the cause of Christ from the Hymnbook fund
> than the wealthiest one of them.

The streak of fear was weaker than the streak of indifference.
Money was transient. At any moment Christ would return to reign
in glory; Moody looked for Him every day. "It's the truth of the
Second Coming of Christ that was used of God to get me out of 'the
world.'" Deeper than these reasons lay Moody's utter scorn at
trading in souls. It seemed to him intolerable that he should get
rich because he was used in a particular line of Christian service.
Introduced to a colorful elderly evangelist called "Uncle Johnnie"
Vasser, who exclaimed, "How glad I am to see the man that God has
used to win so many souls to Christ," Moody replied: "You say
rightly, Uncle John, the man whom *God* has *used*." Then, stooping
to pick up a handful of earth, he poured it through his fingers:
"There's nothing more than *that* to D. L. Moody, except as God uses
him!"

During the first three decades of the twentieth century, when
mass evangelism passed through a regrettably commercialized
phase, men would look back wistfully on Moody and Sankey's
attitude to money.

They did not advertise what they had done. Seven years passed
before Jane Mackinnon knew: "I call it simply a magnificent fact,
the relinquishing of a great fortune, as far as I can judge." An
eminent New York counsel was more blunt. The trustees needed a
legal opinion and selected Charles F. Southmayd, not only for his
reputation but because he hated Christians. At the mention of
Moody and Sankey, Southmayd gave them "all sorts of bad names
and stated they were making large money out of their meetings."

After looking through the papers, he sent for the trustees' lawyer: "Mr. Coffin," Southmayd said, "I withdraw the charge they are rascals but will say instead, they are fools to let such money slip through their hands!"

21

All America Stirred

"We will all go East in a week," Sankey wrote to Hitchcock of Chicago from New Castle, Pennsylvania, on October 13, 1875, "and I cannot tell when we will be able to go to your city much as we love you—" He asked if his "stoves, tables, sofa, etc." could be sold and the "bedclothes, pictures etc." be sent to New Castle. "The reason for this move is that we have become Religious *Tramps* and in all human probability will never be long enough in one place to have a *home*."

When Moody and Sankey were at Northfield much coming and going of church personages heralded four years of intense campaigning. "Water runs downhill and the highest hills are the great cities," said Moody. "If we can stir them we shall stir the whole country." Whether they would be effective in their own land was in doubt: most of the New York newspapers were skeptical, and even the famous Brooklyn preacher, De Witt Talmage, had wondered whether his weekly journal should support or discourage. America needed religious revival. The decade since the end of the Civil War had seen the North cankered by easy money and the pursuit of wealth, by political corruption that strangled public and municipal life more tightly each year of the administration of the incorruptible but easygoing President Grant. Unceasing streams of immigrants altered the texture of the nation. Americans, new or long

established, strode toward some technological utopia, old morali-
ties discarded. The onward rush had braked sharply on the Wall
Street Panic of 1873 and now in 1875 the trade depression might
make men pause and listen.

Moody, having decided reluctantly not to begin in Chicago, because
"I was rather afraid the ministers would not come together," accepted
a united invitation for a month at Brooklyn. Pessimists were at once
confounded as Brooklyn pressed into and around the Rink on
Clermont Avenue, the *New York Herald* estimating that "twelve—
possibly twenty—thousand were unable to gain admittance." Streetcar
companies had laid extra tracks to the building, and, at the close of the
service, "though cars were run at intervals of only one minute, many
thousands had to wend their ways homeward on foot." "All goes well
here," Moody wrote to Farwell. "Pray daily for me. I never needed the
help of my friends as much as now."

It was soon said that Moody "has held in silent attention and deeply
moved, some of the largest assemblies that any speaker has addressed
in America, at least in our day." Moody knew that many in the crowd
were drawn by curiosity, New Yorkers hurrying across Brooklyn
Bridge to look at the latest lion, that the "selfishness of excitement-
seeking professed Christians" left no room for the great unchurched,
whom he felt at the close he had failed to reach. But Brooklyn
launched him with a bang, and proved that clergy would unite
"zealously and harmoniously and intelligently to carry on the work."

From late November 1875 until January 1876, the evangelists
campaigned in Philadelphia. The mission had been in preparation
since the previous June. Moody's great friend John Wanamaker
shrewdly bought the disused freight depot of the Pennsylvania
Railroad, in a central position at the corner of Tenth and Market
Streets, and gave it rent-free, fully fitted, with the intention of
rebuilding it as his new dry goods store: at that time Wanamaker
was still a man of strict integrity, and there is no reason to accuse
him of having an ulterior motive, though his store would rise on a
site that no one, in that religious city, would forget.

One hundred eighty ministers had signed the invitation. The
story again was of vast crowds and reinvigorated churches, "the
greatest series of religious meetings that Philadelphia witnessed
during the 19th century," according to a YMCA estimate of 1905;
perhaps the convert who became best known was S. D. Gordon,
future writer of *Quiet Talks on Prayer* and other bestsellers. "Moody's

meetings," wrote a Philadelphian to an English friend on January 18, 1876,

> are within gunshot of my home. The doors open about 1½ hours before the time and it takes about 10 minutes to fill—12,000 persons. Sometimes the seats reserved for those who get tickets as the unsaved and the companies from the country by train fill the whole body of the house. It is wonderful.[1]

Moody held special meetings every Friday for alcoholics, of the class all too widespread in American cities of the seventies. He had women's meetings. And he gloried in the special meetings for young men. On December 4 Moody scrawled a note to Henry Drummond in Scotland:

> The work among young men in this country is growing splendidly. I am glad I went to England to learn how to so much and will see that all expenses are paid, I think you would get a few thousand souls on these shores if you should come. I miss you more than I can tell, you do not know how much I want you with me, come if you possibly can.

Drummond wisely declined to interrupt his college studies again. By special request, Moody went for a day to Princeton. Of his reception by the students, he confessed, "I have not seen anything in America that pleased me like what I have seen in Princeton. They have got a Holy Ghost revival there. The President of the college told me he had never seen anything like it in Princeton."

In Philadelphia Moody showed the same unaffected, integrated personality known to his friends in Britain. In work, he was utterly absorbed. One of his church officers from Chicago came to the platform at the close of an evening service as the inquiry meeting began. "I touched Mr. Sankey on the shoulder, and he did the undignified thing of embracing me. After a little conversation with him I went where Moody was, and touched him on the shoulder also, when he turned and quickly and earnestly said, 'Talk to that woman!'"

President Grant and several of his Cabinet, visiting the preparations for the Centennial Exhibition, sat on the platform on Sunday, January 19. Moody made no attempt to be introduced afterwards; he had a bad cold and a hoarse voice, but even if he had been well would not have sought out the President.

---

[1] Robert Pearsall Smith to the Rt. Hon. William Cowper-Temple (Broadlands Papers).

In play, he was utterly absorbed as well. Back at the Wanamakers' mansion, where Emma and the children stayed, too (Willie and Emma's education was peripatetic throughout these years), Moody could relax in a moment. "The thing I remember most," wrote one of the Wanamakers, "was Mr. Moody and father playing bears with us children. Such wild exciting times as we had. They would get down on all fours and chase us. We would shriek and scream and run. It was pandemonium."

The New York campaign, from February 7 until April 19, 1876, had been prepared as carefully as the one in Philadephia. At the end, it could be said that Moody's "position today, whether at home or abroad, is unrivaled."

He reached New York only a day before the opening, but he had let the committee of laymen and ministers know precisely what should be done, and they had organized the campaign with true New York business skill. The treasurer was Pierpont Morgan, the banker, the same age as Moody, and the thirty-two-year-old Cornelius Vanderbilt, Jr., one of the private guarantors who advanced money against expenses; both men were Episcopalians. They leased Barnum's "Great Roman Hippodrome," which stood on Madison Avenue, future site of Madison Square Garden. "On one side of it," runs a contemporary description, "lie the homes of wealth, the avenues of fashion, and the great hotels, on the other the masses of the middle class and, a little beyond, the crowded abodes of the poor and the dens of wretchedness and vice."

The Hippodrome was thought too large for the whole to be addressed at once. "We are fitting up two large halls opening into each other," the chairman, William E. Dodge, had told a friend, "one holding about eight or nine thousand and the other about six thousand." Inquiry rooms were arranged, and an up-to-date touch was an internal electric telegraph, whereby orders could be sent to regulate lighting, heating, and ventilation.

A choir of a thousand led a song service for half an hour before the little door opened at the back of the wide platform and D. L. Moody stepped in. "*Stepped* in, did I say?" recalled James M. Gray, thirty years later.

Yes, literally, for he seemed to cover the space between the door and the pulpit in one step! Mr. Sankey was more deliberate, and tried our patience before he settled at the keyboard and touched the keys to melt our hearts, but Mr. Moody was a meteor. He was at the little railing in front, his hand raised, our heads bowed in prayer and we all saying "Amen" almost before we knew it . . . . How lithe, springy, and buoyant he was. How full of life and spirit!

His weight was still primarily muscle and bone, not fat. He used a "health lift" every day, since New York gave no time for open-air exercise. The press described him as "short, stout-built, square shouldered with bullet-shaped head set close on the shoulders, black eyes that twinkle merrily at times, and a full but not heavy beard and moustache." Few observers correctly noted the gray of Moody's eyes; most remembered them as brown—even some who worked closely with him. The gray of the eyes reflected the light and shade of his surroundings.[2]

Day after day New York responded. "The tone and character of the services here has disarmed all prejudice," wrote William E. Dodge from his Madison Avenue home on March 3 to an English acquaintance,

> and nothing is wanted to prove to all fair thinking men that they are of God. Nothing has ever reached our great masses of non-church going people as these meetings have. Our ministers have been warmed and helped, cold Christians [?] won over, and very many careless brought to Christ. I do not think the work has been truer or larger in any place Mr. Moody has visited. He is staying with me and I find his cheery whole-souled humble consecration a great spur and help.

The details of those ten weeks are not significant. The message was the same as in Britain—Moody said his creed was printed in the fifty-third chapter of Isaiah—the method brisker to American tempo. Yards of newsprint recording daily incidents blended into a haze—crowds converging nightly on the Hippodrome, thousands of voices lifted in chorus, Sankey's songs, Moody's torrent of words.

It was the individual hearer who gripped Moody's imagination. As he faced the serried rows, his mind and prayers and words focused on the inquiry room to follow, for he never forgot that long before becoming a mass evangelist he had relished what he called Personal Work, and he could not bear that any man or woman

[2] The fact his eyes were gray is put beyond dispute not only by Mrs. W. R. Moody's memory, but also by a Passport Application filled out by Moody in his own hand in 1891.

should lack or spurn Christ's friendship. Moody had outgrown the habit of throwing off texts:

> His questionings speedily determined whether an inquirer was sincere and genuine, or hypocritical and evasive. With astonishing rapidity he could turn a man mentally and morally inside out, expose his fallacies, moral inconsistencies, perversions, willfulness, and alienation from God.

"Mr. Moody evidently prefers the inquiry meeting as his place," wrote J. E. Rankin (the author of "God Be with You till We Meet Again"). "And what does he find most lacking? Competent men and women to guide inquirers." Moody taught New York what Rankin called "the laymen's opportunity . . . . Let men and women learn the art of personally winning souls."

As in Great Britain, the value of a campaign could not be gauged by numbers who professed conversion but by skills imparted to lay people, encouragements to ministers, the impact not of evangelism only but of a "Christian convention" held toward the end, and the promotion of Christian unity. Moody did not need to bring forward the idea of unity when Beecher and others had preached and striven for it. Moody proved that unity will not be found in a vacuum; it is not an end in itself, but it grows in the midst of mission.

At the close of the campaign, the *New York Times*, so long an opponent, conceded that

> the work accomplished this winter by Mr. Moody in this city for private and public morals will live. The drunken have become sober, the vicious virtuous, the worldly and self-seeking unselfish, the ignoble noble, the impure pure, the youth have started with more generous aims, the old have been stirred from grossness. A new hope has lifted up hundreds of human beings, a new consolation has come to the sorrowful, and a better principle has entered the sordid life of the day, through the labors of these plain men.

For the rest of his life, Moody on his travels met men and women converted in Philadelphia and New York, from 1875 to 1876, and when in December 1896, there was talk that "little permanent good resulted," the pastor of Faith Presbyterian Church on West 46th Street, James H. Hoadley, wrote to Moody:

> Looking over the statistics of my own church the other day I noticed that in the year 1876 there were received into the church 139 persons.

Of the number 121 were received on confession of faith in Christ. The large part of these brought to Christ under the influence of your great revival meetings. Only a very small percent have fallen away so far. Never since that day have we received so large a number into the church in any one year.

Moody was unhappy at the end of the New York campaign. With spring, several pastors left for vacation. "I thought this rather hard. They should have been as much interested in the conversion of the town as I was. But apparently they were not. So I lost my nerve— and I lost my good sense." In the course of an afternoon Bible Reading, he "pitched into the *New York Ledger*," the society gossip paper to which several fashionable clergymen—including the chairman of the meeting, Dr. Hall—contributed regularly. "I didn't mean to say anything against the paper, but somehow it popped up." The moment he finished his sermon he turned to apologize, but Hall had left the chair in a huff and did not see Moody again before leaving for Europe.

Moody said that the incident with Hall made him decide to close the Hippodrome mission two weeks before the three months were up. Immediately he believed he had done wrong. "I closed the meeting in the Hippodrome. In doing so I grieved the Holy Spirit." He left New York believing that, though this campaign had been "the best he ever had," he would never be blessed there again.

The tiff with Dr. Hall was not Moody's only unhappiness.

He went South, where Emma had already taken the children because New York weather had nearly killed Willie, and on April 22 brought them to Augusta, Georgia. Here D. W. Whittle was in the midst of a mission. Whittle was "stalwart and austere, but there was in him the sweetness and gentleness of John Alden and of Whittier." Whittle had brought his wife and six-year-old daughter, May, a year younger than Willie: they had been babies together in Chicago, and now they became playmates. Moody was supposed to be resting but at once took part in the mission, inevitably overshadowing Whittle, who rebuked himself for a slight temptation to resent the intrusion: "I have considered that Moody is a mighty man of God, the Whitefield of this century, owned and honored of God, and if he has been led of God to come here and speak it is a very petty spirit that would think of self in connection with the work."

Moody opened his heart to Whittle, as they walked on the banks
of the Savannah River in the sunshine of a Southern spring.

> I don't know that I will ever go to England again. I am entirely
> bankrupt as to sermons and material—I have used up everything. I'm
> going to study and make new sermons but, I think it will be three or
> four years before I shall go—if I ever go. You and Bliss had better wait
> until next year before going, and you must study all you can.

"Bankrupt"—that was Moody's inner feeling. At the moment of
reaching a height of influence in the United States, he stood in
danger of spiritual insolvency.

He continued to rise early to study his Bible and pray, for he
could work on a minimum of sleep and drop off any time of day or
night. He had evolved a filing system, using for each sermon a large
envelope into which he slipped a scrawled sheet of headings and
"notes and stories clipped from papers or jotted on paper" for
illustrations. On the envelope he listed the place and date of each
delivery. As Jane Mackinnon wrote in Britain, "the peculiarity of his
preaching was that although one heard the same address several
times it always came quite fresh home to the heart and conscience."

Nevertheless, he was nibbling into his spiritual and intellectual
capital. It was not his only danger. Whittle put his finger on
another. Moody had spoken of his passionate desire for unity "in
getting the Gospel before the people." Whittle noted:

> I think M. in having before him just the one thing of the success of
> his immediate work, may be in danger of sacrificing principle and that
> he magnifies those things that have immediate effect . . . . His heart is
> in the triumph of Christ's cause. Divisions, jealousies, everything that
> hinders success he wants out of sight, and the army to move on with
> united front.

Whittle was shocked when Moody said, discussing the long, drawn-
out scandal of Henry Ward Beecher's alleged adultery with Mrs.
Tilton, "I hope if he is guilty, it will never be known, it would have
an awful effect." Whittle was, however, sure that "if M. knew he
were guilty and the responsibility rested upon him of delivering
him to justice, he would do his duty unswervingly."

One other danger Whittle did not note: that Moody had no anchor.
He had bought the Northfield Homestead merely as a summer home.

He had his own church in Chicago but could not bring himself to settle there again. If he did not anchor he would burn out in a few years of wandering ministry. Wherever he anchored, Northfield or Chicago, would shape the remainder of his life.

His present influence was enormous. A small but significant indication lies in Farwell's advice in June 1876, to McCormick, who toyed with running for the vice-presidential nomination, that $5,000 given to Moody's cause in Chicago and widely advertised would do more "than all the money you could put into the hands of political wire-pullers."

Moody, who told reporters, "I am the most overestimated man in America," considered himself

> only the mouthpiece and expression of a deep and mysterious wave of religious feeling now passing over the nation. The disasters and disappointments of the year, the reaction against the skepticism and selfish greed of the day, the deep religious sentiment lying at the bottom of the American character, and the eternal wants of the human heart have prepared the minds of the people for a profound religious transformation or impulse.

By newspapers, which often reported his sermons in full—in volumes of collected sermons, which enterprising publishers issued without permission or royalty—by "Lives," to which he objected on principle and tried to suppress—although at least one was fair and honorable if inaccurate—the message of Moody penetrated the length and breadth of the nation. In log cabins of the Appalachians, in frontier wagons drawn up fearfully in some remote valley of Montana Territory this summer of Custer's Last Stand, in Texan ranches where men and women lived hard and lusty and a clergyman might be seen twice a year, in the soot and grime of Detroit or Pittsburgh or Cleveland shadowed by unemployment, in Atlantic fishing villages, in Southern plantations, in skid rows, and in millionaire avenues, Moody and Sankey were read and sung, bringing comfort, inspiration, rebuke, and a breath of heaven to an all-too-earthy grind.

Imitators were inevitable. In September 1876, a Methodist minister of New York complained,

> The would-be-Moodys abide and abound. Moody and Sankey meetings are advertised, at which Moody's sermons will be read,

Moody and Sankey hymnbook used, etc., then somebody dashes out like Bro. Moody, or tries to sing a solo like Bro. Sankey—perfect copyist, and always more or less a failure.

Exploiters were worse. "Perhaps you noticed," Moody told one audience,

that there is someone at the door selling photographs of Mr. Sankey and myself. I want to say that this is one of the thorns we have in the flesh. Those are no more photographs of Mr. Sankey and myself than they are of you or anyone else.

With press photography in its infancy, only those who had attended their meetings knew their likeness, and no one could photograph them unless they consented and sat still. Moody had tried to stop the fakes by law and found that "and we can't do it. And now we ask you, if you have any regard for us, not to patronize them . . . . I hope I will never have to refer to it again, for I always feel like a fool when I have to talk about myself."[3]

From Augusta the Moodys and Whittles traveled overnight to Atlanta and, the next day, reversing Sherman's march (Whittle excitedly pointing out battlefields and fortifications), came to Chattanooga where the landlady nearly gave them hysterics by begging Moody to sing "The Ninety and Nine." After a picnic of strawberries and milk on Lookout Mountain, they returned to find a "large number of ministers and Christians who prevail upon M. to speak at Presbyterian Church."

The last half of May was no holiday. Northward and westward: Nashville, St. Louis, Kansas, Omaha, and Council Bluffs into Iowa—they took a sort of whistle-stop tour that laid a trail of illuminated lives across the Middle West. Thus James G. Butler, a man of Moody's age, and a stranger to St. Louis, wandered complacently into an after-meeting there. Butler recalled,

[3] After a year or two, Moody appointed his brother-in-law, Fleming H. Revell, as publisher of his sermons, which were the basis of Revell's rise to being, by 1890, one of the largest publishers in the United States. The early American Moody collections, such as *New Sermons, Addresses and Prayers* (Chicago: J. W. Goodspeed, 1877) and *The Gospel Awakening* (copyrighted L. T. Palmer and Co., 1877; 3d Edition, St. Louis: Scammell and Co., 1878), were all pirated.

[Moody] came down where I was sitting, and said: "Are you a Christian?"

"Yes, sir!" I replied, rather expecting he would say something courteous and cordial. But, no. He only said, pointing to another man just across: "Talk to that man about his soul." I did. There was just nothing else for me to do. If the man was blessed as I was, he is a happy man today.

At Des Moines the ministers were determined to cancel all Sunday services and concentrate their congregations on Moody at the local Rink. F. G. Ensign, Moody's friend from the previous decade, while organizing his tour, warned them that Moody would refuse.

An obstinate deputation met him on arrival.

"Mr. Moody, we have decided—our association has voted—that we will not have any services on Sunday. We want all our people to go to the Rink at 10:30."

"No, I can't do that."

"But we have decided it."

"I can't do it! You will have to have your church services. You must have your church services, and then at 2:30, so as not to interfere with the services, we have the meeting in the Rink."

It was an example of Moody's brisk treatment of committees. "I have often to do a shabby thing," he confided to a friend. "A committee takes a great deal of trouble about something, I see it will not suit, so I cut discussion short by saying I am going to do it another way. It is very mean of me, but would take a tremendous time in committee, and I have to do it." His briskness could cause offense. Whittle described Moody receiving a deputation:

> Some of the committee have been grieved because M. has ignored them and gone ahead with meetings as he pleased. Some fifteen are present. Moody keeps quiet and draws out in full all the complaints and injured feeling and then explains and makes right everything and suggesting what he thinks best draws out the ministers to adopt it as from themselves.

And so the Midwest tour continued. At Jacksonville, Moody, president again that year, led the Illinois State Sunday School Association in its four-day convention. Sankey had rejoined but fell sick and was "still quite ill" when, on May 27, after nearly three years, they came at last to Chicago.

22

Moody's Dilemma

Farwell had half wondered whether Moody was losing interest. "If you can give a poor sinner a little advice if he does hail from Chicago . . . " he had written in jocular vein the previous March. At heart he knew that Moody's "own church has been second only to the all-absorbing idea of making the world feel the power of Christian union in active work for the masses."

Moody called that church his "first love. For years I seldom get on my knees in private but I think and pray for the dear church in Chicago." When one of his deacons had come to Philadelphia, Moody took him to the Wanamaker mansion, "where for more than two hours he went over the membership of the church, calling each one by name and inquiring minutely how they were getting on." At the site on Chicago Avenue, which he had secured before leaving for Europe, stood the new building—still with a debt, despite hymnbook royalties, but one that Moody wiped out by a few masterly solicitations and some indifferent congregational giving. On June 1, 1876, an evening of pouring rain, the church was opened, with Moody preaching. It was formally dedicated on July 16.

The old haunts—changed beyond recognition by rebuilding, yet smoky still and impregnated with that evocative stockyard stench, crowded and bustling and cosmopolitan, where ragged children yelled and thieved and booze ruined more lives than Chicago bothered to count—drew out Moody's suppressed longing. As if to indicate that Chicago might anchor him after all, he decided to postpone a promised campaign in Boston in order to accept Chicago's invitation first, provided they built a large enough temporary "tabernacle."

This condition disturbed Farwell. "I don't think you fully comprehend the difficulty in raising money here to build a building to be torn down," he told Moody. "We have very few men who can give, who are not now pulled and hauled to pay church debts." Farwell therefore allowed the committee to erect, on his company's property at the corner of Monroe and Franklin, a tabernacle with outside walls suitable for a permanent building, which he would buy at the campaign's end for conversion to a wholesale store.

The Moodys returned to Northfield for two summer months, and Emma was "a very busy woman." She wrote to Jane Mackinnon on September 11:

> We are in our own home, as you have probably heard, and though in a most delightful spot with such beautiful scenery it is a place where it is very difficult to get servants, and I have had to act in all sorts of capacities. We have had company every day since we came into our house, and [it] has been a pleasure to my husband and myself, but I found my husband's urgent letters took most all of spare time.

The holiday was slightly spoiled by reports in the British papers, which brought letters from England asking if Moody and Sankey had really quarreled over money in New York. "The whole thing is a wicked fabrication," wrote Emma. "Mr. Sankey and Mr. Moody have never quarreled about anything . . . . I have not seen anything from the newspapers trouble Mr. Moody as this has done."

Moody delighted in the Homestead, and in driving around with Sam, who, despite his weak, epileptic constitution, bubbled with plans for the welfare—spiritual and temporal—of Northfield. Once again Moody's anchor seemed cast there, rather than in Chicago. The drama of those critical years, from 1875 to 1876— Moody's first flush of fame in his own land—lies partly in his own indecision as to where his base should be, an indecision scarcely conscious, absorbed as he was in his immediate surroundings and opportunities. He was even less aware of what the consequences might be, if he cast his anchor in the wrong place.

The Moodys arrived in Chicago on Saturday, September 30, and stayed with Emma's sister and her husband, the Holdens. Moody was "in peace as to the work and has faith that God will bless us."

Six thousand Sunday school teachers and the like, 500 singers, and 100 ministers, filled the Tabernacle at 8:00 A.M. on Sunday. Moody took his seat "and spends a half minute in prayer." After hymns and prayer and reading and Sankey's solos, Moody "rises and commences very abruptly his sermon on 'Rolling Away the Stone.'" Recalled Whittle,

> His talk is as earnest, plain, simple, and practical and as absent from all self-consciousness as if delivered to his own Sunday school teachers. You are interested and inspired, and think he has just begun when he stops as abruptly as he began, offers prayer, pronounces the benediction and the meeting is over.

Chicago had forgotten the "Crazy Moody" days. Chicago raved over its own great evangelist. This campaign, it seemed, would proceed like any other. The first Sunday afternoon service was packed out. The new Farwell Hall was overflowing, too; thousands were turned away. The opening evangelistic service on Monday was filled. The Chicago Omnibus Company had to run special buses, and the horses kept at it every three quarters of a minute to connect with the tram cars. A learned theological professor wrote:

> It is perfectly astounding to me that a man with so little training should have come to understand the public so well. He cannot read the Greek Testament; indeed he has difficulty with parts of it in the English version, but he excels any man I ever heard in making his hearers see the point of a text of Scripture.

Whittle dined with Moody on the first Thursday afternoon and found him "unusually solemn." Moody said, "I could pray today, 'O God search me,' but when it comes to asking God to 'try me' it's a solemn thing. I don't know as I could stand *trying*. Am I ready to be laid aside from my work, to be tried? Am I ready to meet affliction?"

The following day, Friday, October 6, Moody at dinner was again "very solemn with the thought of praying God to try him." That evening he invited the officers of the Chicago Avenue Church to take tea at Brevoort House before the meeting. Whittle arrived a little late, carrying Moody's mail collected at the YMCA, a pile of letters and one telegram. He handed it all to Moody.

> While sitting at the table he opened the telegram and upon reading it made an ejaculation of pain, stood upon his feet and said "Sam is dead" and sat down with his head buried in his hands to cry. In a few minutes he said, "Whittle, you will have to take the meeting tonight. I cannot be with you longer," and went out.

Whittle tremblingly reached the tabernacle and found Moody in the anteroom, surrounded by ministers; he was going east to bury his brother, and Whittle was invited unanimously to lead the meetings "and push right on."

Moody was away a week. "The first thought as I went toward home, Oh, how deep the sorrow! The dear boy was gone for ever"—Samuel for whom he had prayed twenty years, who, at the last, "took a stand for Christ, and went to work . . . zealous work." As the train rumbled through Indiana into Ohio, Moody wept and wept again until heaven's voice "at last made itself heard to my heart: 'Thy brother shall rise again.' The cloud was lifted, and for about five hundred miles on my way to my home that verse rang in my ears."

During travel to and fro, Moody wrote letters that seemed to epitomize two loyalties: to Chicago and to Northfield, each dragging softly against the other.

He wrote to the Chicago Avenue Church from a hotel where he, who never would travel by hired or public transport on "the sabbath," had broken his journey:

> Of late you have been on my mind and heart far more than usual . . . . The only way any Church can get a blessing is to lay aside all difference, all criticism, all coldness and party feeling, and come to the Lord as one man; and when the Church lives in the power of the 13th chapter of First Corinthians I am sure that many will be added daily to the flock of God.

To his mother he wrote after the funeral, waiting for a connection at Springfield:

> A strange and lonely feeling comes over me tonight as I am here for

3 hours. But *dear* mother I know you will miss him far more than any of us who are away . . . . You and Edwin will be lonely I am sure but we will all pray for you that God may give you strength and hold you both up . . . . I must say goodbye now & hope the death of Samuel will draw us all much nearer to Christ than we have ever been before. I feel as if it had drawn me much nearer to Christ than I ever have been before—give my *love* to all & tell them it seems as if God had enlarged my heart to love you all much more.

Samuel's death made Moody want to do all that Samuel had longed for Northfield. Yet he felt compelled to give himself to Chicago. He loved both. To the pastor of Chicago Avenue, W. J. Erdman, he wrote: "I do hope you will hold the people to the thought of love. I am sure that is where the churches have all gone astray. We must have it above all things."

The Chicago campaign bowled on through the bitter, long drawn-out presidential campaign of 1876, over Christmas, and into 1877.

A Presbyterian minister, looking back after twenty-four years, wrote about

that wonderful revival . . . that tremendous audience, and its voice in song like the voice of the ocean . . . the mighty faith and courage of the undertaking. Think what it required to prepare for an audience of ten thousand people, and what failure, in the presence of such vast preparation, would mean!

The campaign reached its closing weeks. It had been a strange and difficult time for Moody: Samuel had died; twelve-year-old Emma had suffered a dangerous attack of scarlet fever; and Mrs. Moody—although she did not reveal it to Moody—had been told by her doctor that her heart was diseased, in critical condition, and that "she might at any time be taken."[1] On top of all that, on a wild night, December 29, Philip Bliss, who, Moody said, was like his hymns, "full of faith and cheer—in all the years I have known and worked with him I have never seen him cast down," was in the Pacific Express near Ashtabula, Ohio, when an iron bridge gave way in a snowstorm. The train plunged seventy feet onto a frozen

[1] Whittle Diary, October 14, 1876.

creek and caught fire, over a hundred were reported dead. Bliss managed to crawl out but went back to free his wife. Not a button or a bone of them could be identified.

These afflictions made Moody, in Whittle's words, "very kind and tender." But when the campaign ended on January 16, 1877, Moody lay no nearer the answer to the unspoken inner question: Where would he anchor and what would follow? Even more pressing, would he burn out in a few more years?

On January 28, a week before Moody's fortieth birthday, the Boston campaign began. Failure at Boston could kill Moody's influence in America. Instead, by the time he finished there on May 1, he had received a new vision.

Unitarians, liberal intellectuals, snobs, and Irish Catholics battled against him. Of his friends, led by A. J. Gordon, the saintly Baptist pastor of Clarendon Street, a large stocky man whose clean-shaven face stood out among Boston's bewhiskered divines, few boyhood figures remained. Kimball had moved long ago and lived in San Francisco; Kirk had died nearly three years before; and Moody's Holton uncles were retired. Ninety churches cooperated to fill the specially-built tabernacle, for which not all the money had been raised when the campaign opened, "the smallest, though one of the pleasantest, of the series of great buildings erected for the Moody and Sankey revival meetings." It seated 6,000 and stood on what was then an extension of Tremont Street, between Berkeley and Clarendon, west of the Common toward the new Boston being built on land reclaimed from Back Bay.

"Boston's a peculiar place," Moody was warned. "You can't expect to do the same as elsewhere." Moody scorned such advice. "Christianity," cried Moody the first night,

> has been on the defensive long enough, specially here in New England. The time's come f'r us to open a war of aggression. Remember during the War of the Rebellion some of the generals kept their armies on the defensive until they got confusticated? I guess a good many Christians here in New England have just got into their cushioned pews and gone to sleep—*Now* is the time to wake up and move forward in solid columns—We want not to be on the defensive but to begin a war of aggression. These drinking shops 'n' billiard halls 'n' gambling dens should be visited 'n' told of Christ 'n' heaven 'n' if

they won't come to the Tabernacle 'n' hear the Gospel let us go to their houses 'n' preach the Gospel to them 'n' it won't be long before hundreds are reached.

Shortly thereafter the *Sunday Times* ("the spiciest paper in New England") complained that "the masses in Boston are undoubtedly becoming permeated with piety." The weekday papers "ran the revival" strongly; the *Globe* even recovered from financial disaster by printing so-called verbatim reports. "We never sold 25,000 copies quicker than we did yesterday."

Everybody sang. The street urchins had their own version of "Hold the Fort":

> Hold the forks, the knives are coming
> The plates are on the way,
> Shout the chorus to your neighbor
> Sling the hash this way.

Photograph hawkers did their usual roaring trade (at five cents), and somebody heard a toy peddler in Tremont Street shouting, "Here's yer Moody and Sankey spiders [skillets]! Two cents each."

The *Sunday Times* sneered weekly in a ribald column by a former Sunday school teacher who hid under the pseudonym "I. A. M. Cumming" and said he believed "man is his own saviour." Some of his jokes and insinuations were clever and amusing; others were obscene. Sometimes he would write loftily of Moody's "cant blasphemous phrase." Or he would assure Boston that Moody, having read Barnum's *Humbugs of the World,* had "found out that the public was an ass, and should be fed with thistles." "Moody is not only a mesmeric but a muscular Christian. And, verily, he is not to be bulldozed by the weak and watery sinners." I. A. M. Cumming professed amazement that "Boston humanity, most musical of all humanity" should "sit and be tortured with this astounding discord" which was the "weird and majestic voice" of Sankey, who, according to I. A. M. Cumming, had discovered his vocation chasing off a charge of Apaches by singing "What Shall the Harvest Be?"

Walt Whitman, the immortal poet, whose humanism and tendency to homosexuality scarcely preconditioned him to Moody, came up in his gray suit from Camden, New Jersey:

> After all, not to be converted only,
> But to see for myself what sort of a man this Moody is

Moody, who has on several previous occasions, innumerable
and often, set the people of other cities religiously crazy,

Moody, the magnet of religion, inventor of legends miraculous
and mythical, the boss storyteller of this year 101 of the
States.

Also to listen to the singing of Sankey, the vociferous and
voiceless, to see him demolish cabinet organs, to hear his
ear-piercing but holy howls.

Wonderful singer, wonderful destroyer of cabinet organs!

I sing the praise of Sankey, sweet singer of Israel,

And what I sing others shall sing and be Sankeyfied and happy.

O Sankey I love thee, my camerado, for voice which you have
not and care not for, you have substituted volume, you sing
on tremendously, incessantly and noisily, paying no heed to
time or tune, but in a large, bold, rugged, unmusical and
unfathomable way, deafening men's ears and singing sinful
souls to eternal bliss.

So not because I lack religion, but for these reasons, do I go
to the Tabernacle.

Whitman scribbled six stanzas in parody of his *Passage to India*:

Wait a moment, O Moody, delay the Chicago man a brief and
ephemeral minute,

Hold the Fort O Sankey, for I Walt am coming . . .

In the last stanza he bared his teeth and tried to forget:

Having heard Moody I am satisfied
But I shall not come to him to be saved.
He is not my idea of a Saviour.
I do not believe in him
Nor his God
Nor his method of swaying sinners nor his stories which sound
like lies.
I Walt tell him he is an ignorant charlatan, a mistaken
enthusiast, and that Boston will ere long desire him to *git*.

Boston did not desire him to git. Not even cultured Boston.
When the famous Thomas Orchestra gave a benefit for the "Old
South" Fund, the hall was reported half empty, while 6,000 heard
Moody and Sankey.

One of the evangelical clergy claimed that privately Moody and
Sankey ranked the Boston campaign with Edinburgh's. Moody

made new friends, such as the six-foot-three-and-a-half-inches of Phillips Brooks, the famous Episcopalian, author of "O Little Town of Bethlehem," who preached on Moody's behalf in his absence one night. Moody, as usual, held a great two-day Christian Convention. He tried, and failed, to get an entrance to Harvard students. He pushed temperance hard, held a Temperance Conference, and, for leader of evangelism among women, brought Frances Willard, the famous Blue Ribbon reformer from Chicago, but she drowned her evangelism in Blue Ribbon water, not scrupling to sit on platforms with Unitarians, to Moody's distress. At length she took her own trail.

For Moody's future the decisive factor was not to be reckoned by sinners saved or drunks redeemed. His host, throughout the campaign, was Henry Fowle Durant. Durant had founded Wellesley College for girls. Durant talked, and Moody listened. It seemed almost is if the dead, beloved Samuel were there, too.

23

The School on the Hill

One day of Sam's last summer, 1876, the two brothers had driven by buggy to look at cattle near Warwick. Sam was a proprietor of the social library, had founded a debating club, and was outspoken at town meetings on Northfield's lack of good education, especially for girls such as his twin sister. And now, leader of the local YMCA, an impromptu evangelist making up for twenty years' hostility to evangelical religion, his hopes and dreams blended with those of D. L., as the townsfolk called Moody.

Returning over the mountain lane, the brothers saw a cripple in a cabin doorway and stopped to pass the time of day. They found him reading aloud the Greek New Testament to his young daughters as they braided straw hats for a livelihood. Horace Parmelee Sikes lay on his couch, a pile beside him: Thomas á Kempis, Madame Guyon, *Pilgrim's Progress*, and "other similar well worn books." He had been four years at Oberlin College in the 1840s, had attended Wilbraham College, and had taught at a select school, but, now paralyzed, was reduced to dependence on the meager earnings of his daughters Jennie and Julia, to whom he could not hope to give an education such as he had enjoyed.

Moody asked him, "How do you get along?"

Sikes smiled. "We don't have much roast turkey or plum pudding, but we get along!"

"We just have to take things right out of the hand of God," said Mrs. Sikes, appearing from indoors wiping soap suds from her hands.

"But we have a *real* home," added one of the daughters.

Moody and Sam drove home deep in discussion. That old cripple taught those girls Greek, yet what could be their future with no education beyond that and the little district school in the hills? They had no means to pay board at Greenfield, fourteen miles off, to attend the public high school. A life of married drudgery on a mountain farm or of dreariness as a factory hand was the most they could expect. A girls' school at Northfield had become Sam's dream. He had talked of it to D. L. already. Now he pressed.

Sam died. The dream became a sacred trust. Yet Moody never might have moved to its fulfillment—nor to all that followed—had he not been guest of Henry Fowle Durant at Boston those early months of 1877.

Durant, a prominent wealthy Boston lawyer who retired from the bar to devote himself to Christian service after the death of his only son, was one of Moody's "old friends and one that stood by me in days before I was much known. All through the Boston work he was with me every night, and did a great work." Recently he had opened at Wellesley, his fine estate on the northwestern outskirts of Boston, a first-class college where girls of moderate means might receive "opportunities for education equivalent to those provided at Harvard." Ten years ago, when he was already thinking of founding either a school or a college, Durant had taken Moody to visit Mary Lyon's famous Mount Holyoke Seminary, and from Mount Holyoke adopted the idea that every girl should do a regular share of domestic service. At Wellesley, he said, he did not want "velvet girls" but "calico girls." The fees were set at $250 a year, half of the cost, the other half being made up by the college. Every teacher was to possess not only academic skill but "vital Christianity"; Bible training formed part of the compulsory course.

Durant and his college for higher education crystallized Moody's determination to organize a preparatory seminary "for young women in the humbler walks of life who would never get a Christian education but for a school like this."

Contrary to one of his favorite proverbs "Don't wait for

something to turn up. Go and turn up something," Moody did not transfer dream to reality with his usual impulsiveness. The Boston campaign ended in the spring of 1877. First moves at Northfield waited until the following year, partly because Moody was uncertain whether sufficient money would come, and partly because of pressure of work.

During the autumn, winter, and spring of 1877-1878 Moody and Sankey held shorter missions in New England cities. The Moodys placed thirteen-year-old Emma (whose hair, cut off in scarlet fever, "[had] now grown in again *curly*") in a "little family school at Amherst." Mrs. Moody wrote to her mother-in-law from Manchester, New Hampshire, on November 9, 1877:

> We left Emma Tuesday morning seeming quite happy. I think I miss her more than she misses me. Mrs. Stearns spoke of her very nicely, and said Emma made her no trouble and was so conscientious in studying. I have put Willie into school here in Manchester. I found there was no private school in the place, so I put him into the public school under a very nice teacher. . . . The meetings have commenced well here, more encouragingly than they did in Burlington, and D. L. is much pleased and especially so with the ministers here who seem very earnest.

The tide had not turned against the evangelists. "The wave of sympathy with them," ran an article in the *Hartford Religious Herald* during the campaign there, "has been so strong that it seems to have flowed out and covered everything. . . . We have come to a time when, for a season at least, Religion has come to the front." They ended with a powerful fortnight in New Haven, town of "grand old elm trees" and of Yale. What Harvard had scorned, Yale's eleven hundred students heard with respect. Mrs. Moody wrote from a hired house on April 1, 1878, to Mrs. Mackinnon in Scotland:

> Many prayers are going up from many anxious parents all over our land, and many are uniting with the parents that God will graciously bless New Haven *and* Yale College. A building has been built specially for the meetings which will contain about six thousand, and the first week of meetings has just passed with marks of success that we thank God for. I am sure Mr. Moody would be glad of you and your husband in the inquiry room, or any Christian "Scotch man with a Bible under his arm." My work is still the *waiting at home* and writing and *little* things.

Early next autumn, 1878, a close friend of Durant, H. F. N. Marshall, a retired merchant who had undertaken much of the organization for the Boston campaign, arrived in Northfield to aid Moody's plans for a school.

Moody showed him about a mile from the Homestead an empty three-storied frame house, at different times a tavern and a school and a horseshoe factory and generally known as the Bee Hive. It had verandas but with no land might have served as a school for thirty girls at most, with their staff, so limited was Moody's vision at this stage.

Marshall said: "This isn't the place you are looking for. The price is too high." In the same area a second place without land for expansion fortunately failed to drop to a reasonable price.

On the high road below Betsey Moody's cottage they poked around a dilapidated house that had once been a tavern and now, with a shed, a pond, Parson Doolittle's grave, and 15¾ acres adjoining Moody's land, belonged to the town tinsmith, who came by just as they decided that this could make the site of the school. They asked the man if he would sell, closed at $2,500, took him into the Homestead, made out the papers, wrote a check, and completed the sale before the tinsmith could recover his breath. In the succeeding months, Marshall quietly bought cheaply three or four neighboring lots of barren, sandy, hilly land above the valley before vendors realized something was afoot to raise values sharply, until he had formed an estate of 100 acres.

Moody by then was away again, making a flying visit in mid-October to Chicago before settling at Baltimore where the family took a house for the winter.

That winter of 1878-1879 represented a period of crisis in the careers of Moody and Sankey.

They never referred publicly to this crisis, which has not been mentioned in any biography and would have remained unknown, had not Moody in London in 1884 told Whittle.

Plans for the school had brought forward Moody's deepening sense that if he were not to burn out he must study. During the past two summers he had spent part of each morning in his library. But not until the autumn of 1878, with the Northfield school emerging toward a reality, did he take himself fully in hand: Northfield Seminary, yet unborn, saved its founder from premature decline. Moody thought that Sankey and he ought to find some city where they could attempt a mission of less intensity, which would enable him to study at the same time. Sankey, however, according to a letter from Mrs. Moody to Mrs. Mackinnon, "urged Mr. Moody to go to Europe somewhere and study instead of staying here." Moody gave a confidential, exciting reason why they could not travel: "We are expecting a new arrival in our family next spring." Moreover, he was not ready to face Europe again until he had burrowed into books and more deeply into his Bible.

Sankey itched to be back among England's notables. If Moody would not come, he would go alone and have a singing campaign. Moody dissuaded. Sankey insisted. And they parted.

Sankey crossed the Atlantic in high expectation, and Moody made a sudden decision to start at Baltimore, to the delight of its ministers, who presumed Sankey's absence to be temporary. But Sankey had walked out of the partnership.

That was the end of Moody and Sankey. It also represented the end of the school project, except as a small affair with day girls of Northfield; Moody would not be able to afford a boarders' dormitory, for, although Sankey had shown no desire whatever to bespeak any of the hymnbook funds for his own interests (their finances had nothing to do with their parting), the trustees obviously could not make disproportionate grants to support Moody's pet schemes. Already they had disbursed $5,000 to found a Wellesley scholarship, for which preference was to be given girls from the proposed Northfield Seminary, and a substantial grant toward the purchase of property. (Marshall paid for most of the land, holding it until the school could buy it from him at cost.)

Sankey failed in England. "He wrote to me," Moody told Whittle, "that if I would take him back, the money might be disposed of as I pleased. With this settled I went ahead with the Schools."

Moody and Sankey reunited. Sankey bought a house in Northfield for the summers and became a hearty backer of the schools. And an enthusiastic if rather improbable man of the country, he went riding in the rain and "was thrown off with his umbrella raised up and left sitting in the road." He fell into a brook "while crossing on a tree bridge in the Catskill Mountains," to Moody's glee. Moody "enjoys having a laugh at Sankey's expense. Sankey reciprocates."

Baltimore in all respects was a campaign with a difference. Not "in any way a prearranged matter," without Sankey, and to an entirely new design. Moody felt that the enormous interest generated in the past by mass meetings in ice rink or hippodrome or converted depot had not been plowed back fully into churches because the public, for all the arrays of ministers on platforms, tended to treat a revival as detached. Therefore at Baltimore he held few meetings in large public halls in the city center. Most were in church buildings, Moody working district by district in close association with each selected.

It took strict self-discipline to keep hours of study in the midst of a campaign. Mrs. Moody, who except for asthma and her "little difficulty in the heart" enjoyed excellent health, wrote to Mrs. Mackinnon early in December:

> We have been here in our home for the winter just two months, and are quite settled, Mr. Moody at study and work in the meetings, the children in school, and I in all sorts of work, writing for my husband, attending to some of his calls, and helping him where I can, besides a variety of other things that don't seem to amount to much and yet make me tired by night. Mr. Moody has made quite a *rigid* rule whereby he takes six hours each day for study. Besides this he has daily except Mondays and Saturdays a Bible Reading in the afternoons, and preaching services in the evening with their inquiry meetings. Sundays he preaches four times besides Inquiry Meetings, so you see he did not come here to Baltimore for *rest*, as some say, but for *study*.

During those Baltimore months, Moody's anchor dropped firmly, daily more deeply at Northfield. Chicago meant much to him: "I wish you would write me often and let me know how you are getting on and all about the church," Moody scrawled to a young helper, Robert Aitchison, on arrival at Baltimore. "I do want to see that church made a power in Chicago for good." The same day he assured Hitchcock: "I have thought often of you and your blessed work since I left you and my earnest prayer is daily that God may lead you to not only get the children to the School but to lead them to Christ."

To Chicago Avenue went regular, long letters; but the breathless unpunctuated scribbles hastening northwards to George Moody, acting as farm manager for Homestead and school lands, revealed where lay his home:

December 2

> . . . did you send a turkey to the Sykes [sic] family I wish you would

have some of the snow forks in the cellar (small ones) given to Joseph Lyman I promised him some seed but forgot it before I left how about Willie's heifer is there any hope have you got any snow did the grass come up north of the house & has rye got up in the school house lot how many turkies did you kill on Thanksgiving write us all the news tell us what you said at the south church & what they said & what they are doing this season give love to all we are well very well your brother D L M.

Willie's very own heifer hoofed its way into letter after letter: "Is there hope for Willie's heifer or shall we have to kill her for beef? . . . p.s. you did not tell me about Willie's heifer."

Farm affairs did not fill the letters. George had at last left the Unitarians, but he reported resentment over his nomination for president of the Northfield YMCA. Moody urged him not to

let any strife get in among the people, you had better get John Fisher to take the Presidency if there is any feeling against the Moodys, do not let the church get down on us take a back seat & it will come all right in the course of time but you see what a fearful thing it would be to have a division just at this time & we must do all we can to keep peace, if there is any trouble in the church let it come from others & not us.

Baltimore felt Moody's impact. Between October 28, 1878, and May 25, 1879, he preached 270 sermons. Beadenkopf and Stricklen, two students of Johns Hopkins University, glowingly recorded the event:

Our city was the scene of a mighty religious revival, whose influence was felt in all classes of society, reaching many who had been untouched by the Story of the Cross, and penetrating into recesses of darkness perhaps never yet illuminated by Bible truth.

One evening as Moody addressed a mass meeting at the Maryland Institute, a criminal or suspect on the run slipped into the anonymity of the crowd. To avoid a disturbance, Detective Todd B. Hall would have abandoned the chase, had not the doorman, an ex-saloon-keeper who knew them both, said, "If you will wait until the service is over I will help you to get him."

The detective took a seat. "Mr. Moody was so plain in his delivery of the message that I was attracted by his earnest pleading. When through with his sermon I was forced to decide in Christ as my Saviour. The Devil said I could not be a Christian and a detective." After the service, the criminal forgotten, Hall went straight to the City Hall "and told the Chief of Detectives and the men what I had made up my mind to do and live the life of a Christian, and asked them for sympathy as I had enough of the tough worldly life I was living."

When he got home to his wife, the man confessed his unfaithfulness and begged her to forgive him.

> We then kneeled down and asked God to help me live the Christian life and be true. When I arose to my feet, to my surprise my wife ran up to me, throwing both her arms round my neck and kissing me, and said, "Nothing shall separate us. If you have made up your mind to live as a Christian I will live it with you and take Christ as my Saviour."

Todd B. Hall wrote in 1900:

> Oh what a happy family ours has been, and what comfort has come to our lives . . . . For twenty years by the grace of God I have been kept in that sweet life being still in the detectives' office and have been a blessing to many poor fellows who have been arrested by me, telling them what Mr. Moody told me.

It would be interesting to know if Detective Hall was shown a scrap of paper found wrapped round a gold watch in a box tied to the parsonage doorbell of the Broadway Methodist Episcopal Church on the first Wednesday in March, after a Mr. Brown had reported losing his watch at Moody's service in the church the previous Friday.

Headed "Mr. D. L. Moody" and addressed to Mr. Stitt, the minister, it ran:

> Dear Sir, please send this watch to the owner I stold it from him in your church ask him to forgive a pour thief Jesus has forgiven me of my sins and I dont want nothing that is stolen Jesus Christ clenseth from all sins he pardoned the thief on the cros and he pardons me glory be to his name his blood clenseth me from all sin. A Christian.

The family descended on Northfield in late spring, complete with the infant Paul Dwight Moody, born on April 11, 1879, ten years younger than Will.

Moody hustled the building of the Recitation Hall on the site of the tinsmith's demolished dwelling. On August 21, before a large company, he laid the cornerstone, not with a proferred silver trowel but his father's old working trowel. Sankey sang "The Ninety and Nine." Durant made a speech emphasizing the need for such a school and its aims and ideals:

> It will be a thorough school, it will be nonsectarian and it will be Christian. Working together the Christian home, the Christian Church and this Christian school will turn out young women of the type greatly needed to do the Lord's work in the world.

They placed in the cornerstone a Bible, national and local newspapers, two histories of Northfield, some Moody heirlooms, and a piece of Parson Doolittle's gravestone, from the early eighteenth-century.

Moody reckoned that if Wellesley College could fix its annual fee at $250, his secondary school need ask no more than $100, half the estimate for keeping and educating. As he begged around for the considerable sums required above the hymnbook money, Moody stressed to his friends the school's threefold basis: first, the Bible a vital part of the curriculum (as Will Moody wrote long after his father's death, "God's Word . . . is indeed foundation, cornerstone and capstone of Moody's whole system"); second, every girl to take regular share in domestic duties whatever her home background, thus inculcating a right sense of proportion while keeping down the cost of running the school; third, the low charge.

On Durant's advice Moody appointed as principal a young Wellesley woman named Harriet Tuttle, who was remembered by devoted girls as "fragile in body, delicate in feature but strong in spiritual force," with "gentle dignity and rare charm and sweetness of manner." When Miss Tuttle arrived at Northfield, the Recitation Hall was rising slowly ("Looks like a jail," said a visitor. "Oh no, you are mistaken," replied one of Moody's friends. "It is an institution gotten upon purpose so to educate the people that they shall be sure to keep out of jail!"), but foundations had not even been excavated for a boarders' dormitory. Moody could not bear to wait until it should be built; he adapted the part of the Homestead above the coach house to form a set of cubicles which, when more girls than expected enrolled, was such a squash that the inhabitants nicknamed it Penny Alley.

The summer sped by; the maples turned red and gold; and the Moodys had left for the winter's work in the Midwest. On November third the first pupils arrived in a record blizzard that laid snow sixteen inches deep, according to George Moody's son Ambert, who next morning coasted down the hill on a sled to stoke the two large boilers. Jennie Sikes from the mountain got the highest marks on the entrance examination.

The recitation hall was unfinished for another month and lessons were done in the Moodys' parlor. "Has the children got into new school building yet," Moody wrote to his mother from St. Louis on November 24, "and how do they like it and how do they like the teachers etc. etc. etc."

All through the Moody and Sankey winter campaign at St. Louis (on the Baltimore pattern), Moody's imagination roved to Northfield, especially during the first weeks when he was without his family, left at Mrs. Revell's. "I find I cannot get on well without them and then they have been sick in Chicago and I think it will do them good to come down here for the winter." He was no less devoted to mass evangelism, but those girls at Northfield . . .

"Mr. Marshall came here on Saturday, and or course we had a great deal to ask him about Northfield," wrote Mrs. Moody in January 1880. "The children have been homesick to get there . . . D. L. is well and very busy." And Moody to his brother Edwin: "Do you think Willie's calf will ever come to a cow is there any signs he is most anxious to know."

At last with the spring of 1880 Moody could see his school in action and the completed recitation hall and watch the first dormitory rising, East Hall, and run races with the girls and address them at school prayers. A hundred girls were on the roll. Despite setbacks the dream took shape.

Moody spoke of that dream at the formal dedication of East Hall during the summer vacation. After remarking, "My lack of education has always been a great disadvantage to me. I shall suffer from it as long as I live," he continued: "I hope after all of us who are here today are dead and gone this school may live and be a blessing to the world, and that missionaries may go out from here and preach the gospel to the heathen, and it may be recognized as a power in bringing souls to Christ." He proclaimed as motto of the school a verse from Isaiah: "I the Lord do keep it; I will water it every moment: lest any hurt it, I will keep it night and day."

Then he prayed. "The words of that prayer," said a Boston man, "burned into our souls." Moody thanked God for the urge to found the school, as well as for the friends whose gifts had raised it.

O Lord, we pray that no teachers may ever come within its walls except as they have been taught by the Holy Spirit; that no scholars may ever come here except as the Spirit of God shall touch their hearts. O, God, we are Thine, this building is Thine! We give it over to Thee. Take it and keep it and bless it, with Thy keeping power!

24

Both Sides of the River

Moody had never forgotten how nearly he degenerated into a harassed organizer of institutions.

> The Chicago Fire was the turning point of my life. I had become so mixed up with building Farwell Hall and was on committees for every kind of work, and in my ambition to make my enterprises succeed because they were mine I had taken my eyes off from the Lord and had been burdened in soul and unfruitful in my work. When the Fire came, as a revelation, I took my hat and walked out!

And now again, eight years after the Fire and the epochal experience that ensued he was immersing himself in institutions. Would they throttle again his "preaching of Christ and working for souls?"

Conscious of this grave danger yet assured that in founding the school he had not mistaken divine guidance, Moody on his way to Chicago and St. Louis undertook a brief campaign and convention in Cleveland, Ohio.[1] One morning, the very week the first girls were

[1] Henry Drummond, having a few days left before sailing back to Scotland following a geological expedition, refused the opportunity to dine with Longfellow and Oliver Wendell Holmes at Boston in order to dash to Cleveland, where he found his friends the same as ever, "Mr. Sankey down to the faultless set of his black necktie, Mr. Moody to the chronic crush of his collar."

starting at Northfield, he entered a Cleveland church for a prayer meeting. Proceedings opened with a brief address by a local Methodist editor whom Moody had not previously known, Henry Burns Hartzler, on "Prayer for the Church." Moody sat exactly opposite in a characteristic posture, head bowed as if too heavy for the short neck, beard nestling on chest. Hartzler was dilating "upon the absolute necessity of the Holy Spirit, in order to succeed in the church, etc."

"Suddenly," Hartzler noticed, Moody

> lifted his head, flashed a glance at me as though struck with a bolt, and then resumed his former position. After the meeting he rushed by, catching me by the arm and taking me into the pastor's study. Abruptly he said, "I want you to come to Northfield next summer. Will you? Want to have a meeting to wait on God. Want you."

In that flash Moody had lost his fears. How had he doubted that the Lord had an answer? The school, instead of dragging his eyes off God, would be a place of greater blessing and deeper joy. For him, for hundreds, perhaps thousands, the round-topped hill should be a mount of transfiguration where they would see Jesus. He had given Bible Readings for his Northfield neighbors, sitting on the porch during long summer evenings, and he had regularly held Christian conventions in cities. But this should be different.

Immersed in the winter campaign, he did little about it until back at Northfield and summer had come. As late as July 2, 1880, he mentioned the idea only casually in a letter of thanks for a check: "I should have said I am in hopes to have a Christian conference here sometime at the close of August & the first of September I would like much to have you come up to be at it." "I do wish," he wrote to Farwell, "you would come and let us wait on God together for a few days . . . . Do come and bring all the hungry Christians with you that you can."

In the first days of August he scattered broadcast a circular calling a "Convocation for Prayer" from September 1 to 10,

> the object of which is not so much to study the Bible (though the Scriptures will be searched daily for instruction and promises) as for solemn self-consecration, for pleading God's promises, and waiting upon Him for a fresh anointment of power from on high.

The invitation was to "all Christians who are hungering for intimate fellowship with God and for power to do His work." To Hartzler he wrote: "Now will you come? I want you above any other man in this *nation* do not say me nay but come & let us wait on God together."

Moody pitched a large hired tent on the hill soon to be known as Round Top. For accommodation he offered the newly completed dormitory (East Hall), put beds in the recitation hall, filled the Homestead, and booked lodgings in the town. Other visitors camped in shady corners. Scores of day visitors from Northfield and the neighboring counties made up the full attendance of men and women (about three hundred) at the main meetings. All thirty-seven states were represented, and Moody had collected Canadians, Britishers, and others from overseas who happened to be in America. (It is almost certain that no visitors crossed the seas especially, as they did to later conferences.) S. F. Hancock of Cleveland, one of those present, wrote in a letter of 1896,

> He sought to concentrate all Christendom, so far as he could reach it, in one earnest cry to God for the recovery of Pentecostal power. For this the Convocation was to wait prostrate before God . . . . The first convocation, "The Northfield Convocation" *par excellence*, met the longing of my heart.

"Don't," Moody pleaded, "think of your homes, your work or your churches now. Don't pray for anything or anybody but yourself. Attend now to your own heart only." He had no formal program and urged Hartzler to conduct the conference, "but I declined, saying he was the predestined leader. He insisted I repeat the lecture given in Cleveland." Day by day the sense of God's presence grew until at one smaller meeting all those present, twenty-six men sitting on the straw in the tent (there were no chairs) rose, clasped hands in a circle and solemnly pledged "a covenant of consecration with God and with one another." In the emotion of the moment, one man suggested they swear to pray for each other every day till death. "No," said Moody, "pray but don't pledge or you'll make an irksome duty out of a delightful privilege."

Moody was adept at keeping the conference steady, pricking any bubble of emotional excess. "Oh!" sighed one man, "I hope to get enough out of this series to last me all my life!"

"Might as well try to eat enough breakfast to last you all your life!"

"I have lived," claimed another, "five years on the Mount of Transfiguration."

"How many souls did you lead to Christ last year, eh?"

At the man's confusion, Moody said: "We don't want *that* kind of mountaintop experience. When a man gets up so high he can't reach down to save poor sinners, something's wrong."

During a conversation hour in the big tent, its flaps upturned to admit the faint breeze of a warm September noon, Moody sat plump against the pole. An Episcopal minister ("presuming and officious") in the front row facing him had aired his opinions for the second or third time that morning.

Moody commented abruptly: "Brethren" (he pronounced it "brearth'n"), "Brearth'n, how many of you have so grown in grace you can bear to have your faults told?"

Up shot hands.

Moody looked straight at the Episcopalian, whose hand waggled high. "Brother, you've spoke thirteen times in three days. P'r'aps shut out twelve other good men."

The young man hotly defended himself. Then a "real old Yankee vinegar face on the outer rim of the circle turned loose and sharply berated Moody for his bluntness."

Moody blushed. Demurely he listened out the tirade, then covered his face with his hands. Speaking through his fingers: "Brearth'n, I admit all the fault my friend charges on me. But brearth'n, *I didn't hold up my hand!*"

One evening in the Orthodox Church, a famous incident occurred, which E. S. Millains in 1907 called "the greatest thing I ever saw D. L. Moody do."

Moody on the platform had begun to speak on the high standards required "of a true minister of Jesus Christ." He castigated failures, etching a picture of unfaithful clergy in blistering words that "searched us all keenly." Suddenly a handsome student from Newton Theological Seminary blurted out from the front seat ("frank and outspoken but not rude"): "Mr. Moody, I don't see any such ministers as you describe!"

Moody snapped: "You will, young man, if you live long. Tarry in Jericho till your beard be grown!" And he continued his address.

The retort, recalled Millains, "was not said savagely but it was said keenly. I think everyone in the chapel sorrowed and the young man wilted. But too good a man was speaking, and there was too much love and prayer in the consecrated room for the meeting to be spoiled." The uncomfortable atmosphere slowly dispersed as Moody unfolded his theme. He reached his close. He paused. Then he said: "Friends, I want to confess before you all that I made a great mistake at the beginning of this meeting. I answered my young brother down there foolishly. I ask God to forgive me. I ask *him* to forgive me." And before anyone realized what was happening the world's most famous evangelist had stepped off the platform, dashed across to the insignificant anonymous youth and taken him by the hand. As another present said, "The man of iron will proved that he had mastered the hardest words of all earth's languages, 'I am sorry.'"

Throughout this first Northfield Conference, which determined those present to set aside the entire month of August the next year, letters and telegrams cascaded through the Northfield post office in response to Moody's request that those in sympathy who could not come should send "salutation & greeting that there may be concert of prayer."

Moody held back these communications until by the ninth day, according to Hartzler, "there were more than three thousand requests for prayers piled up on Moody's desk," and presumably all over several chairs. On the two final days, as fitting climax, he read them out at memorable prayer meetings that shriveled distances right across the United States and over the sea.

For Moody there was one very special subject for prayer. On the last day he announced that Northfield, in addition to the Seminary, would have a school for boys.

Some months earlier, an elderly gentleman of peculiar appearance had called on Moody at the Homestead.

Hiram Camp was seventy and dressed (so Will Moody remembered) in

> black broadcloth frock coat, trousers of curious cut, old-fashioned top boots worn beneath the trousers, a soft-bosomed white shirt with collar of antique style and conventional black tie, a black velvet waistcoat against which was displayed a gold watch chain which twice encircled his neck, and a broad-brimmed black felt hat surmounting a shock of snow-white hair.

He had a white beard, too. Hiram Camp had founded the New Haven Watch Company, which produced most of the millions of "dollar watches," cheap clocks, and nickel alarms that ticked on American waists, stood on parlor mantels, and shrilled Americans awake from California to Cape Cod. His company could really claim to be "the world's greatest clock manufacturing organization." Hiram Camp was a merry old soul, skilled storyteller, judge of good horses, and a benevolent paternalist who, though company president, paid the wages with his own hands every Saturday. The New Haven campaign of 1878 had made him the warmest admirer of D. L. Moody. And now he had come all the way up the Connecticut Valley to take counsel.

They sat in the library. Camp said he had provided amply for his family and wanted to decide on charitable bequests. What, he asked in his slow Yankee drawl, did Mr. Moody advise?

"I'm the wrong man to come to. I couldn't counsel in making a will. Why don't you have the fun of being your own executor and see your money do good? You've had the fun of making it. Now try giving it."

The memorable conversation continued between Camp's New England drawl and Moody's equally Yankee gallop.

"What shall I give to?" drawled Camp.

"What's your denomination?" rapped Moody.

"Con-greg-ation-al."

"Why-don't'y'r-give-y'r-money-t'y'r-own-denom'ation? Look at the ABCFM, Home Board, Ministerial Relief, all the others. Well manned, efficiently run."

"But I would like to give to something specific."

"Well, here's something. I'm being hounded to take boys in the school I've started. I don't want to add to my troubles by going into coeducation. Now you start a school for boys on the lines that I've started this school for girls. There is something specific and you can see it and watch it grow."

Camp laughed his infectious laugh. "I'm too old. I've lost touch with youth. But I'll tell you what I'll do. If *you* start such a school I will give you twenty-five thousand dollars for that purpose."

"*What!*"

Moody was trapped. He had not meant to start a boys' school just then. Yet some such possibiliy must have been in mind, for the previous November when a fine farm of 170 acres in Gill on the far side of the river had been auctioned, H. N. F. Marshall bought it as an investment, giving Moody a year's option at the same price.

It was knocked down ridiculously low. This farm had belonged to the late Ezra Purple, Jr., none other than the son of Betsey's creditor of 1841, who had forced his way into her bedroom after the birth of the twins and tried to turn her out. Moody as a lad, vowing revenge, said he would one day own "the Old Bear's" farm. On the Old Bear's death the place had been divided. Through Marshall, Moody now had the northern half, with the old homestead. The smaller, southern farm had been sold by the younger of the Old Bear's sons to his cousin, John Purple, and the proposed school must lack room for expansion unless he was bought out to give possession of the whole Purple place, some 275 acres.

Hiram Camp attended the Northfield Conference and heard Moody's announcement on the last morning, Monday, September 10, 1880, that an anonymous donor had given $25,000 to start a boys' school. Very early next morning, at about a quarter past four, Moody crept down to his stables, harnessed Nellie Gray to the buggy, and disappeared in a flurry of dust at his usual pace (local riddle: "Why is D. L. so good? Because he drives so fast the Devil can't catch him").[2]

Before five he was banging on the door of his first cousin Jonathan Holton, whose farm bordered the Purple place. He found him in the barn milking, asked him to arrange to buy out John Purple instantly before he got wind of the school announcement and put two and two together about Marshall's farm, pulled from his pocket two prepared forfeit bonds of $1000 for vendor and purchaser to sign, mounted the buggy, and was away.

Jonathan Holton's brother-in-law, L. T. Smith, who kept a meat market at Greenfield, had once spoken of buying John Purple's farm. "By 10:00 A.M.," writes Will Holton, who was then sixteen, "Father had Smith at the place and had introduced the men." The price was settled, the bonds signed, and in ten days the sale to the school completed. On the following morning Moody took Hiram Camp and three other friends to explore. They looked over the buildings, walked to the height of land where they could gaze down the property to the river, and across northeastward to Northfield,

---

[2] Moody once drove P. P. Bliss so fast to a meeting at Greenfield that "when they arrived Mr. Bliss was actually sick, and had to lie down for a time before he was able to sing" (W. T. Holton Ms.).

marked by its elms and Northfield Mountain beyond, then north-ward to the green hills of New Hampshire. They tramped the fields and climbed over a fence into a woodland, where, as they rested on the moss in the shade of a great tree, Moody told them of "Old Bear" Purple, and "spoke most reverently," one of them wrote, "of the way God had ordered events, and said that he regarded the securing of the farm as 'poetic justice.'" In the quiet of the woodland, "each of us in turn besought God to accept and bless the new enterprise."

Back in Northfield they fell to discussing possible names, and Camp, on his way home to New Haven, hit upon Mount Hermon: the biblical Mount Hermon was on the far side of the river; it "shall rejoice in thy name"; and in the great, short psalm of unity, Psalm 133, "there the Lord commanded the blessing, even life for evermore."

Mount Hermon, like the Northfield Seminary, had to be made ready in Moody's absence. In October the family disappeared for the winter, going this year more distantly from Northfield than when in Britain, to the Pacific Coast.

At the Mormon stronghold of Salt Lake City, stopping to pass a Sunday, Moody and Sankey were prevailed upon by Presbyterians to hold services. "The interest," wrote Sankey, "at once became so great that we decided to change our plans and stay here a couple of weeks," and Moody wrote to George on October 24, "I think we will get a real harvest." They reached San Francisco on November 10.

Moody had come primarily to rescue the debt-ridden, aimless, spiritually decadent YMCA. With his usual sense of values he set about reviving church life of "the Wicked West." By the ninth of February, 1881, he could write to Cyrus H. McCormick in Chicago: "You will be glad to know that our work on the Pacific coast has been owned of God." Several churches had received "large acces-sions" to membership. "The work is going very well. But I am troubled about its continuance after I leave here . . . " and since "few of the businessmen and still fewer of the young men are Christians," and McCormick, with his reapers, was "well known all over the coast," he must please send $10,000 at once to launch a fund to secure a YMCA building. McCormick wired back: "Too many undertakings here to meet your wishes," but relented and helped to raise $82,000. At Moody's departure in late March the YMCA had "a building for saving young men," new officers, and new zeal.

As soon as the spring of 1881 made the railway through the mountains no longer dangerous, but merely rough, Moody and his family and team traveled East. In Chicago a conversation with his old friend B. F. Jacobs, the Sunday school leader, showed the direction in which Moody's mind was working:

> Jacobs, I sometimes wonder if you will not get more out of your life now than I will out of mine . . . . I work for the salvation of men who have grown up to years of maturity in sin, in evil habits, in evil surroundings. I perhaps reach one out of ten that I try to reach. And then I am not sure that the one out of ten I think I have reached will stick. I am not sure after all they have gone through, whether it is a real surrender and a real victory. Jacobs, you work with them when they are young, before these habits are formed. You are sowing the seed in that most precious soil. Oh, do not let go! It will last there, and it will spring up. Of those I bring in, I do not know whether one out of ten will ever amount to anything in Christian work, but you can help them not only to Jesus Christ, but to see the blessedness of His service. Nine out of ten that you reach will stand fast and be true to God and Jesus Christ.

The Seminary, with its more than a hundred girls, was proving itself. At Mount Hermon the north farmhouse had been enlarged and renovated, and a matron hired, Mrs. Pratt, widow of a missionary in Turkey. Moody had not secured a teacher. The school at that time being intended for small boys between eight and fifteen, he needed a woman, and could only offer for the present a nominal salary because the purchase and conversion had swallowed most of Camp's gift. He sent a telegram to Mary Louise Hammond, younger sister of a seminary teacher. She brought her trunk in case she should decide to stay.

Applications had piled, a hundred or more. Mary Hammond recalled answering them at Moody's direction,

> with dear Mrs. Moody sitting by (in his library), and helping in her quiet way. You know she was always a "balance wheel." I remember so well reading aloud one from a mother who expatiated, quite at length, on the waywardness of her son, etc. etc., and that she wanted him to be under Mr. Moody's own roof, etc . . . . He dispatched that in a few words by saying, "Tell her it is not a Reform School." Another wrote in such a

way as to make it quite evident that her boy was not of special promise but she wanted to send him there because she did not know what else to do with him, and did not even enclose a stamp, so he said "Throw it into the wastebasket," looking at his wife as he would dispose of *such*, in like manner. I can see her now, as she sat there, looking as if she would make sure that it was the wisest thing to do, and now and then suggest a reply which might lead the mother to some other recourse, even if it were not best for her son to go to Mount Hermon.

The first boy arrived on May 1. Symbolically for a school for boys of small means, his name was Tommy Tomkins. On May 12 Moody wrote to his nephew Ambert, now nearly eighteen, whom he had sent to a short business course in Boston to prepare him as quartermaster of the schools:

> Your father got his sheep to pasture yesterday I bought 25 old ones & 25 lambs for the boys school of him & we turned the cows over to them today from the South barn & from mine so we have 8 cows over there now & will have 75 hens there when yours get there. One of the turkeys that you bought is setting I am going to have some geese over there to make things lively. We have or will tomorrow night seven boys . . . expecting more next week.

He appointed Jonathan Holton's son George as farmer to Mount Hermon and took Mrs. Moody for a few days' discussion with Camp at New Haven.

Tom Coyle, a twelve-year-old boy from Brooklyn, sat miserably in a train approaching Springfield on May 18.

It was his first railway journey, and he was going to boarding school. The kind elderly stranger who had promised to put him on the right train at Springfield had been left behind at the lunch stop and sent a telegram up the line, "calling for a silk hat and a valise but making no reference to a small boy." The big conductor put Tom Coyle and his parcels on the South Vernon train. In the parlor car,

> the only vacant place I could find was one side of a double seat. The other side was occupied by a lady. As I looked into her lovely face I felt assured, shyly ventured in and sat down. The lady after reading my name and destination (Mr. Moody's Boys' School, Northfield, Mass.) written on my small package, smiled and said, "Oh, you are going to Mr. Moody's school, are you? Well, Mr. Moody is on the train, he will be here in a moment." As she spoke Mr. Moody came up the aisle, and in

his hearty whole-souled way made me feel at once that I had fallen among friends.

Lessons began on June 1 with thirteen boys in the upper front room of the north farmhouse. The south farmhouse opened in July with another thirteen boys and two Holton sisters in charge. The basis was similar to the Seminary, with the boys doing most of the manual work on the farm and clearing the land. Deep in her heart, Miss Hammond thought this hard: "knowing that the most of them were from the city and not accustomed to exposure in sun, heat and cold, I used to fear the consequences often times." Moody had no such fear. He drove Nellie Gray there frequently and the boys "would rush down the hill and shout to see him coming. Any one of us would run across a ten-acre plowed field to unbar a gate for him, if his gray mare started that way." Plow, pasture, or road were one to Moody in his buggy. Sometimes he disrupted work hours by taking them for a swim in the river, his passion for cold water being unsated, whether to splash in or to drink almost by the bucketful—four or five glasses during a meal. He watched their lessons, set them competitions, and brought scores of visitors from the second Northfield Conference to see them in the new frame schoolhouse between two hickory trees on the hillside.

The boys and the girls were as sons and daughters, and Moody— far in advance of the whitewashed walls, plain deal tables, and poor food of most contemporary schools, especially those that did not ask high fees—created a homelike atmosphere. Early improvisations differed only in degree from the later school buildings where an English visitor would be

> charmed to see the comfortable fittings Mr. Moody had used in fixing up these houses: each room was occupied by two students, who each had a bed and chest of drawers, everything built on a better scale than any similar school or home which I have seen elsewhere.

Moody had no regrets that he had founded a second school. He wrote to Hiram Camp on July 12, 1881,

> If you . . . could see the boys as they are at their studies, work and play I am sure you would feel well paid for all your trouble & you would see it is much better to give than to receive it does not cause any sleepless nights to give to the Lord but think of the pain, troubles etc. in making $25,000.

As Moody and Nellie Gray sped back and forth between the Seminary and Mount Hermon, he had only one sense of unfulfillment. Chicago had dropped to second place. During the 1876 campaign he had talked about founding "a school for training evangelists, pastoral helpers, etc." But nothing had been done.

But the Northfield schools were established. Moody now could respond to insistent invitations to revisit Great Britain, and on September 22, 1881, the Moodys and the Sankeys sailed from New York.

The founding of the schools and what they had wrought in their founder ensured that the ultimate outcome of Moody's second British visit, 1881-1884, would be more than a national mission.

PART FOUR

"The Power of Christian Union," 1882-1899

25

Dan'l at Cambridge

John Edward Kynaston Studd of Trinity College, Cambridge, eldest son of the late Edward Studd of Tedworth Hall, sat writing in the Pitt Club at Cambridge on February 2, 1882, while outside down Jesus Lane the wind blew raw from the fens.

Kynaston Studd was twenty-four. He was a cricket blue.[1] His younger brother George ("G. B.") was Captain of Cricket; their next brother, Charlie ("C. T."), though only twenty-one, was an all-England cricketer who would have the highest batting average that summer of 1882 and be reckoned by the mighty W. G. Grace "the most brilliant member" of the family. C. T. would be Cambridge Captain next year, and J. E. K., though eldest (he had come up late), in 1884, a family record never since broken. To be a Cambridge cricketer in the 1880s carried great glamour and prestige, and, despite their father's death, the Studds also were wealthy.

Kynaston Studd's pen scratched away:

> We have already (in October last) asked Mr. Moody to come here in March and he replied that it was uncertain if he would be in England then or rather if he would have come south by that time. Last time he

[1] A member of the University cricket Eleven. The term comes from the blue blazer.

was in England a petition signed by three hundred undergraduates was presented to him asking him to come & if he should require such a thing now we could easily get that number of members of the university and probably a great many more to sign the petition. We fear that it would not be of very much use Mr. Moody's coming up next term as the men are all very busy with reading and athletics.

Studd was president of the Cambridge Inter-Collegiate Christian Union, which had been formed a few years earlier, and remembering how his father had become "a real live play-the-game Christian," as Charlie put it, he was determined to bring Moody to Cambridge.

On February 13, Moody replied from Glasgow to the friend acting as go-between:

> Your kind letters with others from London and Cambridge enclosed came to me a few days ago. Thank you very much for sending them. I feel much interested and gratified with the invitation to visit Cambridge and especially so from the fact that one of the letters comes from a son of my friend from a former visit, Mr. Studd.

After further correspondence, Moody and Sankey accepted an invitation—signed by undergraduates, town clergymen, and dons—to visit Cambridge for eight days in November 1882.

One who signed did so reluctantly. Handley Moule, future Bishop of Durham, saintly and learned principal of Ridley Hall, the new theological college, and leader of Cambridge's numerous evangelicals, admired Moody warmly but feared that the most intolerant and difficult audience in the world "would not be reached." Cambridge in 1882 numbered about 3,500 undergraduates, nearly all of them raised in homes of real or comparative affluence and bred in the arid religion of the British public school. Many had no need to study hard, for they would not have to earn a living. Despite the force of "pious" undergraduates inheriting the tradition of a daily prayer meeting, unbroken in term time for twenty years, and the CICCU, what treatment would Moody receive from arrogant intellectuals or the breezily intolerant "fast set"?

On the afternoon of Saturday, November 4, a beautiful autumn day, Moody and Sankey boarded the Cambridge train at St. Pancras Station, with Mrs. Moody and Paul (little Paul, taken round

King's College Chapel that week asked, "Where's the 'quiry room?'").

"There never was a place," Moody said afterwards, "that I approached with greater anxiety than Cambridge. Never having had the privilege of a university education, I was nervous about meeting university men."

A year had passed since Moody and Sankey and their families had landed at Liverpool, where, as Mrs. Moody had written,

> even the custom house officers came and shook hands with D. L. as soon as he got off the boat and told him they were glad to see him back again in this country. At the railway station officials came and welcomed him and told him that they had received good when he was in Liverpool.... We have been having quantities of letters of welcome.

The evangelistic campaign began in Newcastle, followed by six weeks in Edinburgh ("The meetings here are being much blessed and D. L. is very much encouraged") and, early in 1882, the start of five months in Glasgow.

This time they did not normally stay as guests in private houses but took lodgings. Young Emma at seventeen was still having lessons from her cousin, Fanny Holton, who acted also as Paul's nurse, while Willie, "a fine tall lad devoted to his father," was put in day school. Paul, not yet three, fell seriously ill in Edinburgh: "dear little fellow has been real sick," Moody told his brother George. "I was afraid for a few days that I could not keep him, that he must sink, we could not get any doctor that could reach his case but he is now on the upgrade."

Paul's illness caused Moody to begin at Glasgow without his family. This deepened Moody's homesickness. "I like America so much better than this land," he wrote on a bleak January day, "we seldom see the sun in this country & it is so cloudy & dark most of the time but the days are getting longer now & I am not so lonely as I was." He corresponded regularly with Northfield, where though keeping down expenses they had already installed a telephone, an instrument barely known to Glasgow, and, busy as he was, he answered letters from the girls and boys. "I wish you would tell the boys I would be glad to hear from them at any time," he wrote to Master George Cragin.

Jane Mackinnon, in raptures at having her old friends again in

Scotland, found Moody, with his beard trimmed a little shorter and his hair a little thinner, but with barely a trace of gray:

> the same, simple straightforward and affectionate man .... His style is also the same but quieter. We think he is quieter altogether—probably the difference between thirty-seven and forty-five. But . . . there has been a mellowing power at work, not all of nature. One feels that he has grown more heavenward.

She continued:

> I have missed much, this time, those little peculiarities—partly American, partly personal—which used to attract and amuse us so much. I dare say it is all in the way of improvement, but it has carried away some of the uniqueness and piquancy that we loved so well.

She noticed that Moody "seems to carry about with him now a little library; how he can have time to read, I cannot think." She thought also that he "is not quite so frolicsome as he was previously." But she should have seen Moody, Sankey, and Whittle chasing a rat (and each other) with a poker in an Irish hotel in 1883!

Their return to Glasgow after eight years produced an outburst of popularity. The *Christian* reported that the crowd

> blocked the streets for hours and the excitement penetrated the meeting to such an extent that an inquiry meeting was not even attempted . . . other revival movements seem to have flourished on excitement, but this is at once killed by it; and instead of taking advantage of heated occasions, Mr. Moody waits for the night of quiet power and the whisper of the still small voice.

During the months of widespread campaigning with united churches Moody did not attempt to carry a load as crushing as that of 1874. Mrs. Moody wrote to Edwin in Northfield on April 19:

> D. L., though working very hard, is *very well* and having much less headache than usual. He has been very much less in the work here in Glasgow. He is now preaching in the very poor district of Glasgow and among people such as you have never seen. It would make your heart bleed to see the wretchedness here and it is most of it caused by drink .... People living in Northfield would hardly imagine such wretchedness as is to be met with here in the poor parts of the large cities. Fanny and Emma have gone to the coast for a breath of fresh air and they will get it pretty direct from the North Pole I imagine.

The Scottish mission was less spectacular than that of 1873-1874. "There weren't such outward and visible results," John McNeill wrote. For one reason, evangelistic emphasis, startlingly fresh in 1874, had been accepted as a regular winter feature in many parishes. Adversely, much energy that might have been brought to evangelism was absorbed in increasingly bitter wrangles over higher criticism, which itself, in a strident overconfident phase, embarrassed.

The early summer of 1882 they spent in northern Scotland. Moody had received invitations from all over Great Britain "to last a lifetime" and agreed to give, after a fortnight's holiday in Switzerland, a series of shorter missions from September until April 1883, in Welsh and English provincial centers. His trail is marked by YMCAs or mission halls, raised as thank offerings in almost every city he visited.

Down the corridor of time, the most significant event, both for Moody and for the world, is seen to be the week's adventure in Cambridge.[2]

The Cambridge visit was planned for town and gown.

On Sunday morning, November 5, at a mass prayer meeting of church folk, sprinkled with University men who were staunch Christians, Moody delivered what to Handley Moule seemed "a very admirable and searching address on the Spirit's power for service," but a row or two behind Moody sat J. E. K. Studd, whose "heart sank when I heard him, for his way of speech was not our way of speech, his accent was not our accent, and I feared what

---

[2] He took a fortnight's mission in Paris in October. British cities included Swansea, Cardiff, Plymouth, Bristol, Portsmouth, Brighton, Liverpool, and Birmingham. Interesting unpublished evidence from Plymouth is the letter of fourteen-year-old Tommy Bewes, youngest of the twelve children of a lawyer, to his sister Evy, on September 29, 1882: "I am writing to tell you some good news which you will be glad to hear. I went to one of Moody's and Sankey's meetings on Tuesday and then I was saved. He spoke from the 9th verse of the 3rd of Genesis. It is where art thou? He said that that was the 1st question that God ever asked man in the bible, and that it was the first question that people ought to ask themselves and he said that there were two more he was going to speak about and they were, Where are you going? and How are you going to spend eternity? I don't think he could have chosen better ones. Thank you very much for praying for me." Tommy became the Reverend Canon T. C. Bewes (1868-1949). (Letter in the possession of his son, the Rev. Canon T. C. F. Bewes.)

undergraduates, full of spirits and ready to make fun of anything, would do." To make matters worse, November 5 was Guy Fawkes day,[3] and though the annual merrymaking—with its fireworks and bonfires, and its fights with town lads and police—would take place on Monday, the Gunpowder spirit was abroad.

As the Cambridge night filled with a symphony of chimes from the clocks of colleges and churches, striking eight, the new, ugly, cavernous Corn Exchange, which had been the scene of packed, decorous town meetings, began to fill with rowdy undergraduates. "In they came, laughing and talking and rushing for seats near their friends." Seventy students who had braved sneers to form a choir ("I wouldn't join that lot for 200 pounds," said one new arrival to another) sang hymns. They were countered by music-hall songs. Several lighthearted men tried to build a pyramid of chairs. A firecracker from outside exploded against a window. Seventeen hundred undergraduates in cap and gown, about half the junior members of the University, had been counted entering.

The choir stopped. A door opened. Handley Moule, John Barton, Vicar of Holy Trinity in the center of the town and University, Professor Babington (professor of botany; he caught a severe cold because of Moody's passion for fresh air), and other dons and clergy led Moody and Sankey to the platform. They were met with hoots and cheers. After "Jesus Lover of My Soul," Barton offered prayer. Some "ill-mannered youths," as Mrs. Barton called them when she heard about it, responded with "Hear! Hear!" Sankey began "The Ninety and Nine," which had never failed to quiet and move an audience. "The students," he said, "listened to the first verse in perfect silence, but at its conclusion they vigorously beat the floor with canes and umbrellas, and cried "Hear, hear!'" Each verse produced cries of "encore!" When they ruined "Man of Sorrows," Sankey came near to tears. Two or three dons quietly warned the worst offenders off the premises and stayed at the back to keep order, while Moody courteously pointed out that this was not a political meeting. "The service is God's and such proceedings are irreverent."

Moody preached on a favorite and suitable opening subject, Daniel in the lions' den, with its theme of faith and manly courage.

[3] The annual commemoration of the defeated plot to blow up James I and Parliament.

His monosyllabic *Dan'l* was "too much," wrote young Barclay Buxton of Trinity, "for the disorderly spirits who had come for fun, and they called out, 'Dan'l, Dan'l,' whenever that unfortunate name appeared." Scattered guffaws greeted Americanisms or un-British intonations; the "unconscious click in his throat before saying certain pithy remarks" induced imitation. Bursts of loud laughter were accompanied by pert shouts of "Well done!"

The University's weekly journal, the *Cambridge Review*, reported that "the majority paid every attention to the service, and marked their displeasure of the minority in no uncertain manner." The rowdies remained unabashed: "We went meaning to have some fun and, by Jove, we had it!" Moody fixed his eye on a particularly elegant young man in the front row, who was fooling hard and evidently leading the others. To a generation less colorful and more indifferent, whose reaction would likely be to stay away in lazy scorn, the undergraduates of 1882 and their full-blooded hounding of Moody must seem astonishing. Had he lost his temper, the history of that week and of all that flowed from it would have been different. Moule's young nephew thought "Moody was visibly affected," but his anecdotes and teaching flowed on, somewhat smothered by the Corn Exchange acoustics, which even his voice could not defeat.

Moody would have closed the meeting immediately after Sankey's final solo, but John Barton whispered to him: "Call a prayer meeting. Ask any who wish to pray to stay behind a few minutes."

Four hundred stayed, many from a sense of sportsmanship and fair play: among them some of the rowdiest, by now "quiet, impressed and apparently ashamed of their recent behavior." Moody spoke again briefly, still in good humor and still on Dan'l.

The Christian Union men returned to their colleges "with heavy hearts." Their opponents laughed. "If uneducated men *will* come to teach the Varsity they deserved to be snubbed," said Gerald Lander, the elegant youth from the front row, as he entered the Great Gate of Trinity. Moody and Sankey, accompanied by Studd, returned to their hotel. "Well, Sankey," said Moody cheerfully, as he removed his sweat-saturated collar, "I guess I've no hankering after that crowd again." Studd says that "Mr. Sankey was greatly upset at the reception his singing had received. What Mr. Moody's feelings were I do not know, but he was a man of great courage and determination." Studd joined the evangelists as they prayed with fervor and in faith for days ahead.

During Monday morning a bellboy knocked on Moody's door and handed in a card: "Mr. Gerald Lander. Trinity College." "Show him up," said Moody.

"I want to apologize, sir. And—I've brought a letter of apology from the men."

"Come right in!" Moody warmly shook his hand.

Mrs. John Barton says that some of the "more gentlemanly (though not yet at all of Mr. Moody's way of thinking) were so indignant at their companions' rude behavior that they got up a memorial to apologize to Mr. Moody." They prevailed on Gerald Lander to present it. He went simply as an English gentleman who upon reflection realized that he had overstepped the bounds of decency.

They had a long talk. Lander agreed that to prove his apology sincere he must attend the next meeting. Could Moody have peered into the future he would have seen this young man, then interested in little but racing and cards, striding through South China as a missionary bishop.

In Market Passage, close under Great St. Mary's Church, a gymnasium had been adapted to hold 500 for the weeknight University meetings. Monday night was wet. When "we assembled in the Gymnasium," writes W. H. Stone, an undergraduate who had been converted during Moody's Swansea campaign two months before, "the sight was enough to depress the spirits of the most sanguine." The bare hundred included most of the seventy men of the choir. But Lander kept his promise, subdued and attentive. And the sparse attendance enabled Moody afterwards to move around the hall to speak to every man in turn. Moule noted in his diary the next day: "Last night it is said 5 men were brought to Christ at the University meeting. Lord make it *stand* and carry it on."

On Tuesday town and country folk packed the Corn Exchange an hour before the start, but at the Gymnasium Moody felt "we've come up against a brick wall." An old lady staying at Professor Babington's for the mission suggested: "Why do you not call a prayer meeting of mothers?" Moody regularly dodged inviting mothers to unite in prayer for their sons. He had never attempted to ask them to pray for other mothers' sons.

Wednesday afternoon, while college men were digesting a restrained and well expressed letter of protest from Studd in the *Cambridge Review*, Moody, at the close of the town meeting, "with infinite tact and feeling," was collecting some hundred and fifty mothers for a prayer meeting. He would recall that prayer meeting as unique in his experience: "mother after mother, amidst her tears, pleaded for the young men of the University." And Wednesday night, wrote G. E. Morgan, the undergraduate son of one of Moody's earliest British friends, "exceeded our strongest faith and showed us how little we really had."

The Gymnasium was fuller. Moody spoke, in Moule's opinion, "with great power—a remarkable difference from the very discouraging occasion on Sunday night." Moody sensed that the mothers' prayers were being answered. He determined to prove it. He began,

> I have not yet held an inquiry meeting for you gentlemen, but I feel sure many of you are ready and yearning to know Christ. When you are in difficulties over mathematics or classics you do not hesitate to consult your tutors. Would it be unreasonable for you to bring your soul-trouble to those who may be able to help you? Mr. Sankey and I will converse with any who will go up to the empty gallery yonder. Let us have silent prayer.

The gallery, the Gymnasium fencing room, was up a clattering iron staircase "in the center of the hall in full view of all." No man would reach this impromptu inquiry room without a deliberate noisy movement before friends. In a Varsity quick to ridicule eccentricity, where men hated to show their feelings, it could hardly have been chosen better to prevent shallow decisions.

Not a man moved. Moody repeated the appeal. "There was no response," Studd writes, "till the third or fourth appeal," and then a young Trinity man, "amidst an awful stillness," left his place and, "half hiding his face in his gown, bounded up the stairs two at a time." Another followed. Soon the Gymnasium reverberated with clatter, man after man. The choir sang again. Moody said, "I never saw the gowns look so well before," and led Sankey up the stairs. Of fifty-two men counted in the gallery, one was Gerald Lander.

Cambridge. Nov. 9. 82

... When you get the cattle out of quarantine will you let me know
how much it cost I have three more to send but I do not want to send
them until I hear how much it will cost. How much did you get for your
wool & have you sold the sheep that belong to the boys school? ... Will
it be so Paul's heifer can have another calf by spring I think it would
please him much & Willie's pony if it could have a colt it would please
Willie but I do not know but it is too late now .... I hope you will keep
your eye on Ambert & see that he makes a good deal of manure.

Moody's letter to George on Thursday made no mention of the
sudden change in Cambridge's spiritual weather. "Never," a local
newspaper affirmed, "within the recollection of the oldest inhabi-
tant have there been such immense gatherings in Cambridge for
religion." Moody drew every rank and age to the Corn Exchange or
the Gymnasium. All over the University, in rooms or strolling along
the Backs or coming up from river or field the most unlikely men—
heavy smokers, racing enthusiasts, and idlers—were talking and
thinking. Those who resisted, respected. They recognized "a true
tinge of manliness" in Moody's preaching.

Arthur Benson of King's, whose father became Archbishop of
Canterbury a few weeks later, went to the Gymnasium on Thursday
"led by sociable curiosity." To him Sankey seemed

> an immense bilious[4] man, with black hair and eyes surrounded by
> flaccid, pendant, baggy wrinkles—who came forward with an unc-
> tuous gesture and took his place at a small harmonium, placed so near
> the front of the platform that it looked as if both player and
> instrument must inevitably topple over; it was inexpressibly ludicrous
> to behold. Rolling his eyes in an affected manner, he touched a few
> simple chords, and then a marvelous transformation came over the
> room. In a sweet powerful voice, with an exquisite simplicity combined
> with irresistible emotion, he sang "There were Ninety and Nine." The
> man was transfigured. A deathly hush came over the room, & I felt my
> eyes fill with tears; his physical repulsiveness slipped from him, and

---

[4] Sankey had certainly put on weight, but no other observer suggested that he had
lost his good looks. Benson was writing twenty-two years later, and in a semific-
tional context. Neither Sankey's nor Moody's name is mentioned. The account
appeared in A. C. Benson's book of *Essays The House of Quiet*, which was published in
1904 anonymously, and under his own name later. In the original edition, Benson
pretended to have found the story in a manuscript of "a distant cousin." Afterwards
he acknowledged it to be based on his own experience.

left a sincere impulsive Christian, whose simple music spoke straight to the heart.

Moody's address that night, on "Sowing and Reaping," Moule called "a noble masterpiece of Christian faithfulness, courage and wisdom; I take it to have been the most solid contribution to moral influence that has been made, by way of public appeal, for many a day." Moody "had not spoken half a dozen words," Arthur Benson writes,

> Before I felt as though he and I were alone in the world . . . . After a scathing and indignant invective on sin, he turned to draw a picture of the hollow, drifting life with feeble, mundane ambitions—utterly selfish, giving no service, making no sacrifice, tasting the moment, gliding feebly down the stream of time to the roaring cataract of death. Every word he said burned into my soul. He seemed to me to probe the secrets of my innermost heart; to be analyzing, as it were, before the Judge of the world, the arid and pitiful constituents of my most secret thought. I did not think I could have heard him out—his words fell on me like the stabs of a knife. Then he made a sudden pause, and in a peroration of incredible dignity and pathos he drew us to the feet of a crucified Saviour, showed us the bleeding hand and the dimmed eye, and the infinite heart behind. "Just *accept* Him," he cried; "in a moment, in the twinkling of an eye you may be His—nestling in His arms—with the burden of sin and selfishness resting at His feet."

Benson did not go up the iron staircase but "into the night, like one dizzied with a sudden blow . . . my only idea was to escape and be alone." He did not seek out Moody or speak to anyone of the spiritual conflict and "intolerable depression" that led him through weeks of misery, never, in a long and honorable career at Eton and Cambridge of teaching, writing, editing, and the Mastership of Magdalene, to find the peace of heart offered that November night.

Others, like Arthur Polhill-Turner, a gay spark of Trinity Hall, crept away to face the fact that life would have "to be a good deal adjusted." Thirty mounted the staircase, including several who had been "cynical and careless."

On Friday and Saturday Moody had a stream of callers, and each night Christian Union men were amazed and humbled to see the iron staircase draw outstanding intellectuals and athletes, admired or popular, of whom most had given little previous thought to religion, and also to see that those who clattered up one night would show by the company they brought on the next that they had followed Moody's advice, "No one can have really received Christ in his heart if he does not confess Him to his friends."

The final University meeting filled the Corn Exchange on Sunday night.

Of that frosty, murky November 12, 1882, a newspaper reported "four such meetings as have never before been witnessed in this town." Yet for all the massive impression on town and countryside, "success has been greater, and as far as can be judged, more real amongst the students of the University than amongst the general outside public."

Moule called it a "strange and unprecedented phenomenon in Cambridge life." Studd, the following week, "sent out a notice to say that any who had reason to be thankful for the visit of Mr. Moody might have the opportunity of writing their names in a book which would be on the table in my room at a certain date and hour, when I myself would not be there." Among the signatures were "the names of many men who made their mark in the world afterwards." In 1884, at the close of his Second British Mission, Moody said, "We have experienced the advantage of the Cambridge visit through the whole of our London Campaign," and Moule that same year remarked to a friend as they breakfasted with the Ridley Hall theological students, "I think there is not one man here whose life was not influenced more or less by Moody's Cambridge mission." In 1906 Bishop Moule could state: " . . . and among the scores of true, deep, lasting conversions were not a few of men well known and of powerful influence. I could name more than one College whose morale was lastingly raised after Moody's week."

The comment that, if extravagant, clearly points to the wider consequences that were to involve Moody, came from James Hope Moulton, a distinguished New Testament scholar, who was a freshman at King's in 1882. In 1914, a year or two before his death in the First World War, Moulton wrote to Will Moody: "I regard that week as the most momentous week in the religious history of this country during my lifetime, for it is certain that it was then the Student Christian Movement was born."

All of this shrouded the future, as Moody, on Sunday night,

November 12, before nearly two thousand Cambridge University men, preached from the text in Luke's gospel "Good tidings of great joy . . . a Saviour." His address was heard without a "shadow of opposition, interruption or inattention." At the end he said: "One last word. I shall never forget this week though you may forget me. I thank God I ever came to Cambridge, but I should like to give you one text before closing. "Seek ye *first* the kingdom of God.'" He finished with the words: "Believe the Gospel and make room for God in your hearts."

The choir sang "Just as I Am, Without One Plea." Moody prayed, every head bowed. Then he asked that all who had received blessing should rise quietly in their places, silent prayer continuing.

Two hundred rose. Moody, looking up, murmured: "My God, this is enough to live for."

26

Seedbed of a World Movement

Moody was now mountainous. "Nothing will fit him he is so broad of back, so large of paunch and so destitute of neck," wrote Whittle after he had gone with Moody and Sankey shopping for an overcoat. "We tell him it would take a land surveyor to lay out a coat for him, his back is so broad!" He did not look obese, for the massive flesh lay hard on his frame. His step was springy, and his strength bull-like as his neck. He could not, however, be quite as prodigal of energy, and, had he not returned for the summer of 1883 to Northfield, would probably have collapsed during the following eight months in London.

And Northfield needed him. Miss Tuttle had left for an administrative post, and the next principal had married the minister, so Moody referred back to Wellesley to discover Evelyn Hall, who became a very young but very able principal from 1883 until her death in 1911, and was reputed the only woman other than his wife who could manage Moody; he was even slightly in awe of her. Mount Hermon had new cottages, and Moody arranged for twelve boys from Manchester to join the growing number of Americans. He appointed a somewhat elderly gentleman as principal and would have ordered the building of a recitation hall if money had not been short.

Both schools were hindered by the lack. The hymnbook fund grew, but during this summer of 1883, in Moody's words privately to Whittle next winter,

> Sankey's relatives in New Castle got around him and persuaded him that he should be allowed to have some of the money to do something for his town and not let it all go to Northfield. So we met the Trustees and $20,000 was voted to him. I could not oppose it, nor did I wish to—I have always wanted him to do something for his town, but he never seemed to care to do so . . . in the meantime, I am pressed for means to carry on my Schools. I am praying for money and believe it will come soon.

Sankey gave New Castle a library, a Methodist church, and, to Moody's satisfaction, a YMCA building. Moody asked a New York multimillionaire, the Huguenot Commodore Cornelius Garrison, for a million dollars for Northfield, "and nearly got it." Later Moody believed he was wrong to seek an endowment.

Work for the schools made the holiday the more invigorating. Lapping up Northfield air, Northfield scenes, and Northfield friends, Moody saw to it that his family members enjoyed themselves. Paul's earliest distinct memories of his father were from this summer,

> as a nearly ideal companion for a very small boy . . . . He had a most engaging way of treating a child, at least he always did me, as if I were more or less his equal in years. He never talked down to me, but flattered me with the constant assumption that my opinion was sought and that he was interested in what I thought or had to say.

They reached London in November 1883, after a short mission in Southern Ireland.

Moody rated the eight-month London Campaign of 1883-1884 "better, better in every way" than that of 1875, an immediate verdict substantiated by long-term effects. He had revised his opinion that London in 1875 had not been "of much value," when all over the south and west of England in the early eighties, and in London, "I found so many of the best workers to be the fruit of these labors," but he saw more brotherly feeling in 1884-1885, increased spiritual life in the churches:

> The Church of England especially is more alive than it used to be. The number of ministers, Established and non-Established, that

cooperated with us all through has been much greater . . . less newspaper sensation, more meetings, better meetings, and the work has been of a more satisfactory character every way.

Thousands of words were written about this London Campaign. Archives and books teem with records and anecdotes. Viewing the campaign from the perspective of more than two generations, it is obvious that its importance was as a seedbed for the movement growing out of the Cambridge mission.

The London Committee, under its secretary, Robert Paton ("an invaluable man but a little stubborn in his opinion: he and Mr. Moody occasionally clash but Moody has a wonderful control of himself and so controls others"), had hit upon a novel plan. Two portable corrugated iron buildings ("tin tabernacles," they were dubbed) were specially constructed. The first was erected in open ground among the small terraces of middle-class houses, each with its own little garden, in Islington. After three weeks, Moody and Sankey and their helpers ("the caravan") moved south of the river to find the second tabernacle waiting on private land in the working-class area of Wandsworth. Then the first structure was dismantled and reerected— it took about three weeks—in the East End, "the midst of awful poverty," in Stepney, for the mission of December. Each tin tabernacle, which seated an audience of 5,180, with more seats on the platform and a spacious inquiry room beyond, appeared to Whittle, who served overflow and follow-up services, "like three long cattle sheds placed side by side with no partition. Inside it has three separate roofs supported by pillars." Each piece of timber and iron was marked and went back to the same place.

Eleven sites were used in the eight months, most of them within the outer ring of London. The only site in the city itself, at Temple Gardens between Fleet Street and the Embankment, had the least success, though it was crowded almost every night. In some districts, the crush to hear Moody taxed the resources of the committee to the utmost, and the *Pall Mall Gazette* reckoned that in the entire mission Moody had addressed 2,200,000 souls.

Within a few weeks of opening the London Campaign, Moody suffered a severe blow. Willie, now nearly fifteen, had bad lungs. Any illness among his children made Moody "dreadfully concerned," and Paul remembers how his father constantly placed a sympathetic hand on the tiny forehead, a hand "little lighter than a dictionary but . . . all you felt was the weight of affection." ("Once he perched on the side of a sickbed and broke it down.")

Money was short, but the Moodys settled that Emma must take the children to the mountain air of Zermatt in Switzerland. "I am dreading the going away from England very much," she wrote on November 9 to Mrs. Mackinnon, who a few days after they had gone abroad saw Moody at Islington, "looking so tired . . . [he] said to me that this parting was the worst 'pull' on him he had ever had." He was "rather downcast at the prospect of having to go through the whole Mission without her help and the comfort that there is to him in her presence."[1]

He accepted an invitation to stay indefinitely with the Quintin Hoggs, who now lived off Cavendish Square, near Hogg's Polytechnic Institute, "in fine style in a house built by an English Duke. The rooms are very fine with exceedingly high ceilings," Whittle noted, "with stone stairways connecting. Moody has a parlor and bedroom, a servant set apart for his use, and a carriage to take him anywhere and at any time he wishes." Hogg brought politicians and public men "for private interviews about their souls." Among them was the great Liberal statesman, John Bright, whom Moody found to be "nothing less than a Unitarian."

Whittle, dearest, most perceptive of friends, rejoiced at Moody's influence "among this class of people . . . . If I were asked as to direction in which his greatest danger lay, I should say that it would come from his Ambition to lead and influence Rich Men." So far that ambition had not led him "to compromise his convictions." Whittle praised God "every time I think of it that He keeps Moody so level-headed."

Despite this plutocratic base, Moody effectively reached the lowest classes.

Some of the most interesting evidence comes from difficulties in follow-up. At Wandsworth 2,000 names were taken in the inquiry room. In the month after the meetings, regular visitors reported that "the conversions were *real* and the people rejoicing in Christ and turned from sin." Why then for all this success did the local

[1] The Moodys were reunited briefly in Belgium for Christmas.

churches each receive a mere handful? Many of the 2,000 were scattered widely around the district and beyond, but it was discovered that "the large proportion of the converts are from the working class, and that they are attending services in mission halls where they feel more at home than in the churches." The Scripture reader who looked after the mission halls of the parish church found "most satisfactory evidence of the reality of the work." Moody himself had "launched the project of a Gospel Hall to be erected on the site of the Iron Building," as a union endeavor. It continues in service eighty years later.

The London workingman was much exposed to noisy rationalists or "freethinkers." At Stratford in the East End, where the destitution and overcrowding of Stepney had given way to acres of factories and cheerless streets of workers' dwellings, Moody waded into the thick of this militant atheism, which thrived on Bradlaugh and gin and gloried in endless debate, in pelting bricks and stones at Salvation Army processions, but had no foundation of intelligence: "they don't know what they do believe or what they don't believe." Moody had been introduced to the president of a local atheist club, who "snarled and growled at me as I spoke to him, and wanted to fight." The man sent a note daring Moody to preach a sermon to atheists. The resulting famous incident of Thursday, January 31, 1884, has been blown up into the legend of an entire hall of atheists, five hundred of whom leaped to their feet in instant confession of Christian faith, a legend still produced in biographies of Moody. The facts, recounted by him four days later at luncheon with George Williams of the YMCA, Professor Simpson, Robert Paton, and Whittle, who recorded it the same night in his diary, are less sensational.

The front seats were reserved for the atheists, and "hundreds came." Moody's sermon was entitled "Their Rock Is Not Our Rock," and it focused on the emptiness of the atheists' hope, and by a succession of deathbed scenes caught them on their soft spot: the mockery of family love if there be no immortality, a theme to which, that night, his own family's absence abroad gave special tenderness. "One man arose to interrupt, but I held the audience and invited them all to remain to the second meeting, not to run away. I have something you all need and all could have. Many of them remained."

To the after-meeting Moody explained four words: "*Receive* Him, *believe* Him, *trust* Him, *take* Him." "Who will take Him?" he cried. "Who will say 'I will'?" Several responded among the general audience. An atheist shouted, "I won't." Moody, compassionate almost to tears, sobbed: "It's 'I will' or 'I won't' for every man in this hall tonight." He spoke of the Prodigal Son's decision: 'I *will* arise and go to my father.'

> The battle is on the *will*, men, and only there. When the young man said, "I will arise," the battle was won, for he had yielded his will, and on that point all hangs tonight. Men, you have your champion there who said, "I won't!" I want every man who believes that man is right to rise and say, "I won't take Him."

Not a man moved. Moody continued: "Thank God! No man says, 'I won't.' Now who'll say, 'I will,' who will take Christ as Saviour, who will take Him?"

A long pause. "Then one of the atheists," said Moody, telling the story,

> called out, "I will take Him!" It was a bombshell in their midst. Some were violent in anger as the meeting closed. But the backbone of atheism in the club received a terrible twist. I met the man who decided to Christ and found him an intelligent mechanic, and fully turned to God.

Ten days later Moody accepted an invitation to family tea with the president of the atheist club, "the street quite stirred and people at their doors to see if I was really coming." In the course of the tea Moody said: "If I lived in Stratford I should not try by argument to win you over, but I should try by kindness to win your affection and make you respect me."

"You have done that already."

The man came along with Moody to the tabernacle "as mild as a lamb." Moody sat him on the platform and during the sermon aimed several hard hits at him.

Unfortunately, as is often the way, the rest of the man's story is lost.

At New Cross in Southeast London in late February, the crowds were almost unmanageable. One night such a milling flow sought to press into the hall at the end of the meeting, as the audience of 5,000 was leaving, that the police inspector wanted to send for a mounted section. Moody jumped over a hedge, ran across a field to an omnibus on the edge of the crowd, climbed to the top, and whispered to the driver, who gave a shake of the reins. A moment later, people heard Moody's voice boom. They converged on the omnibus, which moved away at a walking pace, Moody using it as a pulpit, until the crush eased.

With all its triumphs, New Cross also brought trials. The Plymouth Brethren pitched a tent upon one side of the tin tabernacle to catch the overflow; the parish church arranged a "ritualistic service" on the other, and both asked Moody to boost them.

> The Holiness people have been pulling strong to get my presence for five minutes at one of their meetings as a testimony I'm not antagonistic to them, and the friends of General Booth have been urging for some expression of endorsement of Salvation Army . . . . And so I have had a time of it this week driving the coach through without upsetting!

Sankey collapsed the first day, and for a week Moody had to depend on his American assistants George C. Stebbins and James McGrana-han and his wife ("Mack and Addy" to their friends). When Sankey came back, he was "crotchety" and would not take second place and sing at the overflow meetings. The local choirmaster hashed the hymns, and some gunners from Woolwich Depot volunteered as a male choir for the men's meetings. Said Moody,

> it was the most miserable failure I ever saw. They broke down and had to commence over again three times on the same piece. Some of the audience hung their heads in shame for them, and others laughed at them. If you ever saw a man whistling through a graveyard, I was that man as I got up after that singing.

By March second, the closing Sunday at New Cross, Moody was visibly tired. At the start at St. Pancras, the tabernacle had been erected close to the Midland Railway terminus, on land cleared for a widening scheme. The noise from trains and the heat caused by the high walls that blocked the ventilation gave Moody such headaches that he drank gallons of tea and then suffered a rare bout of sleeplessness. His strain increased as the campaign lengthened—to St. Pancras, Kensington (the site where Olympia was to be built), and Hampstead.

He found relief in romping with the Hogg children or in telling jokes and stories with his cronies. Laughter was always his safety-valve. During the Irish campaign the previous autumn—when Moody, Sankey, and Whittle were staying, grass widowers, in hotels—"most every night before going to bed M. would as he sat at supper have his laugh, shaking all over and holding his side and entering most heartily into anything funny. He is as natural as a child in this." He knew how far to go, never joked about sacred things, and, if an inquirer called, could turn instantly to serious talk "with perfect naturalness."

Though tired, Moody was a contrast to Spurgeon, a mere three years his senior, whom he found "broken from overwork and prematurely old," and to Booth: "If I were to get into such a state of nervous excitement as General Booth I should have been dead ages ago." Moody admitted that he had "so many things on hand that I used to let little things annoy me," and he was abashed when a prominent London clergyman, with several curates and a large parish, told him that "no man ought to undertake so much Christian work that it wears him out and makes him irritable." Moody would confess, "I know you men are way beyond me in the sweetness and peace of your daily lives and I wish I were more like you," but he preserved a healthy skepticism about perfectionist claims and once answered someone's boast of sinlessness with the blunt comment: "I would like to meet your wife!"

By April his daughter was with him. Good news of Willie's health ensured that the whole family would be back with the sun, and in May the last district site but one opened in Croyden close to the Crystal Palace.

Lady Ashburton, the banker's wife, put at Moody's disposal her nearby mansion in its park of 180 acres, complete with servants and supplies. It was from this stately home that he wrote to Willie on the Continent on May 10:

> You will see by the heading of this note ⅓ of May has all ready gone & the days will soon pass a way that seperates us from our dear home
> I have writen to have them get your garden ready & I think we Will find it all ready when we get home I bought some Bowls so we can have some games when we get back—as spring comes on I long to get home & to get into the green fields & see what is goin on there will be a good many changes in our end of the town Mr Marshall is goin to build two buildings so we will have a grate change & number of things to intrest us I have some cooing doves & a butiful Peacock to take back with me & I am in hopes we will be enabled to keep this one

You must take good care of Ma Ma & not let her loose to much sleep with Paul Can you not take care of him nights if she gets him to sleep & he wakes up mornings early & she does not get enough sleep it will give her a head ache I am afraid you must not let Ma Ma overwork see that she is not weary robbed of her sleep if she does not get enough night times let her go to sleep in the day & you take Paul out walking.[2]

Eleven days later, he met them in London; it was "one of the happiest days of my life." The unlucky family brought Paul back with whooping cough.

Sankey sailed home sick, leaving Stebbins and the McGranahans to sing in his place. The London campaign had brought Sankey two bereavements: his delicate eldest son lay buried in Marylebone cemetery, and his father had died far away in Pennsylvania. "The reality of Sankey's consecration to the Lord," Whittle had written,

is impressed upon me in my intercourse with him this winter. His father's death has been blessed in bringing him nearer to God, and Christ and the Gospel are dearer to him than ever. His prayer with us this morning was *very* real and blessed.

No assistant could fully take Sankey's place. Moody would miss him at Temple Gardens. From the Kinnairds' Mayfair home, where they moved from Croydon, Mrs. Moody wrote on May 27:

My husband began his last district here. He keeps remarkably well, but I do think he has had a very long continuous strain on him and will be so glad when he has finished this district, though he does look well.

And all this time the London campaign nourished the remarkable movement among young men that would have such consequences for the world.

[2] Original spelling given as a later example of Moody's family scrawl. The letter is unpunctuated throughout.

27

Student Volunteers

In November 1882, when Moody had left Cambridge for Oxford—where again disaster ended in triumph, though the consequences were not so harsh—several of the Cambridge converts showed an immediate awareness of the call to overseas service. Moody had said little if anything about the "foreign field," as the phrase was, at Cambridge or elsewhere. Yet within a week or two, Hooper of Trinity thought about Africa, Tyndale-Biscoe of Jesus about India, and Arthur Polhill-Turner of Trinity Hall about China.

Shortly after the end of the Cambridge term, Moody held a mission in the mosquelike Dome of the exotically Oriental Pavilion at Brighton, where lived a retired major-general called Hoste, who had one son, William, on vacation from theological studies at Moule's Ridley Hall, and another, Dixon Edward, on leave from the gunners. Dixon Hoste was a subaltern of soldierly bearing, with an utter lack of interest in religion. William dragged Dixon to the Dome where, Dixon wrote, "As Mr. Moody, with intense earnestness and directness preached the solemn truths concerning God's judgment of the impenitent and ungodly . . . a deep sense of my sinful and perilous state laid hold of my soul with great power."

Dixon frequented subsequent meetings in agonized indecision, fearing the cost of becoming a Christian, until on the last night, slipping into the back of the Dome, he yielded, sensed a flooding peace and assurance of forgiveness, and at Moody's call for inquirers went forward radiant. Within a fortnight he wanted to resign his commission to be a missionary. His father dissuaded him. By the spring of 1883, he was reading literature sent by William from Cambridge about the China Inland Mission, then an obscure but valiant pioneering band; and the summer when Moody was in Northfield, Hoste applied to its founder, James Hudson Taylor, a short man of acute perception and extraordinary courage, only to be advised to wait.

Moody's mind also worked in the direction of overseas missions. At the Chicago Convention in September 1883, he had drawn attention to the appalling discrepancy between the world's millions of "Christless souls" and the sprinkling of Western Christians who served overseas, backed by only a trickle of money.

The London campaign saw Cambridge to the fore. "Women had a way of fainting," Jane Mackinnon recorded, "and the young gentlemen stewards—some of them athletes from Cambridge and Oxford—got opportunities of showing their prowess!" At Wandsworth a Cambridge student who felt unfitted for service in the inquiry room told a London cabby that he would "pay your regular fee by the hour if you will go in and hear Mr. Moody preach. I will take care of your horse." For two hours, in Moody's words, "on that cold, bleak night that London gentleman stood by the cabman's horse and let that cabman go and hear the Gospel."

Two slightly older Cambridge men served in the Clapham mission: William Cassels, a curate, and Stanley Smith, a schoolmaster who had stroked the University boat in 1882; Smith's conversion as a boy during the '75 campaign caused him, when he was up for a long weekend during the Cambridge mission and was introduced to "dear old Moody," to give him "such a shake of the hand!" Cassels and Smith had seldom met since Varsity until the tin tabernacle, but the two of them formed a strong bond. "After the meetings," Smith wrote years later, "we had some arm-in-arm talks and heart-to-heart talks about the Lord and China."

Smith spent his free time at the campaign. Moody noticed his skill and invited him to tea during the Kensington mission to put a proposition: he was taking, he said, several young working-class men, mostly Irish (who had asked if he would train them for home or foreign missions, since they knew of no means in Britain), to Mount Hermon to form a specialist class. Stanley Smith must run it. But Smith's heart lay in China. The very same evening, Hudson Taylor dined with Stanley and his parents in their Mayfair home, and that night Stanley Smith wrote in his diary: "Decided to go to China with Hudson Taylor as a missionary, and to go, D.V., via America so as to see Moody's training home."

Smith never saw Mount Hermon. His indirect influence there would be strong, however, and through Mount Hermon have significance for the whole world.

No man under thirty lay more in Moody's affection than J. E. K. Studd, now Captain of the Cambridge Eleven, "of fine ability and promise, and very popular with the gentry, an out-and-out Christian." The next Studd, G. B., was of J. E. K's stamp, but the youngest, C. T., now at the height of fame as a cricketer, had been spineless and effete as a Christian when the campaign began. In December, G. B. fell desperately ill, and by his bedside in the small hours C. T. saw the emptiness of his own existence, living only for games, popularity, and pleasure. When his brother was out of danger, C. T. Studd hurried to Moody's meetings, which were then at Stratford: "There the Lord met me again and restored to me the joy of my salvation."

C. T. became a strong worker, his fame and charm and forthright single-track enthusiasm combining to give his words punch. At a subsidiary meeting of the campaign, he and J. E. K. were heard by a young medical student, Wilfred Grenfell. Grenfell previously had wandered into one of Moody's Stepney services, where on the platform an elderly man stood, coagulating a prayer of such long wind that the huge audience was suffocating, and Grenfell, bored, tiptoed toward the door. An American voice broke in across the English. Moody "kindly but ever so cleverly" called out: "Let us sing a hymn while our brother finishes his prayer." This announcement, Moody's usual gambit in the circumstances, stopped Grenfell in his tracks: "his practicality interested me."

After the singing, the address "moved me . . . . It was a personal conversation with my heart . . . It was the real thing," and a few weeks later, at the close of the Studd meeting, one of the brothers—probably J. E. K.—asked those who intended following Christ to stand up. To Grenfell it appeared a very sensible question but I was amazed how hard I found it to stand up. At last one boy out of a hundred or more, in sailor rig, from an Industrial or Reformatory ship on the Thames, suddenly rose. It seemed to me such a wonderfully courageous act for I knew perfectly what it would mean to him, that I immediately found myself on my feet.

Twenty years later, in a letter written to Moody's son-in-law, Grenfell of Labrador said: "Anything with the name of 'Moody' to it has a great call on my affections. You know I attribute my conversion to his work in Stepney years ago." "He started me working for all I was worth," Grenfell wrote, in one of his books, "and made religion real fun—a new field brimming with opportunities."

With summer C. T. Studd felt he "must go into the cricket field and get the men there to know the Lord Jesus—My heart was no longer in the game. I wanted to win souls for the Lord." Under his wing, members of the M.C.C. Test team heard Moody, and several whose names were household words told Studd, one by one, that they had accepted Christ. These young athletes would be invited to Moody's Saturday holidays in spacious grounds of wealthy homes on London's outskirts, where Moody, in Lord Kinnaird's words,

> He'd throw himself into games with as much zest as he took up all his other work and you can imagine that he did not like to be on the losing side, but generally secured one of the brothers Studd or Mr. Steel to play on his side![1] I shall never forget his portly form running in the game of rounders in which he used to take great delight.

The campaign ended. Moody picked up threads at Northfield and Chicago and immersed himself in a fresh round of American campaigns for autumn and winter. At the same time, in Britain, one by one, Stanley Smith, Charlie Studd, D. E. Hoste, Arthur Polhill-Turner and his brother Cecil, Montagu Beauchamp, and William Cassels—all converts or helpers under Moody—offered themselves for China. When it became known that men of wealth, birth, and athletic prowess were to become missionaries, the sensation was tremendous. "The Cambridge Seven" swept across the universities of England and Scotland, stirring students to faith and dedication, especially for service overseas. Where Moody had

---

[1] Allan Gibson Steel, the slow bowler (1858-1914).

plowed and sown, they reaped, and the climax came with a great meeting in London on February 4, 1885, the day before the Cambridge Seven sailed. The missionary call sounded louder than ever before.

The story caught the imagination of America. And it was in the afterglow of the Cambridge Seven that the third Northfield Conference gathered in August 1885.

Moody allotted August 11, halfway through the conference, to "prayer for world-wide missions." The main address was delivered to about one thousand people by Arthur T. Pierson of Philadelphia, a recognized authority, whose book *The Crisis of Missions* appeared the next year.

Pierson urged that this was the hour for advance. An appeal should be sent to the entire church, he contended:

> Let us have an ecumenical council, representing all evangelical churches, solely to plan [a] world-wide campaign and proclaim the good tidings to every living soul in the shortest time! Let the field be divided and distributed with as little waste of men and means as may be. Let there be a universal appeal for workers and money, and a systematic gathering of offerings that shall organize the mites into millions.

Moody jumped to his feet. With force and enthusiasm he called the Conference to vote their approval by acclamation. Then he appointed a small committee of six others and himself to draw up "An Appeal to Disciples Everywhere." Three days later this paper was read out, endorsed by the Conference, and signed by the committee.

"The whole world" the appeal proclaimed, "is now accessible, the last of the hermit nations welcomes the missionary." And so it seemed, with little exaggeration, in 1885. Swift steamships took men across the oceans; the white man's flag had been carried into recesses of Africa; India was at peace under the imperial crown of Victoria; treaties promised free movement in China—the world was destined to peace and progress under Western leadership. If Tibet's gates were fast shut, New Guinea almost unexplored, and Uganda that very year the scene of massacre of missionary and convert, what were these to determined men? "And yet the Church of God is slow to move in response to the providence of God. Nearly a thousand millions of the human race are yet without the Gospel; vast districts are wholly unoccupied."

Northfield appealed for "the immediate occupation and evangelization of every destitute district," aiming for

> a new effusion of the Spirit in answer to prayer . . . . If but ten million out of the four hundred millions of nominal Christians would undertake such systematic labor as that each one of that number should in the course of the next fifteen years reach one hundred souls with the Gospel message, the whole present population of the globe would have heard the glad tidings by 1900.

They called for an ecumenical conference (which met three years later in London) in words that bear the Moody stamp:

> What a spectacle it would present both to angels and men, could believers of every name, forgetting all those things in which they differ, meet by chosen representatives to enter systematically and harmoniously upon the work of sending forth laborers into every part of the world field.

The appeal had been drafted in the Homestead, partly bought with Edward Studd's gift. One of the seven who signed it was J. E. K. Studd. One who acclaimed it as a member of the conference was a thirty-one-year-old graduate of Princeton called Luther T. Wishard.

Luther Wishard, founder of the Inter-Collegiate YMCA, had twice failed to persuade Moody before 1882 to preach in colleges. Moody "almost took my head off . . . if he had a weak point it was an unnecessary abruptness in declining invitations." Despite his impact on Edinburgh students in 1873, his day at Princeton in 1876, and the number of Yale men who came to New Haven meetings, Moody's lack of higher education inhibited him. During December 1884, Wishard "again tackled him" during the Cincinnati campaign.

> While he was still modest, and shrinking, and distrustful of himself, he intimated that if he could be assured that the students themselves wanted to hear him—not simply that somebody interested in students wanted them to hear him—he would seriously consider such invitations. It did not take long to secure invitations from students. They prepared petitions in Princeton, Harvard, Yale and Dartmouth . . . . Thousands and thousands of signatures were obtained.

Moody stopped short of Harvard, but Princeton, Dartmouth, and Yale heard him in 1885. In Battell Chapel at Yale, "he seemed rather ill at ease and not at all at home being introduced in a regular service and obliged to fit into the regular order," wrote a Yale man, Cornelius H. Patton, to Will (in 1925). "In the evening it was far different. Battell Chapel was packed and your father in full control. He preached his famous sermon on 'Whatsoever a man soweth, that shall he also reap,' the sermon that had overturned A. C. Benson at Cambridge and never failed in its freshness and reality; thousands who heard it could echo Sam Higginbotham's verdict: "I never knew any preacher to reveal *sin* as such a hateful thing, and yet that was the undertone. The overtone was that in God's love there was grace enough to cover all my sin." The Yale men listened in utmost silence, and the scene afterwards was reminiscent of the iron gallery at Cambridge.

At best, Moody's college sermons could be few. He wrote of his admiration for Wishard's lonely labors "among our 1,200 American colleges, professional and preparatory schools," and in the summer of 1885 Moody induced J. E. K. Studd to cross the Atlantic for the college year of 1885-1886.[2] Aided by the glamour of his athletic renown, and as brother of C. T. Studd of the Cambridge Seven, J. E. K. exerted wide influence. At Cornell an able law student named John R. Mott attended his address, "an unbeliever . . . I listened to him and was converted" after a sharp spiritual struggle, "with the help of comprehending and faithful counsel from the English visitor."

The Northfield Conference brought Wishard, Studd, and Moody together. One day Moody drove them to Mount Hermon, which now had settled toward its final form as a secondary school for older boys; the Training School for young men was then a part of it. Proper buildings, with more at Northfield, were now being built, for the British had forwarded no less than 20,000 pounds in hymnbook royalties: "Look at that—" Moody would point "—Sankey sang it up."

[2] In 1927, Sir Kynaston Studd told Will that he joined Moody at Bridgeport, Connecticut. "Your father was in difficulty that morning because he had to take a meeting but had also to receive a large St. Bernard puppy. As he had no one to meet the puppy I was told off to do so. While he was taking his meeting I was walking the puppy, who was not at all anxious to come with me, through the streets of the town. I think he caught sight of me somewhere, and you can imagine the amusement that he got out of the incident and the fun he made of this Cambridge graduate leading a dog about the town."

As they drove around the campus, Moody suggested: "Wishard, wouldn't this be a good place for a conference of the general secretaries of the city YMCAs?"

"Yes, it would be ideal."

"Well, how would you like to bring fifty or a hundred of them up here next summer, and let them live in those little houses where the workmen are living? I will give them a Bible reading every day, and we will have a Bible conference." But Wishard did not encourage him, "because I had larger game to kill."

In Atlanta that winter Wishard met Moody again, and again was asked about a conference of city YMCA secretaries at Mount Hermon.

"Mr. Moody, how many general secretaries could you entertain?"

"A couple of hundred. We will let them occupy Crossley Hall and the teachers' houses, and we will have the meetings in Recitation Hall."

"You would be willing to entertain two hundred, would you?"

"Yes."

"How long would you entertain them?"

"A month if desired."

"Mr. Moody, if you are willing to do that for a couple of hundred general secretaries, why won't you do it for a couple of hundred students from the colleges throughout the country and Canada?"

But "the old spirit of distrust," says Wishard, "took possession of him again . . . . It might be a good idea . . . he did not know . . . would think about it." Moody seemed determined to miss this date with destiny.

Within ten days young Wishard rejoined Moody at the University of Virginia to aid him in evangelistic meetings and cannily kept silent on the subject until about to leave for the train. Moody replied in the negative. "I'm afraid we cannot make a success of a conference of college students in the summertime. They will want to go home for recreation."

"Let them have their recreation on Mount Hermon and in the Connecticut."

Moody said he would have to get strong speakers to attract the students.

Wishard brushed the objection aside: "The man who will draw students is yourself. They know you. You underrate your intellectual qualifications. You have a message to the college boys of this country."

Moody surrendered. Wishard rushed to his train and immediately sent out invitations from New York.

Two hundred fifty delegates from a hundred colleges came for a
full month of glorious July and early August weather. On the first
morning, July 7, Moody mounted the platform "with businesslike
step, portly form and slightly graying hair and beard" and had one
hymn sung after another:

> I want to make as much of music as possible here. Music and the
> Bible are the two important agencies with which to reach the world,
> and I've made as much of singing as I have of preaching. I've been
> asked for programs. I hate programs, and I don't have any. Then I
> can't break over 'em. If you want to know what is ahead, we don't know,
> except that we will have a good time. We want to stir you up and get you
> in love with the Bible, and those of you with a voice, in love with music.
> If I find you getting drowsy in hot weather, I'll just ask the speaker to
> stop and we will sing . . . . Our talks are going to be conversational. If
> you want to ask a question, speak out: that's what we're here for, to get
> all the cobwebs swept away, and go back to our college mates inspired
> with the truth.

Moody had brought several eminent lecturers, but, as Wishard
had foreseen, the students wanted Moody most. One of them
wrote, "Mr. Moody's rugged, cheerful, transparent personality
gave a great thrill to me, and I am sure to other delegates," and
John R. Mott said it was the "note of reality" in Moody's preaching
that "appealed strongly to college men. They were impressed by his
downright honesty and transparent sincerity," and his "lack of
sham," his frankness and directness. "He brought religion out of
the clouds and made it a present-day and everyday personal and
practical relationship and experience."

Moody's enjoyment of the conference grew daily: the long hours
devoted to baseball and swimming, the visits to the Homestead,
where he could display his ducks and geese and chickens and the
peacocks and the ponies and the absurd barn built by little Paul out
of packing boxes and boards. Moody would challenge the college
boys to race him, carrying enough ballast to equal his weight—and
beat them over twenty-five or thirty yards.

The conference took on an importance far beyond the expecta-
tions of Moody or Wishard, and brought to a climax the movement
that was first stirred in Cambridge nearly four years before.

One of the delegates, the son of a distinguished retired missionary, was Robert Wilder, who had formed a Princeton Foreign Missionary Society in 1883, its five student members signing a declaration: "We are willing and desirous, God permitting, to become Foreign Missionaries." He and his family prayed that a thousand missionary volunteers should be secured from American universities. At the start of the Mount Hermon Conference only twenty-three of those attending were committed. Wilder, sensitive and quiet, sought out and gathered them each evening under the trees to pray for more volunteers.

To every other person he came across he put the claim of missions, and John R. Mott's experience was typical: "My first meeting with Robert Wilder was when swimming in the Connecticut River . . . . Before the interview was over, which began in the water and continued as we tramped back to the school campus, he had appealed to me to become a missionary." Memory of the Cambridge Seven lay close to the surface; the time was ripe. Wilder went to Dr. Pierson and begged him to give a missionary address. Moody allotted a special evening session, during which Pierson illustrated his theme from a rough sketch on the blackboard and, wrote his son, "voiced the Macedonian call to young men of the Church to give their lives for 'the evangelization of the world in this generation.' "

"Quietly and without forcing, as I can see," a journalist at the conference reported a few days later, "the mission spirit has spread. Each man has settled the question, 'Shall I go?' by himself with his Bible and his God." In the third week Wilder asked Moody if nine students from overseas, and a North American Indian, might address the conference. Moody consulted Wishard, who approved enthusiastically.

The "Meeting of the Ten Nations" was the birthplace of the Student Volunteers. "The delegates," Wilder wrote, "withdrew to their rooms or went out under the great trees to wait on God for guidance." One hundred signed a declaration of willingness to serve overseas.

From Mount Hermon the Volunteer movement blazed across America.

Following the Cambridge Seven pattern, Wilder and John Forman toured universities. "The missionary spirit is rampant among the students now, the interest is strong, vigorous and healthful," a newspaper wrote the next year. The summer of 1887 brought 400 young men to Northfield. "We have more people in town now than ever before at any time," Moody wrote to his daughter, who was then in Europe.

All the street is full, some sleeping in barns, and tents on the riverbank, in the woods and no less than six tents on the round hill back of our house . . . . We are hearing some fine speakers. Drummond is liked best of all . . . . We had in front of the house fireworks like what we had at Denny's in 84 . . . . Last night the Harvard and Yale and Princeton boys had a fire down on the bank of the river in front of our house and Willie and myself were invited down. They sang songs, told stories, and they did have a time.

Thereafter men students came for ten days every year in the month before Moody's Northfield general conference, and at May Whittle's suggestion, he added later a women's college conference.

Moody never attempted to lead the Student Volunteers. "It's my job to get things going," he decided. Once again his genius had touched into life a latent movement, which other men could carry forward.

The Volunteers girdled the globe, their watchword "The Evangelization of the World in This Generation." In 1891, Wilder carried the idea to Britain to blend with the movement begot directly by the Cambridge Seven. Robert E. Speer and John R. Mott followed Wilder, and the missionary roll lengthened in universities throughout America and Europe, as the Christian gospel went out to untold thousands who had remained unreached in Africa, Asia, and South America. If the evangelization of the world by 1900 (the date suggested in the Northfield Appeal), had slipped from the church's grasp, the volunteers of the nineties believed it to be truly possible in their generation that, by the time they were old (in the 1940s or early 1950s), the gospel should have been presented to every soul in the world, by Westerners to nationals and nationals to their own folk, in such a manner that, in Wilder's words, "the responsibility for what is done with it shall no longer rest upon the Christian church, or any individual Christian but shall rest on each man's head for himself."

From the Student Volunteers developed the Student Christian Movement and in its time the Inter-Varsity Christian Fellowship. John R. Mott, after decades of service for students, said that Mount

Hermon was "the fountainhead of a stream which has brought more blessings to the universities and colleges of the world than any which has gushed out in any nation under the life-giving influence of the Spirit of God."

Since early days, Moody had pressed his "all-absorbing idea of making the world feel the power of Christian union in active work for the masses." He had now a worldwide vision. The target of call and dedication had enlarged first from city to nation, from Chicago to Britain and the United States; and from a nation to the "whole present population of the globe." The city, the nation, the world.

The *far outcome* was to be the Ecumenical Movement, of which the chief spring, however many its sources, was Northfield, through the Appeal of 1885 and the missionary conferences of 1888 in London and 1900 in New York, and Mount Hermon through the Volunteers. The streams flowed together at Edinburgh in 1910 under the chairmanship of Mott.

Whatever channels the subsequent Ecumenical Movement may have carved in later decades, its grandfather—in a sense, and unwittingly—was D. L. Moody with his passion, echoed by the Northfield Appeal, "to further the glorious object of a world's evangelization."

28

Slow Birth of the Bible Institute

Miss Emma Dryer of Chicago had an unhappy love affair at an unfortunate time—at least, that was the explanation offered by the daughter of Moody's faithful helper, J. M. Hitchcock, as to why Miss Dryer nearly wrecked her own dearest plan and increased Moody's gray hairs.

Emma Dryer organized the woman's side of Moody's church. Whenever she could pin him in Chicago she asked him to found a "Bible Institute" for training those who had never been to college, and as a center for evangelistic activity in the surrounding slums. She claimed that Moody had uprooted her from state schools after the Fire for this very purpose, yet had run off to Europe and forgotten. In 1876, and again during a lightning visit in 1883, Moody had indeed talked publicly of the schemes, but nothing had emerged beyond a handful of young women selected by Miss Dryer, who housed them at Mrs. Cyrus McCormick's expense in a house on Warren Avenue.

Several Chicago residents who sympathized with Miss Dryer, though, were undecided whether the institute should be an "order of deaconnesses" for city work or a school "for the preparation of workers for worldwide Missions," met weekly in 1883 to pray "for Mr. Moody to come and plan something commensurate with the needs." The clergyman temporarily filling the pulpit of the Chicago Avenue Church, Charles A. Blanchard,

> was often reminded by Miss Dryer of the fact that the Bible institute had not been started, that it ought to be started, and that she was in trouble about it. She one day said that if we could get it started so that it would be evident that the thing would go, Mr. Moody would come and organize it and then we should get it under way.

Blanchard raised $500, and an able teacher was secured to give free evening classes for "fifty young men and women . . . eager and enthusiastic." A second session followed, and, at last, on January 22, 1886, Moody took the matter in hand.

Moody told a public meeting that, in order to evangelize Chicago's masses, they would need to raise $250,000.

> Spend 50,000 dollars on a building, and put out the balance at interest, and from the income you could support a training school for workers . . . who would serve to act between the preachers and the people. They should be taught the Word of God so they could answer every question put to them.

He pictured need and possibilities in his inimitable way until the meeting caught his enthusiasm and when he finished his address demanded more.

> What would you have me to say? For twenty-five years I have made this question of what shall be done for the workingman my study. It has been my very life. People ask me why I do not come back here and stay. Well, it seems I can't. I have a roving commission which takes me all over the world, nearly.

"Oh," he exclaimed, his beloved Northfield forgotten in the emotion of the moment, "I should like to come back and live here. I love Chicago. I love its people, but I must keep at work. But I will promise this: If this work is taken up as I want it done I will come back every year and help it along all I can."

Young Cyrus H. McCormick, son of Moody's deceased old friend, leaped to his feet. "I will give fifty thousand dollars."

"Better make it a hundred!"

"That will require some consideration." McCormick laughed. Within a few hours, he had promised the hundred thousand. Moody told the assembled company, "Let others raise the money and I will furnish my experience and labor."

Nothing happened. The year 1886, dark with industrial strife and bloodshed, McCormick's own factory being the center of the Haymarket Riots in May, brought the absent Moody's Bible institute no nearer; exactly what happened to the hundred thousand dollars is obscure. Few letters or documents survive to unravel the delays and perplexities of those next years in Chicago.

Moody returned for a four months' Chicago campaign from January to April 1887, on the lines proved at Baltimore and St. Louis: working district by district through the churches.

In the thick of it he brought together Farwell, McCormick, Harvey, the lumber king, and three others in his room at the Grand Pacific Hotel on February 5, 1887, his fiftieth birthday. (He felt then what he wrote on his fifty-first: "It seems strange for me to be so old, I feel as young as I did at thirty.") As a fitting jubilee, they founded the Chicago Evangelization Society "to educate, direct and maintain Christian workers as Bible Readers, Teachers and Evangelists who shall teach the Gospel in Chicago and its suburbs especially in neglected fields." This new society would build and administer a Bible institute.

A letter that was on its way from China would forward Moody's ambition, nursed by the rise of the Student Volunteers, that the institute must train not only for cities of America but for overseas as well. On his twenty-fifth birthday, C. T. Studd had inherited a share of his father's fortune, which he promptly gave away. He sent 5,000 pounds of it to Moody, expressing the hope that he would start gospel work at Tirhoot in North India where the fortune had been made. Moody wasted no time wondering how to do that, but he wrote, with the classic American touch that left Studd believing the inception was entirely from his gift, "I will do the next best thing and open a Training School with it, from which men and women will go to all parts of the world to evangelize."

Once more the project stuck.

The Chicago Evangelization Society began operations in the city, acquiring a tent for summers, and visiting saloons, prisons, and slums. One night when the congregation of Chicago Avenue was gathering to hear Moody, a helper named John Morrison found him outside the northwest corner of the building. "Is that you,

Morrison? Do you see that lot? Let us pray to the Lord to give it to us for a school." Moody prayed one of his brief, practical, childlike prayers and went inside again. The lot stayed unoccupied. "Mr. Moody tells me," his wife wrote the following summer, "that he spent more times in committees last winter than in ten years altogether."

Miss Dryer seemed to block every practical move for reasons unknown except that she wanted a free hand, although Moody doubted her ability to superintend. She wanted Moody to settle in Chicago, and she resented his disappearance to responsibilities in Northfield. Entangling everything, if Miss Hitchcock is to be believed, was Miss Dryer's cussedness, bred of being crossed in love. The trouble all dangled on until July, when Moody resigned as President of the Chicago Evangelization Society:

> I have never had my heart so set on anything as on this society, but for six months I have had to oppose some of the dearest friends I have ever had & I am tired & sick of it. I now take it that God is closing the door to me in Chicago & will open some other & will in his own way overrule it all & magnify his grace.

Moody's resignation caused consternation in Chicago, but Mrs. McCormick thought he wanted absolute control for its own sake. Mrs. Moody reassured her in nineteen half-quarto sheets, and Moody telegraphed, withdrawing his resignation: "Tell the trustees to do as they please about the construction and push the building and I will come as soon as it is ready." On October 15, 1887, he wrote from Montreal:

> I find the committee just discouraged & do not know what to do & they think I am standing in the way & if I am I want to get out of the road. I am willing to work at the front or behind or outside or inside & will go where they say only for the sake of the Master let us get the work pushed this season.

Nearly a year later, the site had not even been bought yet, when from Chicago on "the first day of October I started for India."

The Mackinnons, who had lived in India, had long badgered Moody. During a sea-loch trip in Scotland in August 1882, an Indian clergyman, who had come on board at Holy Loch, "stood on the gangway holding Mr. Moody's hand, pleading for a visit to India. Mr. Moody said he did not want to say No, but that he could not promise." The Student Volunteers convinced him. At the Second Conference, in 1887, Robert Wilder wrote,

> Forman and I went to him and said, "God has blessed you greatly to the students in North America and Great Britain and we believe God wants you to go out to India and speak to the students there." He listened attentively but did not say much.

To Japanese students he remarked: "I would like to see the whole world for which Christ died." Later he sent for Wilder to Chicago and "asked [him] many questions as to where the universities were located, etc. He did not think he could stand the climate. However, he did show clearly how deeply he was moved by the call that had come to him from India."

Mrs. Moody, Emma, and Paul traveled from Chicago on the afternoon of October 1, 1888, as far as Turlington, Nebraska, home of the Harveys, where "Papa left us," as Mrs. Moody told Will at Yale, "and we felt pretty lonely. It was hard to let him go but I believe it will be all right."

Before Moody reached San Francisco, prominent ministers boarded the train and reminded him that the year previous he had promised them a West Coast campaign. "They say that they shall hold me to my word . . . so I am in duty bound to stay," Moody said. He needed little prompting to escape seasickness and heat (which brought on headaches), so he wired his wife, whose relief was profound: "It is such a comfort to me not to have Papa go so far from us . . . . Aren't you glad that Papa is not going to India this winter?"

Moody sent George Pentecost in his place. Pentecost was an able assistant, who had not yet revealed his Achilles' heel. Then he moved up into Canada, with George Stebbins as singer. From Victoria, British Columbia, he wrote on October 13:

> The weather is like May at Northfield, the Sound is full of all kinds of fish, splendid fishing smelts cod salmon herrings haddock etc. Just across the bay from here is the snow cap mountain of Washington territory it is the Rocky Mountain range they say they are grand & beautiful but of course they do not come up to dear old Northfield.

"I am having," he told Will a week later, "a grand work here & all the ministers are much pleased with the work & all united & I think will do a good work after I am gone." "I get lonely at times," he confessed from Portland, Oregon, early in December, "& if it was not for the work I would be wild for we do not see the Sun more than 4 to 5 days in a month." At San Francisco all the family except Will joined him for Christmas, catching colds across the Rockies. "The people are kind and do all they can to make it pleasant for them. The work is good here & I am having a much better time than when out here in 81."

Stories abound of that time. Of the young opium smuggler in British Columbia, whom Moody told must make restitution.

> He said, "I have a young wife and a child, and all my furniture in my house I have bought with money I have got in this dishonest way. If I became a Christian, that furniture will have to go, and my wife will know it."
>
> "Better let your wife know it, and better let your home and furniture go."
>
> He said, "Would you come up and see my wife? I don't know what she will say."
>
> I went up to see her, and when I told her the tears trickled down her cheeks and she said, "Mr. Moody, I will gladly give up everything if my husband can become a true Christian."

Of Judge Williams in Portland, who surprised an audience of 3,000 of his fellow citizens:

> I'm seventy-three years old, have sat on the bench forty-three years, have rendered many important decisions, but the greatest of all was rendered this morning when for the first time, in the presence of Brother Moody, I prayed on my knees in my home for forgiveness for my sins and joy came into my heart. Have posed as a Christian, belong to church—all form and sham. Friends, forgive me, didn't know any better, I know better now. I and my house, we'll serve the Lord.

Of the Jewish professional photographer in San Francisco, George B. Rieman, who wanted to add Moody to his collection of actors, politicians, and others.

Moody declined with thanks the offer of a free sitting, saying he had not come to San Francisco to have his photograph taken, but to save Rieman's soul. "The reply made Mr. Rieman furious," according to a man who knew him well and recounted the incident. Each day Rieman would read the newspaper accounts of the meetings "and get madder and madder." When he saw by glaring banner headlines the final day had come, he took his wife, both of them curious

> to see this man Moody . . . . They listened to the sermon and were interested, but not deeply impressed. When the after-meeting was announced, Mr. Rieman said to his wife: "Well, we have been to the circus, let us go into the sideshow also." . . . In there two earnest Christian workers met them and talked to them about Christ. They knelt and prayed.

Rieman became "one of the most earnest Baptist preachers on the Pacific coast, greatly beloved."

The Moodys moved south to Los Angeles early in March 1889. "I am much encouraged with all the work so far and shall hope to close up in good shape on the 25 of this month and may go to the Yo Semite if we can get in by that time if not I think I shall leave my family to go in." Heavy rains stopped them. Moody left the family in Colorado for Mrs. Moody's catarrh and hastened to Chicago.

He would brook no further delay. The Bible institute must be brought to birth.

The previous summer at Northfield Charles F. Goss, the thirty-six-year-old pastor of Moody's church in Chicago, had been riding with him in a buggy up a "beautiful and quiet valley" when Moody began talking about his plans for the institute.

> His eyes kindled and his face glowed. Suddenly he stopped the horse, took off his hat, and said, in tones that sent a positive thrill through me: "I am awfully concerned about this matter. Let us pray God to consecrate ourselves to it!" That prayer went to heaven if anything ever did! It was propelled by a spiritual force that would have carried it across infinity. It filled my mind with an indescribable awe.

In April 1889, Moody told the Chicago Evangelization Society to convene a short-term training school for ministers, laymen, and women, "something like the conference at Northfield." This was "a great success. We had over 500 ministers this spring. They came up from Miss Ala Ark Tenn Ky and all over the northwest and some from Wash territory." In his first address, Moody stated that "Word and Work is the keynote of this convention," as it would be of the residential institute.

During the convention Moody threw himself into establishing the great enterprise that had eluded him for three years. To Goss it was "the most impressive mental and spiritual exhibition I had ever witnessed. The fervor, the intensity of feeling, the prodigious energy of will, the confident faith, were like the mighty forces of nature." To Moody those April and May weeks were "about the darkest 40 days and nights I have ever passed through." He battered at rich men's purses: Farwell started him with $100,000, four other close sympathizers produced $65,000 among them, and those less scrupulous millionaires, Marshall Field and Eli Leiter, produced $10,000 each. Mrs. McCormick gave $25,000 to him and, in a gesture that eased his path, a similar sum to Miss Dryer to enable her to carry on her own work in her own way apart from Moody.

He bought three houses in La Salle Street next to the church to adapt for a women's dormitory. He bought the site, Judge Anthony's lot, which he had prayed for with Morrison "and am now putting up a building that will accommodate 200 young men . . . . So we can take in 250: 50 ladies and 200 men." At the same time, he was speaking at the convention, joining its mission work in street and tenement, and arranging for the Chicago Evangelization Society to work three tent missions throughout the coming summer. The family, back from Colorado and staying at the Holdens, saw him briefly and unpredictably. He slept short hours there, took quick naps at odd breaks, and ate enormously. Goss records:

> Dashing into my house one evening, after a day of terrific effort, he exclaimed, "Have you got anything to eat?" A large dish of pork and beans (of which he was very fond) was placed before him. He sat down, murmured a silent prayer, and, without interrupting his repast by a word, emptied the entire dish as fast as he could carry the food to his mouth. And yet this was done with a certain indefinable grace! He often ate voraciously, but never like an animal nor ever like an epicure.

By May 10, when the convention ended, Moody knew that the Bible institute would open in the autumn.

He had no doubt that it was needed. Urging Whittle, who was in Britain, to hurry to Glasgow and extract 1,000 pounds from Campbell White, he wrote:

The hour is now come for us to lay hold of the ministers and get them stirred up but my plan is to raise up a class of men and women that will go for the 3/4 that do not go anywhere to church, and I am inclined to think I am going to succeed and get a lever under all the churches. I have never been so hopeful about anything I have ever undertaken. I will have some trouble with the seminaries but if a few of my friends will stand by me it will come out all right . . . . If I can get 10,000 pds to run it for three years I think I can convince the church I am right and then I will get all the money I want . . . . I am trying to work out the great problem of this century and we have got to spend some money in training up some men that do not go through the regular schools.

As he said to a newspaper reporter the following year:

There is a class of people whom no man can reach successfully except one of their own number . . . . There is far more demand for trained lay workers than is commonly apprehended . . . . I am not seeking to make any shortcut to the ministry. I do not consider this work to be in conflict with the work of the theological seminaries.

The return to Northfield in mid-May was graced by a charming incident.

Moody had ordered a pony for ten-year-old Paul.

We got home in time and Uncle Ed had Paul's pony and cart at the station. Paul knew nothing of it until he got through the bridge and Emma's horse stood there and the span, and back of the span stood Paul's all on fire. I told him it was his. You should have seen the dear fellow. He stood looking at it for a few seconds and then flew at me and kissed me. I told him to get in and drive home. Sam [Walker] went with him and he got home long before we did.

It was "a black pony," Paul remembers, "and while small in stature he was great of heart and I learned to fall off his back with alacrity and enthusiasm. All summer long he was my inseparable companion. His name was Toppy."

Northfield's summer of 1889—the schools, the college conference, and the General Workers' Conference—had the additional thrill of constant reports from Chicago and letters back ("see if we cannot stir up a fire that will spread all over the city"),

mounting to the climax of Moody's return in time for a second
short convention to inaugurate the Bible institute, beginning on
September 26. Moody wrote to Will that morning:

> We got here last night, & have spent the day in looking around &
> getting things ready for work. I think we will have a good lot of
> workers from all over the country. Mr. Sankey Mr. Hyde Stevenson
> Murphy Harvey Farwell Fleming & a host of others are on the ground
> & a good lot of workers coming from all the churches.

The new building that would be the men's dormitory was still
unfinished, and the staff used part of the women's houses, while the
first male boarders lodged nearby. Moody had secured Reuben
Archer Torrey as Superintendent of the "Bible Institute of the
Chicago Evangelization Society."

Torrey's record and abilities were as remarkable as his looks; he
was nearly as gray in hair and beard at thirty-four as Moody was at
fifty-two, and he had the piercing eyes of a prophet. Unlike Moody,
he was a rich man's son and a college graduate. He had sown wild
oats in his youth and even attempted suicide before his conversion.
Torrey knew the slums: he was head of a city mission in Minneapo-
lis when Moody called him to Chicago. Torrey was a man of
intellect, wide reading, and theological training—Yale, Leipzig,
and Erlangen—who read the New Testament in Greek each day
and the Old Testament in Hebrew: Moody's choice for superin-
tending simple men was certainly no simpleton himself.

A third factor gave Torrey a special attraction for Moody: he had
been a disciple of the higher critics: "There was a time," he once
said, "when I was so wise that I believed so much of the Bible as was
wise enough to agree with me." He went to Germany to learn from
the higher critics—and returned wholeheartedly to believe "in the
Bible, the whole Bible, as the Word of God: an altogether reliable
revelation from God Himself, of His own character, His Will, His
purposes; and of man, his nature, his possibilities, his duty, his
destiny."

The Institute, pioneer of its kind, owed much to Torrey and his
able interpretation of Moody's distinctive plan: free tuition and
boarding at low cost; the blend of systematic Bible teaching and
practical ministry, "daily study with daily practice"; the time given
to music; and the shaping of the curriculum so that a student could
begin at any time.

"I have no trouble with Miss Dryer I think the storm is past & it is clear sailing just now. The meetings are good & all goes well." Moody wrote to Will on November 9, 1889:

> I got a 1000 pds today from Peter Mackinnon. It did me good it is grand to have such good friends I think my dark days in Chicago are nearly over I am getting out all right I think but it has been a hard haul I am so thankful that it is behind me & not before me for I would not like to see another three years like this.

The new building was dedicated on January 18, 1890, and three weeks afterwards, starting a month's mission at Brooklyn, Moody wrote to a fellow trustee, "I think now the old ship has got out on to the deep water let us get up all the steam we can and put up the sails and go ahead."

By the end of that year, in all his schools, Moody had a total of over a thousand students. He wrote to the Mackinnons on December 31:

> The dream of twenty years has at last been reached, and I will always look on 1890 as the year that I reached the top of the hill and you helped me to get there . . .
>
> I want to take young persons at the age of 16 to 20 to Northfield and give them a good English training and when they prove themselves worthy to send them on to Chicago and there they go on studying the Bible and working and as fast as they can prove themselves good workmen, send them out to all lands. I am in hopes if I live to 1900 I will send out a thousand a year.

Looking over Northfield, Mount Hermon, and Chicago, Moody reflected, "My school work will not tell much until the century closes, but *when I am gone I shall leave some grand men & women behind.*"

29

A Dark Valley and the Sea

The Moody children never had any doubts that theirs was the best father in the world. "He was so full of humor—the things done in this house . . . " There was hide-and-seek, with Moody popping up and down the stairs with a student lamp in his hand. There was the day when Emma, thirteen or fourteen, was with her friends in the playroom when Father went by the open window, and suddenly a piglet was squirming and squealing among the shrieking girls.

In early days at the Homestead, Moody spent much time and pride on coaxing his lawn to emulate that of an English country house. May Whittle, afterwards Will's wife, recalls,

> It was just coming up, when some way or other Paul and Will got the horses loose from the barn and they came galloping all over the lawn. Well, Mr. Moody just saw red! That's one time he had to go and ask forgiveness of all he had said to the boys. Oh yes, he had a quick temper, but my husband's and Paul's great memory of their father was when he had lost his temper with them, and after they had gone to bed they would hear those heavy footsteps and he'd come into their room and put a heavy hand on their head and say, "I want you to forgive me, that wasn't the way Christ taught." To them that was the greatest Christian evidence they had seen. Mr. Sankey couldn't do that. He had three sons and I loved Mr. Sankey but he was always right and they were always wrong.

Moody's attitude to his children carried a double but hidden tension.

He wanted them to enjoy what he had lacked—education, travel, toys, and hobbies—yet to learn the discipline of hardship and denial. This went little further than occasional fits of ordering Will, and later Paul, to do an hour or two of weeding a day during vacation and attempting to persuade that it should be done barefoot. The weeding usually lapsed early because Moody wanted them to share his fun with the hens and bees and swans and peacocks and pheasants and deer and all the other animals and things that somehow came to the Homestead and farm. To his sons Moody on vacation "was a stout and bearded Peter Pan, a boy who never grew up."

His heart was set also on his children's being strong Christians, yet he wished, far in advance of his time, to protect them from an overdose. Thus, family prayers never preceded breakfast: "no tantalizing a hungry family by the smell of coffee and bacon while devotions were going on, for Father!"—and if young Moodys grew up in a home devoted to religion there was no constraint or self-conscious pious talk; Moody did not subscribe to the current convention that children should be seen and not heard. Nevertheless, to be offspring of a world-famous religious leader, and constantly among earnest godly adults who expected them to be little credits to Papa and Mama, could not make for a normal childhood.

Moody's letters to Will as a boy were jovial and chatty and only occasionally, as on Will's fifteenth birthday—sending him from London much love and best wishes and a crisp five-pound note—did he add, "May you live to take the place of your father in the blessed work of leading souls to Christ," or, "I long to have you out and out on the Lord's side." Will's spirit progressed intermittently through an adolescence shadowed by frequent illness until during the happy Northfield summer of 1886 he had seemed at last a true Christian.

The spark proved a feeble flicker, and early in December, when he was nearly seventeen and three-quarters, Will wrote from Mount Hermon (which he had entered on its reorganization as a secondary school) a letter stating plainly that he rebelled from the religion of his parents.

Moody's reply from Binghamton, New York, on December 8,

1886, throws a beam of light deep into his character, revealing not only the quality of love and sincerity, but also his vivid sense of Christ as an intimate, living Friend. Had this reply not survived, or permission not been given gladly by Will's widow to publish it, the full savor of D. L. Moody's personality would have eluded a generation that did not know him in the flesh.

Moody wrote:

Yours is at hand & I am glad you told me for I would far rather have you come to me with your faults than to hide them. Of course I am very sorry you were ever tempted to smoke. I was in hopes it would never be a temptation to you but the thing that hurts me worst is that you have no desire to know Christ. Sometimes my heart is so heavy & sad to think that you have such contempt for one that has done so much for your mother & father, all that we are or have has come from him & you have been saved from an early grave I think in answer to prayer & now when you have strength & health given you & are now in a position to do good you turn against the truest & best friend you will ever have. For the life of me I cannot see why you should have taken such a dislike to Christ.

I sometimes think it is my fault, if I had lived more consistent you would not be so disgusted with what is so near my heart. Last Sept was the happiest month of my life when I thought you had really started for the kingdom of God but when I returned home & found you were more indifferent than ever my heart sank within me. I have not talked much with you for fear I would turn you more & more against him whom I love more than all the world & if I have ever said or done anything unbecoming a Christian father I want you to forgive me & would rather *die* than to stand in your way.

The thing that shames me is that I am preaching to others & my son does not believe in the gospel I preach. It was hard preaching last night after reading your letter, it seemed as if I could almost hear a voice saying look to home. I have always felt when a father & mother both were Christians & their children were not that there was something decidedly wrong with them & I still think so & last night I was speaking to parents & how my life condemned me—I have tried not to make religion offensive in my home & if I thought I had neglected to do all my duty towards my three children I think I would rather die than to live. I have tried to make your home life as pleasant as I can & have done all in my power to make you happy. I thought when I started the schools it would bring a good influence into the town for my own family & day & night my desire and prayer has been that we might all be united in Spirit but you seem to hate the things I love. The gulf seems to grow darker & deeper every day between us & I am afraid in 5 years there will be nothing in common between us. If you choose the world for your portion you will die some day a sad disappointed man I am sure. Dear Willie the world will deceive you but never satisfy you. You have not been happy for a year & your discontent has increased & it has hurt your father & mother far more than you will ever know until you become a father yourself.

I hope there is no *sin* that is keeping you from Christ but times I am afraid there is something that I do not know in your life but I pray God to show it to you if there is & may God help you confess it & turn against it. I have never prayed for you as I do now. I think it is a crisis in your life & now dear Willie take this in the same spirit it is written— your Father D L Moody.

Hardly had that letter gone than Moody heard that Will was sick again, and the Christmas holidays were shadowed by his illness and the depression that followed. When Moody went to Chicago for the founding of the Chicago Evangelization Society, he sent affectionate daily notes to his son. "I do wish I could be with you," he wrote on January 7, 1887, "& help cheer you up. You must not lose heart for it may be you will be far better after this is over." Will regained health in the spring, and his father had to rebuke him for overteasing Emma, who, though twenty-three and about to tour Europe with her uncle Fleming H. Revell, was inclined to rise to the bait too easily. In October 1887, Will entered Yale.

On the way to Chicago, Moody called at Yale. Dismayed by the thought of his son's entering college without being a Christian, he was unhappy.

> I am afraid I spoilt my visit to you last night and this morning but I was so burdened that I could not keep cheerful. I have had a good day today it troubles me far more than you will ever know if I did not love you so much it would be different but the thought that you may be cut down unsaved troubles me I do hope you will take the gift of God.

His adored father's unwonted gloom shocked Will into an immediate letter to his mother, who replied by return mail:

> About Papa. I don't think he is changed. I think and know he is anxious about you the same as I am. He does not worry over your going to Yale. He does not mention that to me, but I know that the thought of you being in any college without reliance on the help of Christ, it is to both of us an anxiety that we can only generally pray

about. I have feared to "nag" at you as it might seem and yet it seems often that I cannot bear the thought of you being so unsafe . . . Papa I know is praying, and I am that God's Spirit may lead you to give up yourself to Christ entirely, not to please us but because it is "your reasonable service." You know what you ought to do, then do it, not halfway but out and out. I shall keep praying for you. It is not for dying alone but for right living you will need help stronger than your own.

They were such a closely-knit family. "If you miss us as much as we miss you, you will be quite lonely tonight," runs a letter from Moody on Will's return to Yale in January 1888, and in another, during March when Mrs. Moody left Northfield to join him on tour, "I am thinking that you will all be lonely without Mother but what is your loss is my gain for I am getting lonely without any of you, after I have been away a few weeks it gets lonely enough." This closeness, and the constant concern that sprinkled the correspondence with medical advice ("And now Willie be careful about getting sweaty and cooling off too soon") made Moody the more distressed and puzzled that Will—a charming, well-mannered youth, full of zest and humor when not downcast by sickness—should lack love for the Christ so precious to his parents. If the longed-for Bible institute showed no sign of coming to birth in the early months of 1888, neither did Will's soul, which could not be "pushed for all we are worth" without certain abortion.

In the summer of 1888, when Will was nineteen, Moody saw the dark valley opening. Will began to "take a stand for the Son of God," genuinely but diffidently. His faith matured slowly over the next four years. He relinquished voluntarily an ambition to be a doctor, in order to prepare himself to help his father in the administration of the schools. But not until May Whittle, his childhood friend, returned from Europe in 1893 (they became engaged, and were married in 1894) did Will enter fully on the steady, quiet, and unashamed Christian discipleship that rejoiced his father's last years, a discipleship and faith all the deeper for the long years of uncertainty.

The postscript to that unhappy letter that Moody had written in 1886 is another, written on Will's twenty-fifth birthday in 1894:

. . . for 25 years I have prayed for you & I think the last year you have given me more real joy than any other year of your life. I have had one desire for you & that was you might be engaged in some Christian work & now the time has come & my prayer is answered & I can hardly

[?] return it. And I think May will be a real help to you. You will never know unless you have a son & get your heart above him for some special thing & pray 25 years & see no answer & then have it come about & you will understand what joy you have given your Father in the year of 1893.

It was Will who was with Moody when he was shipwrecked on the Atlantic.

At the Northfield conference in the summer of 1891, Moody was presented with an illuminated scroll of invitation from Scotland, 150 feet long, carrying 2,000 signatures from 50 places and all churches. Moody made no promise, and when he arrived unexpectedly in London early in November with his entire family and Sankey, his intended destination was India. Doctors and British friends of Indian experience dissuaded him: "They say it might cause me a stroke."

He decided instead to tour Scotland and sent the family to the Continent. After hurried consultations among ministers in Edinburgh, with Moody expressing his "great desire to work in country places as well as in large towns," Sankey and he began in northwest Scotland on November 23.

The Scots found him after seven years' absence wondrously stouter: as somebody laughingly put it, "he could lay his Bible on the book-rest which nature had provided him, which he carried with him wherever he went, between two buttons of his waistcoat." His well-trimmed beard showed grizzly to white. At nearly fifty-four, he looked an old man, but his eye was not dim nor his natural force abated. "I do hope the Lord will help me in England as He has here," he wrote to his mother for her eighty-seventh birthday in February 1892. "It is a privilege to live if I can be used as I have been of late."

From Paisley he wrote to Peter Mackinnon:

> I am encouraged . . . . I am happy in the work . . . . I wish you had as good health as I had & could have been with me all this winter I remember what grand times we had in Ireland England & Scotland 18 years ago I have now been in over 50 towns & found fruit in each one in nearly every place I find the ministers were converted at that time.

The family had gone to Venice and Rome. "Paul is much excited & thinks it all great fun. Emma studies up the guide book & helps us, & Will attends to paying bills & all the business & studies Italian." They crossed in January to Egypt, then a great winter tourist resort with special attractions for weak chests and neuralgia sufferers, and Will went on to Palestine. Early in April, Moody met them in Paris and decided after considerable dither to accept the Mackinnons' invitation to visit the Holy Land as their guest, all expenses paid. "Emma did not want to go, Will had just been, so in the evening Paul and Mr. Moody and I started for Rome," Mrs. Moody scribbled to her mother on April 8. Moody greatly enjoyed Rome and the Holy Land "even though he hates the sea journey more and more" (at Jaffa on the return they had to climb onto the steamer from small boats "& as there was quite a heavy sea we had an exciting time. D. L. was too excited or frightened to get seasick"). He preached on Easter Day at a service arranged by the Church Missionary Society at the probable site of Calvary. "I have preached for thirty years," he began, "but have never felt the awe of God as I do at this moment."

Back in Britain for the summer, Moody worked where he had never been, and after Mrs. Moody left for America in August with the family except for Will, who studied in Germany, he took a ten-day campaign in London in September at the Metropolitan Tabernacle,[1] lately bereft of Spurgeon, and went to Ireland, where from Dublin his nephew Ambert wrote home, "The meetings have been grand and my! don't the people think a lot of Uncle D!" Will rejoined his father in London in November. Their passages were booked on the crack liner of the North German Lloyd, the *Spree*.

Before sailing Moody agreed to consult Sir Andrew Clark, the Harley Street heart specialist, who confirmed what a doctor had lately diagnosed: slight heart trouble. Clark asked how often Moody preached.

"Oh, I usually preach three times a day. On Sunday four or even five."

"How many days a week?"

"Six, but during last winter seven."

"You're a fool, sir, you're a fool! You're killing yourself!"

"Well, doctor, usually I take Saturday to rest. This year has been an exception. But may I ask how many hours a day you work?"

---

[1] The future Queen Mary attended his services with her mother. Many years later her son (later the Duke of Windsor), introduced in Chile to a man connected with Mount Hermon, said: "My mother thought Mr. Moody quite a chap!"

"Oh, I work sixteen or seventeen."

"How many days a week?"

"Every day, sir, every day."

"Then you're a bigger fool than me! And you'll kill yourself first."
Which he did, dying almost exactly one year after the consultation.

Will and his father boarded the *Spree* on the following Wednesday, November 23, and immediately heard a hearty American voice, "Why, Moody! The sight of you does me good!" It was the one-armed General, Oliver Otis Howard, who long ago before the Atlanta Campaign had encouraged Moody to preach to his corps. The Moodys had "a lovely cabin," wrote Lady Kinnaird, who had come to see them off. Moody was in "great dread of seasickness" and she naughtily asked, quoting a popular Sankey hymn, if "he felt like singing *all* the time . . . . Will was indefatigable: he let his father have no trouble and seemed so happy in surrounding him with every comfort."

During the first two days, prostrate on his bunk, Moody did some hard thinking, for despite jocularity he had taken the heart specialist's warning.

He reached the conclusion "that I would not work quite so hard." In particular, he would revise his plans for mounting a five-month monster evangelistic campaign at Chicago to run beside the World's Fair, or Columbian Exhibition, scheduled for the coming summer of '93. He had talked and prayed about it, had warned European evangelists to be ready to come over, had engaged a young Irish law student, Percy Fitt, as his secretary—unaware what happiness this would introduce to the family—and had left Torrey and the Institute to enlarge their buildings in preparation. The World's Fair would be the "opportunity of the century," as millions from every American state and abroad would flock to a Chicago already filled with immigrants and, despite churches and ardent Christians, deserving its reputation for wickedness.

On the *Spree* Moody accepted the fact that his World's Fair campaign must be muted.

During the third morning out, Saturday, the Moodys, both on their bunks because of bad weather, were "startled by a terrible crash and shock." Will rushed on deck, and returning said: "The shaft is broken. The ship's sinking, Father."

Moody dressed and went on deck. Passengers were shouting that water was flooding their cabins. Officers and crew kept perfect discipline and mustered everybody, first class, cabin class, and terrified Central European immigrants from the steerage, into a main saloon. The drifting ship settled at the stern. She "rolled from side to side, lurching fearfully" in the heavy sea, for the fractured ends of the shaft had broken the stern tube and pumping failed to empty the three after compartments beyond the promptly closed bulkheads.

Captain Willigerod at noon told the passengers the water was under control and that they could expect to drift in the track of a steamer by midafternoon. Night fell without sighting a ship. Alone on the open Atlantic before the days of radio—lights blazing, rockets firing to no avail—drifting steadily away from the sea lanes, "that was an awful night, the darkest in all our lives—several hundred men, women, and children waiting for the doom that seemed to be settling upon us . . . . No one dared to sleep." During the long hours Moody wrestled with his soul. He felt seasickness no longer—the accident cured him permanently—and his mind ran clear.

He heard as it were the voice of his Lord: "Were you ready to let up, to go slow? Then I will take you to myself. You are no use to Me unless you are out and out."

Moody later related:

> No one on earth knows what I passed through as I thought that my work was finished, and that I should never again have the privilege of preaching the Gospel of the Son of God. And on that dark night, the first night of the accident, I made a vow that if God would spare my life and bring me back to America,

the World's Fair campaign should be undertaken with "all the power that He would give me." He would work till he dropped, a year, five years, seven. Let the weak heart look to itself, he decided.

Sunday dawned with seas high, sky overcast, ocean empty. Passengers were allowed to move more freely. Thirty years earlier, the immature Moody would have shouted the announcement of a revivalist service. This Sunday, sensing that such talk might create a panic by suggesting the end, he did nothing until the evening. With the Captain's permission ("Certainly! I am that way myself") General Howard and Moody held a service in the dining saloon, with almost every passenger attending. "With one arm clasping a pillar to steady myself on the reeling vessel," and a German translating, Moody read the ninety-first Psalm, the words, "He shall give his angel charge over thee to keep thee in all thy ways," coming with fresh vitality, "like a voice of divine assurance." Then he prayed.

Moody had no fear of death. "There was no cloud between my soul and my Saviour. I knew my sins had been put away, and that if I died it would only be to wake up in heaven." But he had been thinking all day of his dear Emma, his two children in America, his schools, his friends, "and as I realized that perhaps the next hour would separate me for ever from all these, so far as this world was concerned, it almost broke me down . . . I could not endure it. I must have relief, and relief came in prayer."

Moody prayed in that lurching saloon, and his prayer echoed the deepest thoughts of all present, that God would still the storm and bring them safely home, but above all would do His will. "Thy will be done!"

Peace flowed across the room. Hearts were brave again. Peace filled Moody's heart: "Northfield or heaven, it made no difference now." He went to bed and fell sound asleep.

About three in the morning Will shook him awake. "Come on deck, Father!" and Will's voice was excitedly happy. They saw, far away, a light rising and falling, slowly drawing nearer. Passengers began to cheer.

The rescue ship was the Canadian Pacific freighter *Lake Huron*, Captain Frank Carey, bound from Montreal to Liverpool, which had seen the masthead flares and closed on the *Spree*. A *Lake Huron* passenger related the events,

> Twice during the darkness an effort was made to get a cable aboard, and each time we had almost gripped it when the force of the waves snapped the rope as if it had been cotton thread. Then the captain signaled: "I'll stand by until morning!" and for five hours we kept steaming around the helpless vessel.

At dawn, the wind and seas dropped, "as though God spoke to the elements as He had done years ago on Galilee," and an officer of the *Spree* could board the *Lake Huron* to consult Carey, who said he would attempt a tow and if necessary try to transfer the *Spree*'s passengers.

> The operation of getting the tow lines aboard and made fast was accomplished and about nine o'clock we again started on our journey to Liverpool with the great ship dragging after us. For six days we

traveled on without a mishap, covering 130 miles a day. Steamers passing us in either direction showed by their appearance that they had experienced rough weather, yet the storms did not come near us.

As they saw the hills of Ireland, Will confessed to his father that he had always doubted if direct answers to prayer ever came, "but I am no longer doubtful."

30

The Incomparable Moody

The World's Fair campaign, running from May 28 to October 31, 1893, drew a total attendance of 1,933,240 of every state and almost every nationality, according to the register kept at the Bible Institute.

Architect, speaker at scores of the hundreds of meetings, soul and brain of the entire operation, Moody worked right through the heat of a Chicago summer as if his heart were sound as an athlete's. Unlike any other campaign, Chicago 1893 was not sponsored or directed by a local committee but by himself through the Bible Institute. "I think it would have been utterly impossible to have carried on this work without the Bible Institute," he said at the close.

It was the headquarters and nerve center. Moody used the 220 men and women students and augmented staff as shock troops: "If there was any part of the city where we needed to throw a detachment, we could send fifty men over and placard and ticket the whole neighborhood and fill a building." The campaign steeled and cemented the infant Institute, stamped it with its president's personality and ideals, and

> deepened the love for souls and earnestness in Christian effort, of the students, has made them more than ever convinced that it is the preaching of the old gospel that draws men and lifts them up, and has

given them the advantage of contact with the very best preachers in
the world

This last was an overstatement, but Moody had brought good men:
John McNeill from Scotland and old Henry Varley from England,
Spurgeon's son, Thomas, on his way home from New Zealand, A. J.
Gordon of Boston, and a galaxy of American evangelists. For
immigrant groups and foreign-tongued visitors he had Theo
Monod the younger from France, and a controversial (and after-
wards reprehensible) German, in addition to a Swede and a
"Bohemian," as Czechs were then known.

The Chicago churches, dispirited by the concomitance of high
summer and the dazzling counterattraction of the Fair, were slow to
assist until Moody's campaign gathered momentum. The city was
evangelized systematically. Churches, theaters, and halls were
filled. Moody rented Forepaugh's Circus Tent the two Sundays it
was in Chicago and was half-amused, half-annoyed when he saw
the proprietor's placard: *"Ha! Ha! Ha! Three Big Shows. Moody in the
Morning. Forepaugh in the Afternoon and Evening."* Down near the
stockyards he took Tattersalls, where the political conventions and
Wild West shows were held, saying, "We have got something better
than Buffalo Bill and we must get a bigger audience than he does."
Moody drew 7,000—about half-filling Tattersalls—on a warm
June Sunday afternoon at the beginning of the Fair. He refused to
attack the Fair authorities for opening on Sundays but said the
gospel would be stronger. Few believed him until, in August, the
Fair decided to stop Sunday opening because of indifferent
attendance while Moody's campaign, Sunday by Sunday, was rising
above 40,000 and 50,000 and, on October 15, the last Sunday but
two, reached a peak of 62,000 at forty-three major meetings.

Moody certainly could claim at the close of the Fair: "Thousands
have apparently been genuinely converted to Christ . . . . Fires have
been kindled in many parts of this land as a result of the summer
campaign."

The year 1893 inaugurated six years of unceasing activity.

Moody seemed like a juggler, keeping six or seven balls in the air
at once. J. H. Harwood, his Chicago friend since early days,
"expected that [he] might at any time hear that [I] had died

suddenly," but Moody did not care. No resting on fame or achievement, no self-satisfaction, Moody's attitude to himself and his enterprises was expressed in two favorite phrases: "We must grow or go to the wall" and "Let us push out in all directions."

He gave the whole of himself to whatever occupied his mind. Bible institute, Northfield schools, evangelistic campaign committees—each cause found it hard to believe that *it* was not his prime interest. His approachability, sympathy, frankness, and bluntness drew scores of people to consult him in trouble or difficulty and count him intimate. But none of his colleagues or associates—not even Whittle, and certainly not Sankey—saw the whole of him. He wanted Will to be his biographer after his death, "because so many friends will think they knew me better than anyone else and they don't!"

George F. Pentecost accused Moody searingly behind his back and, after his death, of betraying his friends: "the moment they ceased to be useful or were in his way he dropped them, and even flung them away," but Pentecost had himself been disloyal. Having reached considerable eminence through association with Moody, Pentecost allowed incipient pride, love of ease, and an uncontrollable temper to turn him into an open embarrassment and hindrance at Northfield, where he had his home.

Moody did not drop close associates who drifted in outlook but remained true to Christ. Charles F. Goss, the lovable but too socialist former pastor of Chicago Avenue, kept Moody's staunch friendship after they had ceased to work together, and Goss's brief biography came very near the real Moody. Yet it failed to show the whole of him.

Moody was like a gem of many facets, the light catching now one color, now another.

Religious leaders down the centuries have been molded generally in the pattern of the apostle Peter, Paul, or John. Moody was much of each. He had Peter's impulsiveness, full-bloodness, quick temper, and rough humanity; he had Paul's single-mindedness, strategic skill in evangelism, strong church centeredness, and hardihood, if without the scholarship; and he had John's love, spiritual appetite, and steady growth in devotion.

The years fell into a busy pattern. At some time during every twelve-month period, Moody would descend upon Chicago like a whirlwind.

If I should speak on Friday night at the church I should want tickets got out and all the work done to get the people out.... Get all the press to work at once & all the Institute men and women & let it be known it will be my only night in the city. All the houses within a mile of the church should be visited at once with tickets.

He would stay at the Institute, interviewing officers and administrators and making lightning decisions. "His perception of the right and wrong in things, the true and false, the thing to be done in any circumstance, were almost like inspiration," Harwood thought. "His intuitions were as quick as a flash and almost absolutely accurate." "All he seemed to require," Charles F. Goss wrote, "was to have a given problem set before him in the clearest light possible, and he instantly saw the answer in all its bearings."

No one could doubt what the Institute meant to its president. "We must make the Institute a mighty power," was a constant theme. On his travels he picked likely candidates and nearly drove the business staff to despair by insisting that "we must take all that come, that is, if they are worth taking . . . I do not want it ever to go out that we are full . . . I want to see 1,000 students and we must all work for that end."

A. F. Gaylord, business manager since 1891, received a stream of brisk letters in the familiar large scrawl filling a sheet of hotel paper or, more often, at the foot or on the back of the letter Gaylord had written to him. If Moody thought of a point, he would dash off a note, perhaps several a day. Thus from Charleston and Savannah in March 1896, Gaylord had eight letters in six days.

Moody's mail, always forwarded, reached enormous proportions, by the scale of the 1890s. "His pen was kept constantly busy," wrote Percy Fitt, close to him as secretary and, from 1894 on, as Emma Dryer's husband. "He always wrote his letters by hand. I never knew him to dictate to a stenographer." He opened his own mail and dealt with it at once, handing many letters to Mrs. Moody. The less important ones he would flip to a member of the family or a guest if at Northfield, or when on tour to a local friend or a secretary or his singer. If somebody asked him what to say, he would look at him over his glasses poised on the end of his nose and, as Paul recalls, "playfully snort, 'I gave it to you to answer! I don't intend to hire a dog and do the barking.'"

A letter was answered, a decision was made, and it was finished.

"He never procrastinated," says Fitt. "His mind was not cluttered with heldover matters," and through disappointments, financial burdens, and perplexities, "he never lost his faith and nerve . . . . One could not be downhearted or defeated in his presence. He could always pray if no open door presented itself." Gaylord said that Moody's "*prayer life* was the one thing above everything else that made an impression upon my life."

He always sought means of expansion.

> How would it do to send out a Gospel wagon into the towns of the West (small) and load them down with books and let them preach and sell books. Could they not go into towns where there is no bookstore and sell enough to keep them going. They could preach evenings and sell books from house to house daytimes.

That letter to Torrey from Baltimore, written on March 8, 1893, was the germ of the Bible Institute Colportage Association, which grew to become Moody Press.

Moody's discovery in the fall of 1894 that the entire state of Wisconsin held one store that sold religious books turned his idea into reality. He was told that such books were not in demand unless they were cheap, although the vast sale of his own collected sermons, authorized or pirated, would contradict this. Early in 1895 he launched, with Revell's help, an edition of 100,000 copies of *The Way to God*, Moody's equivalent of Billy Graham's *Peace with God*, and thereby founded the Colportage Library of popular religious authors and well-produced cheap paperbacks. He then organized the Colportage Association to distribute them.

No sooner had Institute men in gospel wagons packed with books pushed out through the Midwest than Moody learned that three-quarters of a million Americans were passing in and out of prison, or serving long sentences in rigorous, soul-decaying conditions, and that except in the great state penitentiaries libraries were almost nonexistent. Moody had long been concerned about prisoners. He had preached in scores of jails; the most trusted deputy in the sheriff's office at St. Louis in 1895, and a valued local preacher, was a one-time old jailbird called Valentine Burke, who had spent half his life in prison until he was converted in 1880 by reading a newspaper report of Moody's sermon on the Philippian jailer. Moody began to flood testaments and colportage books into every cell of every county jail and state penitentiary.

When the Spanish-American War broke out, and Moody united with the YMCA for Christian activity at the military base in Florida, he ordered the Colportage Association to "turn our forces now on to getting books for the army & let up on the prisoners a little . . . I am now going to push hard to get books into the camps."

Moody books quickly became important. In the tooth-and-claw jungle that was American publishing of the nineties, Moody insisted that the colportage practice be unimpeachable: "I would rather close up the business than to have anyone be able to say we had not been *Honest*." When an allegation of cruelty to the gospel wagon horses reached his ears, he was grim: "If the men were cruel they should be dealt with by Mr. Torrey, it is a shame that young men on a mission like that should do a thing of that kind."

Moody never wrote a book. His gospel sermons, Bible characters, and devotional and doctrinal studies were all compiled from his spoken word, those after 1893 by Fitt: "I came to know his vocabulary and mannerisms of language so well that I could do him justice and reproduce his true flavor." Moody read every book and article before signing.

Moody had already circled the globe in print, as John R. Mott soon found. By 1902, Mott could say he had not

> visited a country in Europe, Asia or Africa where the words of Mr. Moody are not bearing fruit. Next to the words of the Bible, and possibly those of Bunyan, his words have been translated into more tongues than those of any other man.

"I am in hopes God will use the books to stir up the nation," Moody wrote in 1896. If astronomical figures of distribution are any guide, God certainly did.

Every autumn, and again if he had spent Christmas at Northfield, came Moody's time to "turn my back on the most beautiful home on earth."

A Chicago Congregationalist said,

> He went from end to end of this land, calling multitudes away from mere earthliness of interest and the greed for wealth and prosperity to

the problem of individual salvation and the concerns of everlasting life.

He traveled between 1893 and 1899 throughout North America, from Canada to Mexico, no longer staying for months at one city, though occasionally remaining for several weeks, as in New York and Boston the winter of 1896-1897. In most seasons, however, he moved through a wide area, spending two or three nights at each center, until there was scarcely a city of importance that had not heard Moody.

In his travels, "he was such a good sport in regard to hardships, laughing at them," wrote Paul. Moody liked to be comfortable but not luxurious, preferring small temperance hotels. He enjoyed scenery, always soaked up information on local background and personalities, and pumped people about their families and work and interests. Occasionally the rush snapped his patience, which was never very strong. "I'm so ashamed of myself," he confessed after losing his temper with porters. "Some of these men may have known me, and if so I have dishonored my Master."

Once while Moody was on a train with the singer D. B. Towner, a drunk having a badly bruised eye recognized him and started bawling hymns. "Let's get out of here," Moody said, but Towner knew the other cars were full. When the conductor came along Moody pointed out the drunk. The conductor quietly took the fellow, bathed and bandaged his eye, and sent him back to the car, where he fell asleep.

"Towner," said Moody after a while,

> that is an awful rebuke for me! I preached last night to that crowd against Pharisaism and exhorted them to imitate the Good Samaritan, and now this morning God has given me an opportunity to practice what I preached and I find I have both feet in the shoes of the priest and Levite.

For the rest of that tour he told the story publicly against himself.

In the campaigns of the nineties, Towner was often with him, or George C. Stebbins, P. P. Bilhorn, or H. H. McGranahan, the nephew of "Mack and Addy." Sankey's voice and physique no longer could keep abreast.

None equaled Sankey. Sankey in his prime had lasted entire campaigns with few breaks, but now Moody would wear out two or three singers on a tour. Moreover, none had that extraordinary, indefinable quality that could still cause a hearer to exclaim: "I would rather hear Sankey with his wornout voice than the greatest prima donna in the world." Sankey tried all the harder and became, Paul recalled, "a little heavy and pompous, and mannerisms grew upon him at which some of the thoughtless used to laugh, and this never failed to hurt my father . . . . There was never any lessening of affection." Sankey survived Moody some six years and went totally blind: the legend that he lost his faith at the end has no basis in contemporary sources.

Moody's voice had lost nothing with the years: "Thank God, when the Almighty created me," he once chaffed, "He set my head so close to my body that He hardly gave me any neck, and what little there was He macadamized!" Nor had his power to sway audiences lessened. The chronic crush of his collar had gone, for on tour he now dressed carefully, in black or dark blue, well-cut to offset his girth and unadorned by watch chain or gold cuff links: "he wanted nothing about him to distract in any way the attention of his hearers," Will said. Eye and tongue retained their astonishing power to command; in the 1890s, rising sixty, he was at his zenith.

A massed audience packed shoulder to shoulder, and well prepared by song, lay in the hollow of his hand. Charles Goss, who knew him well during that period, wrote,

> The fact that he meant *business* and not fireworks, oratory, or theatricals was apparent. He was there to convince and persuade men, and for nothing else whatever. Nothing could be more impressive than his determination to secure the results he aimed at. The evidences of a supreme and terrible resolution were manifest in every move.

Occasionally, he reached a real height of unintended oratory. In Detroit, Gross heard his sermon on Elijah,

> when it appeared to me that supernatural things were actually occurring in the room . . . . In the final outburst we actually beheld the chariot swoop down from heaven, the old man ascend, the blazing car borne through the still air; and when the impassioned orator uttered that piercing cry, "My father, my father, the chariot of Israel and the horsemen thereof!" the excitement was almost unendurable.

Those close to him on the platform thrilled to the contagion of Moody's expectancy and his joy of victory.

> Was he not about to see avaricious men abandon their love of gold, defaulters restore their ill-gotten gains, adulterers abandon their lust, drunkards dash down their cups, the captives loosed, the bowed down lifted up? As the words poured in torrents from his lips he knew that those eternal deeds were being done. He pierced the mask of those faces and saw the operations of the souls. He beheld Christ moving among them.

Moody's expectancy, with his belief that no person present was too foul or too hard to be beyond the reach of God's love, had not dimmed but increased with the years, so it was small surprise that men and women, as a Hermonite recalled, "rose so easily and went forward to confess Christ." Once more Moody would hurry to the inquiry room. In the quiet, broken only by the murmur of converse between "personal workers" and "anxious souls," Moody was like some doctor after a battle or a mine disaster.

Once a woman journalist seized the opportunity of a brief pause as Moody mopped his brow, to accost him on his future plans. Moody, always courteous to the press in its proper place, "turned on me like a wounded lion, and said, 'I have no time to talk about myself. I have to deal with these souls,' and dashed back to his work."

"People gathered round him like moths around a candle," said Goss about Moody on campaign. "They made absurd excuses to approach him." Moody's influence seemed almost hypnotic, but when Goss asked him if he thought he had mesmeric gifts, Moody dismissed the idea with a toss of the head: "Not if I know myself! If I thought my influence was owing to that I would quit preaching tomorrow. Any power I have comes from the Spirit of God."

As ever, the campaigns were deliberate expressions of Christian unity.

"I am more and more convinced of the importance of sustaining and working with the Church," Moody wrote in a private letter at that time. "Every effort is going to be put forth to arouse the churches to greater activity," he said before starting his 1897 campaign in Boston, where he urged every minister to cooperate "by conducting gospel meetings in his own church." "If the Church was built up it would reach the world" was a constant theme. He wanted the churches to work together and deplored the multiplicity of sects falling over each other when wide tracts of America were barely churched, and any divisive tendencies among his supporters he suppressed rigidly. In his absence, Hartzler and Pierson set up a Northfield Emergency Missionary Fund, which would operate independently of denominational boards. It lasted exactly as long as it took Moody to return to Northfield.

His willingness to cooperate went far beyond the imagination of his friends, who were shocked that he subscribed toward the building of St. Patrick's Roman Catholic Church for Northfield's Irish colony and horrified when he accepted an invitation from a friend who had turned Roman to meet Archbishop Corrigan of New York, to whom he said he "wanted to see New York shaken for Christ and wouldn't it be a grand thing if all the churches swung into a simultaneous effort . . . . The Archbishop had the power to do it for the Roman Catholic churches, and the other churches would follow the lead."

The nineties represented a decade of increasing bitterness between religious groups—but not when Moody was around—and of increasing skepticism—but not where Moody went. "I have not seen so much religious interest in this country for twenty years. I think there will be more than 400,000 come into the churches this year," he recorded in 1894. And in 1897: "Never has America been so aroused over religious matters." He believed that revival could spread everywhere if churches cooperated and ministers were loyal: "What the people want is to be fed, and then they will go to work . . . . If you want a good church feed it on the Word of God."

He would not pronounce on public questions. He was profoundly interested in political and international affairs, being "a great reader of the daily papers," according to his last secretary, H. W. Pope. "He wanted to know what was going on in the world. He wanted to have a hand in it." He had his opinions, but he contended that he lacked time to study up enough to make public comment, and he criticized—sometimes a little glibly—ministers who spent pulpit time, as he said, "discussing topics which are treated far abler in the newspapers and magazines."

His instinct was right. America in the nineties, an age of industrial strife, was a melting pot of economic and political theories. To have pronounced on them would have made Moody partisan. He was a child of his age in economic outlook, with an inevitable leaning toward the captains of industry, many of whom he knew, and a "veiled admiration," in Paul's words, "for men who came to the top in almost any line of activity." But he loved the common man and rigidly opposed oppression when he recognized it.

Harper's Weekly affirmed in 1896:

> He preaches against anarchy, against greed, against extortion and hate. He is the enemy of sectionalism and all hostility of class to class. His mission is to arouse the conscience and awaken the spiritual side of men.

Moody's impact on the social history of America—as of Great Britain—was enormous. His young missionary friend Robert E. Speer was right when he said (in 1931):

> Every community where he worked felt the effect in a better and friendlier community life, in more just and humane economic relationship, in more solicitude for the unfortunate and needy. The Kingdom of God had come nigh.

31

Northfield

Moody's return to Northfield was always a time for rejoicing. In winter each seminary girl would put her oil-lamp in her window "so that all the buildings were brilliantly lighted up," and in summer they would gather woodland flowers to decorate the Homestead and garland the Moody porch. Hermonites crossed the river, and the combined choirs sang a welcome.

At Northfield and at Mount Hermon, stony fields and woods were now well laid out campuses that merged in hillsides of the Connecticut Valley, improving every year through the enthusiasm and vision of Moody and the devotion of honorary administrative colleagues such as young Henry W. Rankin. Moody took intimate interest, avoiding interference in professional affairs but writing continuously to both principals on subjects like the health of specific boys and girls, the farm and its stock, the buildings, information about his meetings, thanks for prayers, and his desire to see an improvement in the students' handwriting—a topic pointed by the unpunctuated misspelled scrawl that conveyed it: he wanted the schools to "give an education that would have done me good when I was a boy."

Mount Hermon, like Northfield, suffered trial and error before Moody in 1890 appointed twenty-eight-year-old Henry Franklin

Cutler as headmaster. Cutler continued in office until 1932; as a man of deep faith and breadth of understanding, he was the chief molder of Mount Hermon into an institute of first-class education. When Cutler took over, the average age of the nearly three hundred boys stood temporarily high at nineteen. Mount Hermon undoubtedly was unique at this time in providing for older boys whose education had been interrupted by poverty; some were orphans, and many had worked for their living in offices or factories or in menial occupations. The school was thoroughly democratic and included Red Indians, Asiatics, British, and Continentals. Cutler defined "D. L. Moody's idea of education" as

> the training and development of hand, head and heart. The work system stands for the development of the hand, the classroom for the development of the head, and the Bible for the development of the heart . . . . It is like the weaving of a braid of three strands; the overdevelopment of any one means the misalignment of the other two . . . . It is the training of the heart that differentiates education at Mount Hermon. Mr. Moody insisted that education was not worthwhile unless the heart was right. To him an educated rogue was the most dangerous man in the world.

"I think dear Hermon is much nearer my heart now than ever before," Moody wrote to Cutler in 1892, "& I am determined if I live, to do all I can to make it still stronger & a greater power for good I am convinced that what the world wants is true men & women not great but true honest & upright persons God can use." When at Northfield he would visit frequently: "His appearance on a rainy day was much like Santa Claus, with his hoary beard, wrinkled, ruddy, kindly, smiling face, rubber boots and corduroy coat," one Hermonite remembers. At the start of every school year Moody would

> make a direct appeal to the boys to give themselves to God. Very few indeed could resist his appeal . . . . Every boy felt that Mr. Moody was personally interested in his fortunes and success. The thought of this often governed our conduct. A boy would refrain from doing some unworthy act with the remark "D. L. would not like it."

He demanded that his students should make full use of their opportunities. If a boy was to be expelled for mischief, Moody would often intercede: "Give him another chance," but if the complaint was "He is lazy," he would dismiss the matter with his characteristic half-grunt, half-snort. "Let him go. We have no room here for boys who won't work." Hermonites never forgot Moody's proverb "The school is not going to spend a hundred dollars on a ten-cent boy." Paul Moody believed that Mount Hermon was never "quite as close to [D. L. Moody's] heart as the first-born of his projects. His boys were five miles away, and added to this Miss Hall was longer in his service than anyone else and certainly more trusted." "He took such an interest in the girls' lives," said Moody's daughter-in-law, May Whittle Moody, who entered the school in 1885, when she was fifteen years old. "And they would love to tell him all their troubles. He broke up a number of engagements of the girls in school if he didn't think the man was worthy. He would investigate. And he was always right." "We all realized that we had in him not only a spiritual adviser, but one with interest akin to that of an earthly father," another girl wrote.

The staff probably would have sometimes dubbed it grand-fatherly, rather, especially when he indulged his boyish delight in suspending all studies once or twice each summer term by calling for a "Mountain Day," as it was known at both schools, when everyone went up Northfield Mountain for picnic and fun.

In the eighties Moody would join the romps and games, literally crushing the opposition and playing pranks such as tying his end of a tug-of-war rope to a tree or a stake. In his last years he pranked by proxy: Dan Sutherland, who worked when he was young as hired man on the Moody place told how one Mountain Day he had driven Moody up to join the girls under the great chestnuts and old apple trees on the mountaintop, and had waited a little below with

> the horse and old wagon. He hollered "Come up," well, I went up. "Do you think you can shinny up that tree?" "Sure." I shinnied up the tree to shake the branches so the apples would fall down, and when he had got me up the tree he called at the girls, "Here, go for him!" Well, all the girls started picking up the apples and they did paste me! I beat a hasty retreat. But it tickled Mr. Moody.

The schools would have died in infancy had not Moody thrown enormous energy and acumen into raising funds, because the hymnbook money could not cover the expense of expansion. Whenever the trustees advocated higher fees, Moody would toss his head, vowing, "Not in my lifetime!" He disliked his institutions' incurring debt; when that happened from time to time, he labored all the harder to bring in necessary gifts and would refuse permission for formal dedication of any building until it was fully paid for.

Millionaires gave to Moody because, they said, "He's one of us." "In the course of a lifelong commercial experience I have never met a man with more business capacity and sheer executive ability than D. L. Moody," Peter Mackinnon said to Henry Drummond.

Moody wrote frequently for big gifts from rich men whom he believed sympathized with the general principles of his schools. At meetings in which the bulk of the audience were active supporters (as at the dedication of a new Northfield or Mount Hermon building) he would sometimes state needs, just as on campaigns he raised money for local needs—a YMCA or a temperance hall— and one time at Mount Hermon he obtained $40,000 in less than twenty minutes On another occasion, having heard of a man in Pennsylvania who was giving money away, Moody hurried to see him, to find that this eccentric philanthropist had decided to scatter $300 each to all worthy applicants. Moody took his place in the queue beside an expressman who had lost his horse. When Moody's turn came and he was asked his name, the philanthropist exclaimed, "What, the great evangelist? Well, I'm delighted to see you here."

"You won't be when you learn what I'm here for." He told him about a building needed at Mount Hermon and asked for $10,000.

"But I'm not giving more than $300 to each case."

"But this is a special case."

"Yes, I know, and I'll give $5,000."

"Don't you believe in me and this work? Why not at once give the money? I can stand in line and beg $300 at a time, but I must be off and build this building." He got the money.

It was a time of great fortunes quickly made, often by men with no sense of responsibility or idea about how to spend it right—a time of swift transitions from cabin to mansion, of absurd extravagances and ostentation. Moody believed implicitly in his right to direct that wealth into service. "When a man makes money by jumps I go by jumps," he told one protesting plutocrat; Moody regretted that "sanctified wealth is a very rare commodity in America," as contrasted with Britain where many families had been born and bred in riches and knew how to use them.

Moody had a slight suspicion of an enterprise run on "faith" without open appeal. He did not understand the circumstances that gave Hudson Taylor his conviction that the China Inland Mission must not ask for money, but the affection between the two men deepened with each meeting. And Moody, who had never asked money for himself from the day he left business, claimed that he did indeed run his schools on faith. "I always have and I always expect to. I believe I show my faith when I go to men and state to them the needs of the Lord's work and ask them to give to it."

"Now make some room for faith," he would tell the trustees if they wondered where the money was coming from. The story was sprinkled with incidents of donors suddenly remembering Moody, who would receive an unexpected check at a critical moment. In 1897, during an evangelistic series at Chicago's Auditorium, he prayed alone in his room at the Bible Institute: "Oh Lord, you know I have been so busy preaching that I haven't time to go out after money. I need $3,000 to pay the bills and must leave it to you to send in." During the afternoon meeting, an envelope was thrust into his hand, which he opened later to find $3,000 from Mrs. McCormick. She told him when he called to thank her that it had occurred to her he would need money for the rent of the Auditorium, and that she wrote a check for $2,000 but immediately felt strongly that she should increase it.

He could have raised an endowment for the schools, and his unsuccessful solicitation in the eighties for a million from Commodore Garrison proves that he thought of it, but, although he liked big gifts with which to put up buildings, for the day-by-day expenses he grew to prefer a large number of small amounts, in order to widen and sustain interest. "And a good part of the time when not otherwise occupied," his son Paul explained, "he would be signing, literally by the thousand, typed begging letters."

He would not have his signature rubber-stamped and disliked blotting paper. "He wanted the ink to dry, and the room, floor and furniture would be covered by these myriad letters."

Northfield proudly gave Moody honor in his own country. Town

and family alike benefited from its attraction to a widening world as
a center of education and conference in surroundings of natural
beauty. Men around Moody bought or built houses at Northfield,
and a New York capitalist friend named Schell was raising a huge
French chateau. Moody had erected the Hotel Northfield, in
Ambert's charge, and during the winter months used it for a
women's training school, which Moody counted as a third Northfield foundation: it did not long outlast him. In 1894 he built the
auditorium seating 2,000. F. B. Meyer thought it too large. "Do you
think you can fill it?" he asked.

"God is marching on," Moody replied, "and I must keep pace
with him."

At conference time, Moody put a bushel basket of apples at the
bottom of his drive, free for all. "The capacity for apples among
attendants at the Conferences was amazing," records Paul, who in
boyhood had to keep the basket full; he was also expected to devote
hours, laboriously preparing ice cream "for the hordes who would
be invited in after the evening service." Once he got his own back in
true Moody manner by freezing the ice cream so hard that at
serving time he had "my father looking more and more baffled."

At Northfield, Drummond wrote that Moody "gathers round
him the best men he can find . . . but when one comes away it is
always Mr. Moody one remembers," yet he never sought to
dominate. "What a time we had year after year in getting him to
consent to speak," John R. Mott writes of the college conferences.
At the General Workers' Conference, Moody would leave the
platform after introducing a speaker, and sit at his feet, "always
with his Bible open," as Charles Blanchard noticed, "always with a
pen or pencil in his hand, and if anything was said which was
particularly good he noted it and used it without hesitation."
Moody was no longer a great reader, and the conferences were his
filling stations. If a man had something to give, Moody wanted it.
"On any other subject he did not care a button for my opinion," the
aged President Weston of Crozier Theological Seminary wrote to
Will, "but when I opened to him the Bible which was so precious to
him, the tears would come to his eyes and he would say, "Say that
again, Doctor.' "

"The central idea of the Northfield Conference is Christian unity
. . . but it is understood that along with the idea of Christian unity
goes the Bible as it stands."

Moody's theological views were, in Speer's words,

> the simple central convictions of the evangelical tradition, the
> Wesleyan evangelistic warmth appealing to human freedom, and the
> sinews of the Calvinistic reverence for God and His will which Moody
> felt and knew as a will of love.

His was a biblical theology. As Dr. James M. Gray, of the Bible
Institute, Torrey's future successor, explained, "The brain of his
theology was the grip he had on the authority and integrity of the
Bible as the Word of God." Sankey gave as one of the reasons for
Moody's phenomenal success "that he believed absolutely, implicitly in the message he gave to men . . . . No doubts ever dimmed
his faith in the Word of God. To him it was the truth, and the whole
truth." "To the Bible he went continually with the spirit of a little
child," Dr. Weston wrote. When he preached he held his Bible in
his hand through much of the sermon, "often adjusting his glasses
to read in a manner that made every hearer feel "these are the
oracles of the living God."

Moody was already established when the superbly confident
stream of higher criticism broke out of the confines of German
theological schools. "The storm of literary criticism began to beat
upon the Bible and many people were frightened, but Mr. Moody
was not frightened," said C. I. Scofield, the Southern ex-lawyer that
Moody brought to Northfield as pastor, who was later to become
eminent as the editor of the *Scofield Reference Bible*. Higher criticism
in its extreme literary stage busily dissected the Bible into a
haphazard collection of documents expressing human aspirations
in ancient times; its opponents responded with piecemeal defenses
to support each biblical point. But Moody saw that the battle had
already been won on a different part of the front.

Moody had depended upon promises, obeyed commands, and
proved the Bible as God's Word in his own life and by its influence
upon others beyond any force of critical theories to detract. He
could trust the Bible as he could trust a man, without needing to
know exactly how the man had come to be what he was, biologically
or in development of mind or character. Moody had seen the power
of the Bible. And therefore, as Speer said, "he believed in the living
Book, the living message to men, as complex and varied as all the
problems of life."

"If you ask," Moody explained in one of his books,

do I understand what is revealed in Scripture, I say no, but my faith bows down before the inspired Word, and I unhesitatingly believe the great things of God even when reason is blinded and the intellect confused. Now what we want is to be so sure of the Word that the Spirit coming upon us shall bring to mind—bring to our remembrance—the words of the Lord Jesus.

Moody knew and trusted the Christ of the Bible. He wrote to Will about a controversial point:

> I am sure Christ believed it, & shall the servant be above the master? I hope you will have the courage to stand up against any man that does not preach all the truth. I have little sympathy with any man that would attempt to undermine any man in the Bible.

Moody stressed the positive power of truth. Certain that criticism could not shake the gospel—lesser men feared that it would, fearing that such criticism vindicated contemporary confidence in man's upward march, the moral evolution that would leave redemption redundant—Moody regarded such critical problems as less important than soul-winning and the increase of churches. He may not have appreciated the strength of intellectual pressures, but he knew that the way to fight error was to emphasize truth, for which the common man hungered. He said in 1897,

> The masses are sick and tired of speculative theology in the pulpit. That is why our churches are half empty and also why millions never darken a church door. People are not fed. They are hungering and thirsting for the pure Gospel and they get pulpit essays and discussions of questions. They go away empty and disgusted and then they stay away.

Time proved Moody right. Had the clergy been in less of a hurry to trot out the latest undigested critical theory, the churches of America and Britain probably would not have sunk into the trough of the twenties and thirties.

Moody refused to indulge in personalities. "The critics raise questions which do not help the spiritual life, their opponents retort with bad temper and personal recriminations," he complained. And after Torrey had been ungracious to George Adam Smith at Northfield, Moody exclaimed to Will and Percy Fitt: "Awful! awful! They often put us to shame by their more Christian attitude." He found it hard to understand how an evangelical of deep personal loyalty to Christ could absorb himself in the literary origins of the Bible when a world needed saving. "Why talk of two Isaiahs when most people don't know of one?" he asked G. A. Smith. Or, he would question, why attempt, like the later Henry Drummond, to reconcile Darwinism with the Bible's view of life? But if a man's fundamental loyalty was to Christ and the gospel, Moody heard him gladly. He stood by Drummond, although he deplored "the unscriptural things he is now teaching."

Upon hearing about Drummond's untimely death at age forty-five, in 1897, Moody, then at Goss's house in Cincinnati, "cried like a child. 'He was the most Christlike man I ever met. I never saw a fault in him,' he said over and over again through his sobs."

Moody was his own best testimony to the Bible's power.

Gamaliel Bradford, the agnostic who attempted a biography, sympathetic but puzzled, in the late 1920s, wrote that Moody had "reduced the population of hell by a million souls." Moody would not have put it negatively (and would have puffed away the numeral), but he would have said that God had used him to bring them to the joy of life in Christ here and in eternity, so that Christ had not died in vain for them. And no man in the nineteenth century put more of his fellow beings to service for God and humanity, an inspiration that continues through his foundations.

Drummond called Moody "the biggest human I ever met." And again: "I had no idea of the moral size of the man, and I think very few know what he really is." An early Hermonite, George L. Cady, looking back after thirty years, described him in an article, perhaps with a pinch of hyperbole, as "human in the sense that one can hardly tell where the human leaves off and the divine begins, when God really has a chance to do His Will with one." An Englishman, T. Farmer Hall, referred to Moody in 1899 as

> the only friend I utterly believed in . . . . I never heard him without feeling the strongest desire to love and know Christ . . . . He was that rarest man in the world, an absolutely (in my opinion) consistent Christian. The same, wherever he was, with only one thought in his life, how to bring glory to Christ by loving and working for those whom Christ loves and died to save.

Woodrow Wilson, when he was president of Princeton, was in a

barber shop one time when another customer entered and, he
related,

> sat in the next chair to me. Every word that he uttered, though it was
> not in the least didactic, showed a personal and vital interest in the
> man who was serving him; and before I got through with what was
> being done to me, I was aware that I had attended an evangelistic
> service, because Mr. Moody was in the next chair. I purposely lingered
> in the room after he left, and noted the singular effect his visit had
> upon the barbers in that shop. They talked in undertones. They did
> not know his name, but they knew that something had elevated their
> thought. And I felt that I left that place as I should have left a place of
> worship.

32

The Grandchildren

The Homestead at Northfield never was sweeter to Moody than during his brief vacations.

Each summer dawn, he would put on his outrageous "Bumblebee" suit: his yellow Donegal tweed trousers and waist-coat, his brown velveteen coat, "an old pair of rubber boots and an utterly disreputable hat"—and go out, sometimes to sit and study his Bible, and sometimes just to drive around. He did not spend long hours on his knees. At the mention of Luther's having prayed all night, Moody said that he had tried that once "and woke up a very stiff Moody." Young Paul, sharing a hotel room with him, was quite shocked by the extreme brevity of his father's devotions.

Moody prayed anywhere, "all the time," Mrs. W. R. Moody remembered. "Everything that came up, he'd say a dozen words perhaps, I never heard him make a long prayer." Christ was so close to him. "How dark this world would be without Jesus Christ!" he once exclaimed to a friend, as they walked out into one of Northfield's most beautiful mornings.

Strolling around—or over—his own small farm and the school estates, he would first visit his pampered and overfed hens. "Father loved them, not individually but in the mass . . . he held endless wordless communication with them . . . . It may have been that after

331

a winter of crowded meetings their very unresponsiveness made an appeal to him."

He kept acres of vegetables, because he liked to watch things grow. He had several cows, including a few Jerseys for their milk, along with pigs and bees; and he even tried sheep unsuccessfully. Dan Sutherland, who was expected to leave a cow half-milked so that family prayers should start on the dot, thought Moody "amateurish, very much of an amateur," as a farmer, but he grew things for fun and gave quantities of fruit and vegetables away, racing around to backyards of relatives and neighbors "in the most uncomfortable of express wagons." "Many a time," George's daughter Mary said, "has my uncle driven into our yard and would call out, 'Come here, I have something for you.' And it would be three or four baskets of home-grown strawberries."

Farming was a hobby, and he thought up others. Paul wrote,

> You never knew where he would break out next . . . . He shamefacedly did things he knew he would be lovingly scolded for doing. But he had a perfectly wonderful time both doing them and defending himself afterwards. And he actually seemed to enjoy the remonstrances of the family and particularly those of my mother, who was, before everything else, practical and orderly.

Moody had fits of mild megalomania, such as ordering barrel loads of china when he thought the house short, and Paul would swear that his father, impatient at finding himself out of a pair of suspenders, once bought a gross, 144 pairs, large size, all white.

His impulsiveness once nearly ruined him. To save a quarrel over a barn, he offered $10,000 for a farm he did not want, which was worth $2,500; the option was to run until the following Wednesday. "The words were hardly out of Father's mouth before cold fear assailed him." The Yankee neighbor figured that if Moody offered $10,000, he must want the place enough to give a few thousand more and realized his mistake only when the option had expired. "Father gave gigantic sighs of relief." Paul watched the neighbor, sitting on the sofa in the library and desperately bringing his price lower and lower, "and Father sitting at his desk pretending to read his mail and refusing every offer."

Every day Moody called on his aged mother in the cottage until her death in February 1896, at the age of ninety-one. Since her conversion from Unitarianism, old Betsey Moody kept an intense interest in her son's work and remained a cynosure of pilgrimage for the good and great who visited Northfield. The younger generation found her forbidding. No cookie jar or sweets, "she seemed to be afraid of spoiling us . . . remarkably undemonstrative . . . suffered our filial kisses with a sort of grim resignation," wrote Paul, and May recalls accompanying her father-in-law on a visit:

> I sat there and watched them, they may have said good evening and good night but if they did that was all they said. They just sat, never spoke, and he came home saying he had had a lovely call on his mother. It seemed strange to me, but that's the way, they were very close, they could just sit together and not have to talk at all.

Back at the Homestead, Moody hurried over supper, in order to be in time for the sunset. He would sit on the front porch and drink in the superb view of the Great River bending in a sweep of an S, and watch the sun sink slowly behind the wooded hills beyond.

The only person in all the world who really knew D. L. Moody was his wife.

"Aunt Emma and Uncle Dwight were so perfectly *one*," his niece Mary recalled, "that no one could possibly tell which was *the* one." "I have never seen anything more idyllic," Paul wrote toward the end of his life, "nor do I believe two people, young or old, were ever more completely wrapped up in each other."

White-haired, calm and self-effacing, efficient, touchy about nothing except detraction of her husband, humorous without Moody's boisterousness, but with an occasional gentle sarcasm, "which we both enjoyed and feared," Emma was the "balance wheel." Dan Sutherland said he was "more sold on Mrs. Moody than I was on Mr. Moody, to be strictly honest," and Paul found her easier to confide in. Moody never took her for granted. He looked up to her until the day of his death, and for her and no other would he drive quietly and not swerve off the road across a field.

She had seen him in his raw form, had polished and brushed him until, for all his abrupt directness, he had courtesy and social grace. "Only the closest and oldest of his associates know the extent to which he leaned upon her. She did not intend they should."

Arthur Percy Fitt was "a good Irishman, blunt and forceful, always came straight to the point, very popular in Town," a Northfield resident described him.

Moody's pleasure at Percy Fitt's engagement to his daughter Emma is prettily reflected in a joke letter that he wrote from a hotel in Providence, Rhode Island. Moody had called Emma out to see a cousin and found she had paper ready to write to her fiancé. Moody did it for her:

> My dearly beloved Piercey I cannot tell you with pen how very much *I love you* you will never know in this world how very much *I do love you.* Your last letter lifted me up into the clouds, but I expect the dentist will pull me down again.

Emma and Percy were married in May 1894, and Will and May Whittle followed in August. The W. R. Moodys went to live in a little house at Mount Hermon, where Will assisted in the administration.

Early on a beautiful morning of August 1895, a horseman crossed the ferry and pounded up Northfield main street on the old white mare, Ouida, having already called at Major Whittle's house. Moody heard "me coming and stuck his head out of the upper window. Says he, 'Is it good news?' 'Yes.'" Moody had the buggy out and was away. "D'you hear I have a granddaughter?" he called to any neighbor he passed. "I'm taking her a present." "What is it?" "Doughnuts!" He bought her a Bible, "for the last forty years the dearest thing on earth to me."

The birth of Emma Moody Fitt, in December 1895, made Moody a doting double grandfather. He sent nonsense letters to the new grandchildren. He wrote from Georgia to three-month-old Emma:

> I have just heard that the milk you get at your house doesn't agree with you . . . . It must be your parents' fault . . . . You slip down to Miss Johnson or Florrie and they will give you some hot doughnuts and ice cream that will agree with you if bottle milk does not.

And to little Irene:

> When summer comes I am going to have Emma and yourself at our house and I will show you some little pigs chickens ducks turkies and lots of things . . . . I want you to keep things lively till I get back, do not let them bother you about sleeping after daylight, keep good natured but laugh crow and make the rattle go hard so all the house will be stirred up.

Moody seldom drove in good weather without one or both grandchildren. The arrival on November 7, 1897, of Dwight Lyman Moody, Jr., added to the fun. Nobody guessed that grandchildren would precipitate the final crisis in Moody's life.

In 1898, aged sixty-one, Moody rode the crest of the wave in campaigns, institutions, and home. He warned Gaylord, who had been ill, "you cannot be too careful of life. When a man gets into a position to do what you are doing you should aim to live as long as you can for one year now is worth ten years before you got started," but Moody did not abide by his doctrine. Far from placating his weak heart, "I asked the Lord to give me a hard field" for the winter of 1898-1899.

He went to the wicked West with Mrs. Moody, taking D. B. Towner with him to sing; they traveled through Colorado, New Mexico, Arizona, and up the length of California. At Denver, Colorado, the welcoming committee could not find Moody; he "had escaped unnoticed to the rear of the train and now appeared with a suitcase in his hand, and a slender consumptive young man by his side," with whom he had become acquainted on the train; the welcome committee was ignored until Moody had put the man in a cab for the sanitarium.

Denver crowded to hear the evangelist, but of Arizona, Towner wrote, "We were in the midst of iniquity such as I never read of in a civilized land. I was real surprised that Mr. Moody at his advanced age should think of working there with as little prospect as there was." At the mining town of Tucson, with 6,000 inhabitants, thirty-six saloons, and four churches, Moody and Towner had to distribute the tickets themselves.

On November 30, Moody received a tragic telegram: baby Dwight had died, after being unwell for some months. Moody was desolate. "How I wish I could be with you and comfort you," he wrote to May, "but the Lord will comfort you, my heart aches for you and Will more than I can tell."

He invited Will and May to bring three-year-old Irene to the West, and in the Los Angeles area, Will served as his associate evangelist. Stebbins replaced Towner, and Moody ventured to use a lady singer, named Miss Boole, whom the *Los Angeles Times* described as "exceedingly pretty" and "a treasure, for the lady not only has a powerful voice, but she can throw more "tears into it than any other sacred singer who has ever appeared on the Coast."

While in Los Angeles, Moody received an invitation to preach in Australia and New Zealand. He was obliged to decline, but the 15,831 signatures on the petition were a happy assurance, nonetheless.

After three days in Pasadena, the Moodys began to work northward. At Santa Barbara, on March 1, Irene caught pneumonia. Moody was miserable; at Stockton and Sacramento he waited impatiently for the daily telegrams he insisted Will should send. "I got a wire today saying she was better," he wrote to Torrey on March 11, "but the danger is not past, I wish you would pray for them, if they lose her it will be a terrible blow & my heart aches for them."

"If I do not get better news soon," he wrote on March 14 from Santa Rosa, "I shall close up the Mission and go down there—if they lose Irene I do not know what will become of them they are so fond of children."

The fever broke, and the mission was completed with six days at San Francisco. The tug of love and uncertainty had been hard on Moody's heart.

33

Heaven Opens

On his way east, in April 1899, Moody addressed his own church in Chicago, where a reporter could see "no sign of added years; no evidence of faltering strength; no trace of failing vigor."
The sermon made a veritable tract for the times.

> I'd like today to speak about the book of Acts. People nowadays seem to think they should get as far away from the Bible as possible—it is my opinion that the closer we can keep to the apostolic times the better . . . . Human nature has not changed in the last 1900 years. Preach a different gospel from that which was successful in apostolic days? Oh, bosh!

He talked of deep clouds darkening the horizon, foresaw riots and revolutions all over the world—1914 lay only fifteen years ahead. "What can save the life of the nation? Only the strength of a quickened church, and the church can only be quickened by a visitation of power such as the old apostles knew!" He said, laughingly, that he had been criticized for not bringing his preaching into line with modern beliefs. "If my theology wasn't the same now as I preached thirty years ago I would bundle it up, drop it into the Mississippi and let it drift down to the Gulf of Mexico!"
Moody reached Northfield after a day campaign at Detroit, "all

tired out but had to go out & stir things up to keep things goin.'" The Colportage and Prison Fund needed support, school benefactors had to be met, and next winter's campaigns discussed. Phrases such as "the load is heavy at times" crept into his letters.

He seemed his brisk self to all of Northfield that summer. At the college conference his stories by the campfire were the best. But Irene was wasting away with tuberculosis. Moody brought Will, May, and Irene under his own roof. The August Conference started. Few present detected that his thoughts strayed continually to Irene, and at Chicago Gaylord and Norton wondered why their letters remained unanswered. Every day Moody deserted the company of important speakers to give Irene a little air, driving her and her mother unwontedly gently, "and he'd stop his horse and he'd make a prayer and he'd drive on." Once he came back with Irene asleep in his arms and would not dismount until she woke, but took a nap himself.

A day or two later, Dan Sutherland milked in the barn, "and Mr. Moody was in the grain room praying and I heard him distinctly say, 'The Lord's will, the Lord's will.'" When he was showing F. B. Meyer Irene's pet lamb, he broke down. He "poured out his heart in prayer as a number of us knelt in the drawing room in definite entreaty that her life be spared if it was God's will."

Irene died on August 22. May remembered Moody's response: "He was with us in the room and he said to my husband: 'Will, there is a lot of work to do. Come on,' and got him out and put him to work." At the open-air funeral, Moody rose unexpectedly and spoke of Elijah,

> waiting in the Valley of Jordan so many years ago, for the chariot of God to take him home. Again the chariot of God came down to the Connecticut Valley yesterday morning about half-past six and took our little Irene home.

On the auditorium platform for the remainder of the conference, sitting next to Torrey and Meyer and Wilbur Chapman and young Campbell Morgan, "[Mr. Moody] looked so weary and troubled," a Northfield girl thought. On September 11, Moody wrote to Gaylord from Philadelphia: "I am sorry I got behind but my dear little grandchild has taken up nearly all my thoughts for months."

The visit to Philadelphia was in itself a strain, because John

Wanamaker had plans for a winter campaign like that of twenty-three years ago. Wanamaker, Moody's dear friend, had, for the past year or two, been committing adultery in secret with another man's wife. There was no open scandal. Wanamaker's position as a leading Christian remained, along with his enthusiasm for the gospel. Moody, having discovered the facts, had brought Wanamaker and the woman to talk the matter over in the Murray Hill Hotel in New York. Wanamaker refused to give her up. "That's where your grandfather broke his heart," Emma Fitt declared to her daughter, in the same hotel many years after. Moody had not seen much of Wanamaker since, but wondered what the right course ought to be, when Philadelphia wished to follow their honored citizen's lead and have Moody to preach in January 1900.

Moody's body seemed to weigh more than its 250 or 260 pounds, as he pushed on to Chicago for the autumn convention at the end of September. "I do not want to speak next Sabbath afternoon," Gaylord read to his surprise, and on Monday or Tuesday Moody handed the preaching to Gray at the last minute. "I'm not feeling well," he explained.

Back in the East, he threw off a heavy cold; he spoke at Boston, traveled back and forth in New England, and spent two days in New York, speaking with force and foxing even Mrs. Moody into believing that he was again well and strong, until the day came, in the second week of November, to leave Northfield for Kansas City, Missouri, where three Hermonites had persuaded the city to book the enormous Convention Hall for an eight-day campaign.

On the Sunday before he left for the West, he preached at Mount Hermon in the chapel that had been given him as a sixtieth birthday present, and on the day he traveled, shortly before Dan Sutherland drove him to the train, Moody addressed the 400 seminary girls on a favorite text: "Search me, O God, and know my heart, try me and know my thoughts."

He walked slowly out, the girls singing softly the Northfield benediction, "The Lord bless thee and keep thee." Outside, he stood at the foot of the steps, tears trickling down his cheeks, until the last note died away.

Wanamaker walked with Moody down a Philadelphia street toward the depot. "I coaxed him very hard to defer his journey as I thought he wasn't very well, and to go home with me; but he resolutely set his face to carry out his program." Moody uttered a deep sigh:

> My great longing has been to get a good hold upon one of the cities on the Atlantic coast. If I could just get under New York or Philadelphia, and lift them to God, I believe I could sweep the country to the Pacific.

He traveled West alone because Mrs. Moody was needed at Northfield, where May would be having a baby within a few days, but he took comfort in the thought of the three Mount Hermon boys at Kansas: Charley Vining, doing very well in the Union National Bank; Syd Bishop, head of the city YMCA; and English-born David Baines-Griffiths, a pastor. Moody stopped over at Chicago for one train, checked up on administration, and addressed his beloved Bible Institute:

> He stood before us in the lecture room, and as he closed, resting one hand on the desk and using the other in slight gestures, the tears running down his cheeks, he said: "I need power! Pray for me that I may have the power of the Holy Spirit. Power is what I need."

Kansas reporters, meeting Moody's train on Saturday, November 11, 1899, thought he looked well "and [he] says he feels equal to the campaign," but when Charley Vining went to the Coates House hotel,

> [Moody] excused himself from rising, when I shook hands with him, saying he was tired. That afternoon he, Baines-Griffiths and myself, went driving through the city; while he seemed in good spirits, and joked some, I noticed that he was not himself.

Vining told the other Hermonites that they must keep people from Moody. "The boys thought that I had better accompany him to the hall."

Convention Hall, a huge building used for horse shows and grand opera and balls and the Megaphone Minstrels, twice drew, on the Sunday, its capacity of about fifteen thousand, "the great arena like a valley filled with upturned faces, and the balconies thronged like receding hillsides covered with a countless multitude." Moody "preached with his old fire and spirit," his voice sounding "as though he was talking confidentially to a man in the eighth or tenth row, and without effort it carried to every part of the building." For both services he took "my old text," "Whatsoever a man soweth, that shall he also reap." Afterwards, he said happily that it was like the great days at Philadelphia in the seventies.

In his hotel room that night, a little lonely, he slipped into reminiscence and, drawing a sheet of hotel paper, wrote to Jane Mackinnon:

> I am off here all alone thinking of the past & you & your good husband have come into my mind & I just long to see you both once more it would do my eyes good to see you all & ride down that western coast once more I wonder if I should like your new house as well as the old one.
>
> I cannot tell you how much I miss dear Drummond it does not seem possible I shall not see him again on earth what a good time we shall have when we get to heaven only think what a lot have gone home since 1873 when we first met I get homesick for them sometimes & yet I would not be off until the work that the Lord has given me to do is finished the work is sweeter now than ever & I think I have some streams started that will flow on forever what a joy to be in the harvest field & have a hand in God's work.

On Monday he told Charley Vining that he had not slept well "but I must not let it get out, as he did not wish the papers to know it." There was no falter on the platform that day, and the pain in his chest (he had said nothing of it to his wife, lest she had stopped his going to Kansas) lifted as he preached, until he returned to his room, where he was grateful for the services of a masseur engaged by Vining last thing at night. The man failed. Moody tried sitting up in a chair. "I had a dreadful night," he admitted.

His singer, C. C. Case, at breakfast "saw he looked pale and he didn't eat much . . . . Of course I knew if he could not lie down he was a sick man," and at length Moody allowed him to telephone for Dr. Schaufler, whose mustard plaster on the chest relieved some of the pain. "After that he preached six times but I could see being with him all the time that he was all the time growing weaker."

A telegram was thrust into his hands. Mary Whittle Moody had been born. "Thankful for good news," Moody wired back. "Dear little child," he wrote on Tuesday to Will, "I already feel my heart going out towards her . . . . Thank God for another grandchild." Soon he was busily scribbling to his other grandchild about how they would all play together.

Vining sat with him Tuesday and Wednesday nights, and Moody slept rather more. When he was awake, he chatted about the school and Will and the grandchildren. He now had to have a carriage for the two-block ride to the Hall.

The campaign was reaching the heights: Moody told Case he was enjoying it "as much as any I have ever had." The deep interest assured him he would be used yet, once he had thrown off this weakness and pain. "Look at the other world!" he cried to the massed thousands, his arm pointing heavenward in the old familiar gesture.

> No death, no pain, no sorrow, no old age, no sickness, no bending forms, no dimmed eyes, no tears. But joy, peace, love, happiness. No gray hairs. People all young. Think of it. Life! Life! Life without end! And yet so many men choose this life on earth instead of life in heaven. Don't close your heart against eternal life. Only take the gift only take it. Will you do it?

After Thursday night's sermon, Moody was "in a dripping sweat—I had never seen him so exhausted," Vining wrote, and Moody had to rest and lean on the gate on the short way over to the after-meeting, in which he took no part. In the carriage he said to Baines-Griffiths, "David, I'm finished," and on reaching his room sat in his chair for two hours without moving. He was a little delirious in the night, but the next morning he kept assuring Vining that he should pull through.

Not until Friday afternoon did he let them telegraph Northfield, arrange to take him home, and send for Torrey to complete the campaign.

A chapel car, "Messenger of Peace," was placed at Moody's disposal by Dr. and Mrs. S. M. Neil, field secretaries of Railway Evangelism, who accompanied him as far as St. Louis. Moody left Kansas at 9:45 p.m. on Friday, with Vining and the doctor looking after him for the whole journey of two nights and a day.

He improved immediately. Hopeful telegrams kept the family abreast of his progress. The train on Saturday evening reached Detroit late, owing to engine trouble, and Vining feared the next connection would be missed. When the engineer who was to take

No. 4, the next stage, heard that Moody was on the train and failing, he sent a message back to him: "Tell him I was converted under him fifteen years ago and owe everything to him. Tell Mr. Moody one of his friends is at the throttle, and just hold your breath!" The train covered the stretch from Detroit through Canada to St. Thomas, including stops, at a mile a minute.[1] Mrs. Moody and Will had gone west to meet Moody but missed him. Paul, hastily back from Yale, went to Greenfield early on the Sunday afternoon "and felt greatly reassured when in his old manner he chided me for having brought the slower horses . . . and laughed at my old fogeyness at being cautious." At the Homestead Moody rested at the bottom of the stairs, then mounted them at usual speed to prepare for tea, but then decided to go to bed, instead.

Letters and telegrams poured into Northfield. On Sunday prayers were offered all over the nation. "Even up in the Adirondacks," one friend wrote, "the rough men in that region are deeply interested in your condition. It is a joy to know that God has given you the hearts of the people as He has." America and the world hailed the news that Moody's illness "is not as serious as we feared at first." Perfect strangers wrote to him. He received a letter from a woman of Granby, Massachusetts, saying,

> I might not agree with you in all your views, but I believe in you with all my heart. Your genuineness, honesty, sincerity have helped me more than you will ever know. There isn't an atom of sham in you.

Moody hated being bedridden. Impatiently he counted the days until he would return to work, if at a slower pace. In his chair, much of the time facing the favorite view over the valley, he chatted with whichever of the family kept him company, asked news of boys and girls, and played with baby Emma a little each day, planning with her for Christmas. He tried to get a laugh, or at least a smile, out of the heart specialist's "doleful but efficient" nurse. When Paul returned to college, and at the start of the vacation, "we were still hopeful."

---

[1] This fascinating incident is verified by the reply from the Superintendent of the Wabash Railway Company, Peru, Indiana, to W. R. Moody, November 24, 1899, acknowledging his letter of appreciation.

To Moody the past sixty-two years were merely a prologue. "Some day you will read in the papers that Moody is dead," he had said at New York on a hot Sunday in August 1899. "Don't you believe a word of it. At that moment I shall be more alive than I am now . . . . I was born of the flesh in 1837, I was born of the Spirit in 1855. 'That which is born of the flesh may die. That which is born of the Spirit shall live for ever.'" It would not be eternity merely but eternity with Christ. The thin veil would drop. On the evening of December 21, lying on his bed at Northfield, Moody wrote in pencil in his usual bold hand, barely palsied by weakness: "To see his star is good but to see his face is better."

As the next winter dawn broke, Friday, December 22, 1899, Moody stirred from an hour's deep sleep that had ended a fitful night of increasing weakness.

Suddenly Will heard, "in slow measured words": "Earth recedes, heaven opens before me!" Will hurried across the room to his father.

"No, this is no dream, Will. It is beautiful. It is like a trance. If this is death it is sweet. God is calling me and I must go. Don't call me back!"

At that moment, Mrs. Moody entered.

"Here is Mother, Father!"

Moody said "rather faintly but clearly, 'Mama, you have been a good dear wife,'" and began to slip into unconsciousness, murmuring, "No pain, no valley, it's bliss."

Dr. Wood, who had stayed overnight, came in and gave him an injection. Emma and Percy, Paul, and George Moody gathered round the bed, as the room brightened with the growing daylight, reflected from the snow outside. Moody revived and wondered why they were there. In Mrs. Moody's record, made the same day:

> Then he said, "What does it all mean? I must have had a trance. I went to the gate of heaven. Why, it is so wonderful, and I saw the children!"
>
> Will said, "Oh, Father did you see them?"
>
> And he said, "Yes, I saw Irene and Dwight," and then when Will cried, he said: "You must not cry, Will, you have work to do."
>
> Will said with anguish, "Oh, if I could only go."
>
> But he said, "No, Will, your work is before you."

Moody had another spell of unconsciousness, and, when he

came round, he divided the oversight of his institutions among the children. When Emma asked which their mother should look after, a flash of the old wit brought the instant riposte, "Why, Mother, she's like Eve, the mother of us all!"

"Don't leave us, Father," young Emma cried.

"I'm not going to throw my life away. I'll stay as long as I can but if my time is come I'm ready." Then he said: "I think I'll get up! Perhaps I may not die. If God wished he could work a miracle. I'll get up. Doctor, I can die in a chair just as well as in bed can't I?"

He waved away the fussy nurse, who was busily applying warm cloths. Once again his wit flashed like summer lightning: "The first thing I suppose we should do would be to discharge the doctor!"

He rose, crossed to his chair, almost unaided, and sat a few moments. His head swam, and he allowed them to lead him back to bed.

He had received his signal for eternity. Nothing need keep him. The chariot was in the room.

List of Principal Sources

MANUSCRIPTS, ETC.

The Moody Papers

At Chicago:

(a) *Washburne Collection.* Early letters of Moody, etc., collected by his younger sister, Mrs. Franklin Bryant Washburne, whose daughter left them to Moody Bible Institute.

(b) *Bible Institute Correspondence.* Principally letters between Moody and R. A. Torrey and A. F. Gaylord.

(c) *Colportage Correspondence.* Principally letters between Moody and William Norton.

(d) *Miscellaneous,* including many manuscripts and typescripts of Moody's early Chicago friends, and photostats of McCormick correspondence.

At Northfield:

(a) *Mrs. W. R. Moody Collection.* Principally early family letters, letters of Moody and his wife to W. R. Moody, letters from American and British friends, especially on Moody's death and in connection with the biography of 1900.

(b) *Mrs. E. M. Powell Collection.* Principally family and other letters to and from Moody, collected by his daughter and enlarged by Mrs. Powell, including correspondence between the Moodys and the Mackinnons, the manuscript of Mrs. Mackinnon's *Recollections,* and Mrs. Moody's diary of 1873-1875.

(c) *Schools Correspondence.* Letters of Moody and others in the archives of Northfield and Mount Hermon schools.

(d) *Diaries of D. W. Whittle,* 1875-1876, 1883-1884. Manuscript in possession of Mrs. W. R. Moody.

(e) *Recollections of May Whittle Moody* (Mrs. W. R. Moody). Tape-recorded by author.

(f) *Recollections of Mr. and Mrs. Daniel F. Sutherland.* Tape-recorded by author.

OTHER UNPRINTED SOURCES

The Diary of the 7th Earl of Shaftesbury (manuscript in Broadlands archives).

Memoirs of John Barton and his wife (loaned by the late Miss Jesse Barton of Cambridge).

Higginbotham, Samuel, *Recollections of D. L. Moody* (paper read at Landour, N. India, 1929). Mount Hermon archives.

Holton, W. T., *D. L. Moody as I Knew Him* (T/S, Mount Hermon archives).

Powell, Elmer W., *Moody of Northfield: A Re-evaluation* (T/S, 269 pp., with annotations by author. Crozier, 1940).

PRINTED SOURCES

(This is *not* a bibliography, which space excludes, nor does it list every work consulted.)

Bibliography

Smith, Wilbur M., *An Annotated Bibliography of D. L. Moody,* copyright 1948 (with some omissions, very full up to 1948; also printing some unpublished documents verbatim).

Short List of Sermons, etc., by Moody

Addresses by D. L. Moody, London, 1875 (anonymously edited by Henry Drummond).

D. L. Moody's Addresses, revised by himself, London and Chicago, 1876.

New Sermons, Addresses and Prayers by Dwight Lyman Moody (unauthorized, edited by Henry G. Goodspeed), Chicago, 1877.

The Gospel Awakening: Sermons and Addresses of the Great Revival Meetings Conducted by Moody and Sankey (unauthorized, copyright L. T. Palmer), 1877, 3d ed., Scammell, St. Louis, 1878.

Moody's Talks on Temperance (edited by J. B. Dunn), New York, 1877.

Notes from My Bible, by D. L. Moody, New York, 1895.

Daily Gems: The D. L. Moody Year Book, selected by Emma Moody Fitt. Chicago, n.d.

Echoes from Pulpit and Platform, edited by C. F. Goss, Hartford, Conn., 1900.

(For an extensive list of shorter works by Moody, including variously revised editions of *The Way to God, Heaven,* etc., see Wilbur M. Smith, above.

Many are still in print from Moody Press and Fleming H. Revell.)

Biographies of Moody

(Books are listed in chronological order. This is not a complete list, nor does it indicate relative reliability of the works included.)

1875   Daniels, W. H., *D. L. Moody and His Work*, London and New York.
       Clark, R. W., *The Work of God in Great Britain*, New York.

1876   Goodspeed, E. J., *The Wonderful Career of Moody and Sankey in Great Britain and America*, New York.

1877   Boyd, R., *The Life and Labors of Moody and Sankey*, Toronto.
       Daniels, W. H., *Moody, His Words, Works and Workers*, New York.
       Nason, E., *Lives of Moody, Sankey and Bliss*, Boston.

1900   Moody, W. R., *The Life of Dwight L. Moody*, New York and London.
       Chapman, J. Wilbur, *The Life and Work of Dwight L. Moody*, Philadelphia and Chicago.
       Davis, G. T. B., *Dwight L. Moody: The Man and His Mission*, Chicago.
       Drummond, Henry, *Dwight L. Moody: Impressions and Facts*, articles of 1894-1894. Edited, with a Personal Tribute, by George Adam Smith), New York.
       Fitt, A. P., *The Shorter Life of D. L. Moody*, Chicago (original edition listed Paul Moody as co-author).
       Goss, C. F., *Echoes from Pulpit and Platform*, Hartford, Conn. (with biographical sketch).

1905   J. M(ackinnon), *Recollections of D. L. Moody* (priv.), Edinburgh.

1907   Farwell, J. V., *Early Recollections of D. L. Moody*, Chicago.

1915   McDowell, John, *Dwight L. Moody, Discoverer of Men and Maker of Movements*, New York.

1923   Torrey, R. A. *Why God Used D. L. Moody*, Chicago.

1927   Bradford, Gamaliel, *D. L. Moody: A Worker in Souls*, New York.

1928   Erdman, C. R., *D. L. Moody: His Message for To-Day*, New York.

1930   Moody, W. R., *D. L. Moody*, New York.

1931   Speer, Robert E., *D. L. Moody: Founder's Day Address*, Northfield, Mass.

1936   Day, Richard Ellsworth, *Bush Aglow*, Philadelphia.

1937   Fitt, A. P., *Moody Still Lives*, New York.
       McDowell, John (ed.), *What D. L. Moody Means to Me*, Northfield, Mass.

1938   Moody, Paul, *My Father*, Boston.

1943   Powell, Emma Moody, *Heavenly Destiny: the Life Story of Mrs. D. L. Moody*, Chicago.

1962   Curtis, Richard K., *They Called Him Mr. Moody*, New York.

Periodicals

Periodicals of Moody Foundations:

The Hermonite (1887-   )
Moody Monthly (formerly *Institute Tie,* 1891, 1900-1910)
   Christian Worker's Magazine (1910-1920)
   Moody Bible Institute Monthly (1920-1938.)
Mount Hermon Alumni Quarterly (1902-   )
Northfield Schools Bulletin (1912-   )
Northfield Echoes (1894-   )
Record of Christian Work (1881-   )
(A large number of general newspapers and periodicals, American and British, have also been examined, either in files or in collections of clippings. Special mention should be made of *Advance* (Chicago, 1867-   ), the *Christian* (London), and the special Moody number of the *Congregationalist and Christian World* (Boston), 12 November 1914. Newspapers and periodicals in 1937, Moody's centenary year, are an especially rich source.)

Pamphlets

Chicago Young Men's Christian Association Ninth Annual Report, Chicago, 1867.

"I. A. M. Cumming," *Tabernacle Sketches,* Boston, 1877.

Dale, R. W., *Mr. Moody and Mr. Sankey,* London, 1875.

_____, *The Day of Salvation: A Reply to the Letter of the Archbishop of Canterbury,* London, 1875.

Kennedy, J., *Hyper-Evangelism, "Another Gospel" Though a Mighty Power,* Dingwall, 7th ed., 1875.

Manual of the Illinois Street Independent Church, Chicago, 1867.

Moody, W. R., *The Story of the Northfield Schools,* Northfield, Mass., 1930.

Popham, J. K., *Moody and Sankey's Errors Versus the Scriptures of Truth,* London, 1875.

Varley, Henry, *Souvenir Account of Conversation with Mr. D. L. Moody in 1872,* Boston, 1902.

Books

Aberdeen and Temair, Lord and Lady, *We Twa,* London, 1925.

Anon., *Harriet Ford Cutler,* Northfield, Mass., n.d.

Benson, A. C., *The House of Quiet,* London, 1910.

Blanchard, F. C., *Charles Albert Blanchard,* New York, 1932.

Braithwaite, R., *Life and Letters of Rev. William Pennefather,* London, 1878.

Brown, W. A., *Morris Ketchum Jessup,* New York, 1910.

Cook, Fred K. Francis, *Bygone Days in Chicago,* Chicago, 1910.

Cooke, Sarah A., *Wayside Sketches,* Grand Rapids, n.d.

Coyle, Thomas, *The Story of Mount Hermon,* Mount Hermon, Mass., 1906.

Cuyler, Theodore I., *Recollections of a Long Life,* New York, 1902.

Dale, A. W. W., *R. W. Dale,* London, 1899.

Davidson, David, *Memories of a Long Life,* Edinburgh, 1890.

Davidson, R. T. and Benham, W., *Archibald Campbell Tait*, London, 1891.

Day, R. W., *A New England Schoolmaster*, Bristol, Conn., 1950.

De Remer, Bernard R., *Moody Bible Institute: A Pictorial History*, Chicago, 1960.

Dodge, D. S., *Memorials of William E. Dodge*, New York, n.d.

Farwell, Abby, *Reminiscences of John V. Farwell*, Chicago, 1928.

Gammie, A., *John McNeill*, London, n.d.

Gibbon, H. A., *John Wanamaker*, New York, 1926.

Grenfell, Wilfred, *A Labrador Doctor*, London, 1919.

Grubb, Norman, *C. T. Studd*, London, 1933.

Hartzler, H. B., *Moody in Chicago*, Chicago, 1894.

Hogg, E. M., *Quintin Hogg*, London, 1904.

Howard, O. O., *Autobiography*, New York, 1907.

Hutchinson, W. T., *Cyrus Hall McCormick: Harvest*, New York, 1935.

MacEwan, A, R., *Life and Letters of John Cairns*, London, 1895.

McLoughlin, W. G., *Modern Revivalism*, New York, 1959.

Macpherson, J., *Henry Moorhouse*, London, n.d.

Mears, D. O., *Edward Norris Kirk*, Boston, 1877.

Morgan, G. E., *A Veteran in Revival*, London, 1909.

Morse, Richard C., *History of North American YMCA*, New York, 1913.

——————, *My Life with Young Men*, New York, 1918.

Moss, L., *Annals of the U.S. Christian Commission*, Philadelphia, 1868.

Needham, G., *Recollections of Henry Moorhouse*, Chicago, 1881.

Parsons, Herbert C., *A Puritan Outpost*, New York, 1937.

Phelps, William Lyon, *Autobiography with Letters*, New York, 1939.

Pierce, Bessie Louise, *A History of Chicago*, vol. 2, New York, 1940.

Pierson, D. L., *Arthur T. Pierson*, New York, 1912.

Pollock, J. C., *A Cambridge Movement*, London, 1953.

——————, *The Cambridge Seven*, London, 1955.

Runyan, W. M., *Dr. Gray at Moody Bible Institute*, New York, 1935.

Sankey, Ira D., *My Life and the Story of the Gospel Hymns*, New York, 1906.

Shanks, T. J., *Gems from Northfield*, Chicago, 1881.

——————, *D. L. Moody at Home*, New York, 1886.

Silverthorne, M. E., and Moody, P. D., *Life Story of Evelyn Hall*, New York, 1914.

Simpson, P. Carnegie, *Life of Principal Rainy*, London, n.d.

Smith, G. A., *Henry Drummond*, London, 1899.

Stebbins, George C., *Reminiscences and Gospel Hymn Stories*, New York, 1924.

Stuart, George H., *Life, Written by Himself*, Philadelphia, 1890.

Trumbull, C. G., *Life Story of C. I. Scofield*, New York, 1920.

Varley, H., *Henry Varley's Life Story*, London, n.d.

Weisberger, Bernard A., *They Gathered at the River*, Boston, 1958.

Wells, J., *James Hood Wilson*, London, 1904.

Whittle, D. W., *Memoirs of Philip P. Bliss,* New York, 1877.
Wilder, Robert P., *The Great Commission,* London, 1936.
Willard, Frances E., *Glimpses of Fifty Years,* Chicago, 1889.

Other Books by John Pollock

BIOGRAPHY

The Cambridge Seven
Way to Glory (Havelock of Lucknow)
Hudson Taylor and Maria
Billy Graham (2 vols., 1966, 1979)
The Apostle
A Foreign Devil in China (Nelson Bell)
George Whitefield
Wilberforce
Amazing Grace: John Newton's Story

HISTORY AND TRAVEL

A Cambridge Movement
Shadows Fall Apart
The Good Seed
Earth's Remotest End
The Keswick Story
Faith and Freedom in Russia
The Siberian Seven

Moody Press, a ministry of the Moody Bible Institute, is designed for education, evangelization, and edification. If we may assist you in knowing more about Christ and the Christian life, please write us without obligation: Moody Press, c/o MLM, Chicago, Illinois 60610.